lest Edito
& 20

The Elephant
and the
Polish Question

The Elephant
and the
Polish Question

Maurice Craig

THE LILLIPUT PRESS
DUBLIN

First published in 1990 by
THE LILLIPUT PRESS LTD
4 Rosemount Terrace, Arbour Hill,
Dublin 7, Ireland.

ACKNOWLEDGMENTS
This book is published with the assistance of
The Arts Council/An Chomhairle Ealaíon, Ireland.

British Library Cataloguing in Publication Data
Craig, Maurice, 1919–
The elephant and the Polish question.
1. Ireland. Social life, 1900– – Biographies
I. Title
941. 7082092

ISBN 0 946640 59 9

Jacket design by Jarlath Hayes
Set in 11 on 13 Erhardt by
Seton Music Graphics Ltd of Bantry
and printed in England by
Billings & Sons Ltd of Worcester

FOR
AGNES
WITH LOVE

CONTENTS

AUTHOR'S NOTE

A number of people of various nationalities wrote books on the elephant. The Englishman wrote one called *Elephants I Have Shot*; the Frenchman's was a slim and elegant volume called *Les Amours de l'Éléphant*; the German book was in two volumes, called *Prolegomena zu Vorskizzen zur Elephantenwissenschaft* with most of the verbs huddled together in *Band II*; and the contribution of the Pole was called *The Elephant and the Polish Question*.

In the most recent form in which I have encountered this tale, in an Argentinian newspaper, the animal was the camel and the country, needless to say, Argentina. But it is the same story, and it is of universal application.

Some passages in this book, written between 1984 and 1987, may read strangely in the light of recent events. I have left them as they stand, as a truthful record of what I felt and thought. The ends are not yet, and the wheel may take another turn.

MACHINERY AND MORALS

THE GENESIS of this book is very simple. For a long time I have thought about, and have wanted to write about, a great many subjects which found no place in any of my published books, all of which are on comparatively restricted themes and all of which, except the first, were written because a publisher asked me to write them. A great deal of this material might, in other times, have taken the form of essays, or, had I been a novelist, might have been put into the mouths of characters or passed off as commentary. Some of it might have been cast into the form of broadcast *causeries*, and indeed some of it was. But literary forms have an inevitable tendency to solidify and become rigid. I recall that the word which we now know as 'sermon' started life meaning no more than a string of casual ruminations on this and that. That is what it meant in Horace's time, and his '*sermones*' have come to be known indifferently as his 'satires': another word which has since acquired a narrow meaning.

I am as open to the temptation to sermonize as others are, and sometimes tempted, also, to a satirical vein, but reluctant to be confined by too narrow a form. *The Life and Opinions of Tristram Shandy, Gent.*: now there is a title for you, however ill it fits the book it belongs to. My life will hardly by itself engage a reader's attention, though my opinions may, particularly when they interact with experience.

A friend who has read the bulk of this work has complained that it is lacking in urbanity, a quality which he is good enough to say he has found in my previous books. I think that I can see why this is so.

Urbanity is the fruit of ease. When you are at ease with your subject-matter you can afford to be urbane. In writing my books I have usually been in command of my subject. I have mastered it to the extent of thinking I know how it is or was and how I should present it in a coherent way. The subject has usually been a rather small one, at least by the standards of the world at large. And, good or bad, my books have reflected, I hope not complacency, but at least some confidence that I had a package to deliver.

But now my attention has been turned to those discontinuities and contradictions, in myself and in the world at large, which have troubled me and which I want to explore and probe.

A book which sets out to be about one thing can, as we all know, end up by being about something else, and this can be true even of a paragraph. When I was at school I was often reproached for being 'tangential', because in the middle of discussing something I would see an analogy with something else and would be diverted by this. This still happens to me in conversation, but in my books I have always had to suppress it. Now, perhaps, is the time to let it have its head. After forty years between the shafts might not the draught animal be turned out to grass? No longer bound to draw its load to or from the market, might it perhaps roll on its back and wave its hoofs in the air? or at least canter round the field for the fun of it? Engines, it is true, always run better under load. But, to vary the metaphor, there are things to be picked and gathered in the course of a country walk which may be worth the trouble of bringing home.

Much, though not quite all, of this book was written at the Tyrone Guthrie Centre at Annaghmakerrig, Co. Monaghan, a place where it is possible to lay aside all worldly things except tobacco, the wireless and one good meal a day.

Nobody can expect to find here any thoughts which have not occurred to other people. But, just possibly, there may be some juxtapositions of thought which have not occurred or been recorded before. A tangent, it will be remembered, is a prolongation in a straight line of the course which the body was pursuing immediately before its release. As a child I used to think that if I swung a chestnut on a string round my head and suddenly let go, it would shoot straight away from my head. I now know that this is not so, and that its course, if extrapolated backwards, would miss me by a distance equal to the

4

length of the string plus that of my arm. To that extent, perhaps, the trajectory of a thought may have some independence of its author.

Metaphors of this kind come readily to me. Though completely without training in mechanics or physics, and having done no 'science' at school, I am at heart a Victorian mechanistic materialist, a dealer in rods and levers, billiard-balls, lines of force and moments of inertia. I love machines, but only when I can understand them, and everything I think I understand I tend to see as a machine.

Little boys, they say, want to be engine-drivers when they grow up. At least they used to, in the days of steam locomotives. I cannot imagine that the inducement is nearly so strong nowadays when the engine is simply a long nondescript box giving out a loud thrumming noise and, usually, a bad smell also, even when stationary, in a station.

I did not grow up, in this sense, till I was sixty-two, when the small model engineering club to which I belong resumed operation of its railway, newly laid out in the foothills of the Dublin mountains with money provided, I am glad to say, by the EEC. The locomotives and the rolling-stock are provided and operated by us, on Saturday afternoons, ostensibly for the benefit of all comers aged between nought and about ten, but in fact, of course, for our own amusement.

This was where, and how, I finally learnt to drive a coal-fired steam locomotive, how to keep the four or five variables: steam-pressure, height of fire, water-level, throttle-opening and speed, in harmony with one another. The problem is not unlike that of making a speech in public: managing the elements of tone, vocabulary, speech-rhythm, syntax and, last but not least, sense and content, without coming a cropper.

I have lived a very quiet life and it is extraordinary that I should be writing about it at all. But now that I have finished writing about buildings what else is there for me to write about? At least I am not doing it at anyone else's insistence, so it has perhaps the merit of an *acte gratuit*. In any case, when the general noise level is lowered, some quiet things get heard.

5

One of the achievements of which I am most proud was not achieved by me at all but by someone else. When the Four Courts was restored after the devastation of 1922 they did several things which they ought not to have done, and left undone some which they ought to have done. Until I drew attention to these (in an appendix to my *Dublin*) I do believe that nobody noticed them. Everybody repeated, parrot-wise, that reinstatement had been scrupulous and complete etc. etc.

Most of what was wrong could not be put right. But there was one thing which could. The dies (recessed rectangular panels) in the centres of the blocking-course above the cornice on the wings had been, doubtless through ignorance, omitted, giving them a bald and meaningless appearance.

For something like twenty years I pestered successive architects in the Board of Works. Then, to my delight, in the early seventies, Gerald McNicholl, then Principal Architect, put them back, having first, with characteristic courtesy, told me he was going to do so.

Every time I pass the Four Courts I get a lift from seeing and remembering this. But I do not suppose that one person in ten thousand notices it.

That is one great advantage which buildings have over printed books: they can be put right even after they have, so to speak, 'gone to press'. They can also be corrupted in the course of their working lives, and this, alas, is what more often happens.

II

I do not greatly care for children and I very much resented being a child myself. I was always very impatient to be delivered from that status. My own children have given me much more pleasure since they grew up than they ever did when they were small.

It is the same with animals. Kittens are all very well, but the company of an adult cat is incomparably more rewarding. I am well aware that according to Konrad Lorenz all domesticated animals are in some respect fixed in an infantile mode with respect to their owners. No doubt this makes up some part of the pleasure of 'owning' them. But it is much less true of cats than of other creatures.

I agree with the schoolboy who wrote that 'the pleasures of youth are as nothing to the pleasures of adultery'. People who do not share my enjoyment in playing with toy boats and driving toy trains no doubt think that I have never grown up. Let them. If that were the only respect in which I have not grown up as I ought to have done, I would be more contented than I am. Perhaps if I were as fully grown up as I should be, I would take more pleasure in the society of children.

III

I have noticed something about Annaghmakerrig. Not just the peace, the solitude, the freedom from interruption – no post, no television, virtually no telephone – not even the fact that it is so skilfully and unobtrusively run. It is the size of the rooms. The room I have at present is about 27 feet by 15, and they are mostly about this size. It is sparsely furnished: a bed, a table, three chairs, and against the walls a bookcase, chest of drawers and wardrobe. As a result, I can walk about in it, backwards and forwards. To me this is even more important than the view out of the windows, though others might put these advantages in a different order.

At home in Sandymount my library, where I work, is so small and so full that I cannot move about in it without tripping over something. It is, consequently, difficult to think in it. When I have the house completely to myself I put my typewriter on Agnes's* father's desk in the drawing-room. The drawing-room, though also somewhat too full of furniture for comfort – my comfort I mean of course – is at least long and has, at one end, a view over a large open green space and, at the other, a view straight out to sea.

When I lived on a top floor in Merrion Square over forty years ago I had two very small rooms, but the view I

* The author's present wife.

commanded was of the whole length of the square as far as Leinster House about 800 feet away. In the evenings this vast space would be flooded with a deep sapphire-coloured light. My cat had the run of the roofs of Merrion Square East and the whole of the North side of Upper Mount Street, while, as I lay in my bath of a Sunday morning, I could hear a sound denied to the rest of Europe: the retired opera-singer Margaret Burke Sheridan, singing in *her* bath. Neither the *lumière* nor the *son* were reflected in the rent, which was twenty-five shillings a week.

But there is no doubt that indoor architecture cannot be made to work without a much more generous allowance of space than is nowadays customary. I once spent a fortnight at a summer school in one of the newly built colleges of the University of York. It was like being in gaol.

Of course I have been spoiled. I returned recently to Magdalene for a dinner. They could not put me in my old rooms as they had done once before, because they are now part of the enlarged library. They accommodated me in a reasonably sized (old) bed-sitter; but I did get a glimpse of some of the new rooms. Though well designed, they had more of the cell than the room about them and I did not envy their occupants.

What must it be like, to live in Leningrad, where indoor space is so sparsely rationed while outdoor space is provided with such lavish splendour? Back to Merrion Square I suppose, only more so. Maybe if I were a state-favoured writer I would be given a dacha: an Annaghmakerrig all of my own? I doubt it.

IV

There is a great difference between what one would like to do and what one would like to have done. For example, when I saw on the television Mr Aspinall sitting on the grass beside his enormous female tiger a small part of me envied him because I love cats, and tigers are the grandest possible kind of cat. When, a minute or two later, Mr Aspinall, still sitting on the ground, was playing with the tiger's kittens while Mrs Tiger prowled around in the same enclosure, I envied him rather less (and also rather more) and I trembled for him, even though I knew that had anything terrible actually happened I would not be watching the film. Yet, at the time when the film was made, only a day or two earlier, it was all perfectly real, and Mr Aspinall was perhaps in great danger. Certainly at the back of my mind was the knowledge that two of his keepers had been killed not long before. My motive in watching had little if anything in common with that which impels people to watch a man being pushed in a wheelbarrow on a wire stretched across Niagara Falls. From that I would have averted my face in horror. But Mr Aspinall's tiger was sublime: beauty and terror incarnate.

It is much more pleasant to be somebody who has written a book than to be somebody who is going to write one. But both conditions are much more agreeable than that of the man who is actually writing. One longs to be safely out of the enclosure with the door locked and the tiger on the other side of the wire.

V

Among the few recollections of my childhood is that of a holiday or holidays taken at Ballynahinch Spa. Though less than twenty miles from Belfast, the small town of Ballynahinch was then very rural indeed, and the Spa still more so. Through the grounds of the small hotel, which was an old whitewashed house belonging to a Mr Flynn, there wound a small river, slow-flowing, with level banks, from which we launched our paper boats. Near it, I seem to recall a circular or octagonal pump-house from which we once – and once was enough – drew glasses of murky water tasting of sulphur.

Like all small boys, we preferred the back parts of the hotel to the front. Butter, in those days and in that place, was still made in a dash-churn, a large round tapering wooden vessel closed by a wooden disc through which protruded the handle of the dash. By prolonged agitation butter was produced, and this fascinated us.

9

Even more fascinating was Mr Flynn's performance on Saturday nights. He must (I now suppose) have had drink taken. He would plant himself in the middle of the hotel lounge with his feet apart, hook his thumbs into the armholes of his waistcoat, throw back his head and sing:

> Yield not to temptation
> For yielding is sin,
> Each vict'ry will help you
> Some other to win.
> Fight manfully onward,
> Dark passions subdue,
> Look ever to Jesus
> He will carry you through.

> *(chorus)*   Ask the Saviour to help you,
> Comfort strengthen and keep you,
> He is willing to aid you,
> He will carry you through.

Never since then, in any place or at any time, have I seen or heard those words or the tune they go to, which is as clear to me now as when I first heard it at the age of six or seven. If the purpose was to impress the juvenile mind, success was complete. I was dimly aware that my elders (not my parents, who were at the time doubtless cruising in the Mediterranean, but our governess and others) were somewhat embarrassed by Mr Flynn's performance, and this is probably part of the reason why I remember it so vividly. It has also helped to suggest my later opinion that his afflatus was not only evangelical but alcoholic as well.

Once, when I was between the ages of eight and thirteen – I cannot be more precise – I decided that I would remember a chosen moment for the rest of my life. There was nothing particular about the moment except that I had decided to choose it. I was on my way back to school. The train was somewhere between Dundalk and Drogheda. I was standing up in the middle of the compartment, facing North with a bit of West in it, looking down at the seat I had just been sitting in, which was the seat in the North-West corner (the train was of course going South). 'I shall always remember this moment,' I said to myself. And I have.

VI

I can think of no pleasure greater than that of visiting a railway-works, such as many railways formerly maintained but which no longer exist except perhaps in India. When I was quite young I visited two. The father of my school-friend Michael Booth was an engineer in the Great Southern Railway so that at the age of twelve or so we had a memorable visit to the great works at Inchicore, while at about the same time or a little later, thanks to my father's friendship with the Chief Mechanical Engineer of the Belfast and County Down Railway, we had a similar visit to the works at Queen's Quay.

In such works locomotives were built, rebuilt, repaired, re-boilered and serviced: there were drop-hammers for forging, hearths for smiths' work, giant lathes for turning and skimming wheels, and most dramatic of all, you could see, hear and smell the red-hot steel tyres being lowered and shrunk on the driving-wheels.

Many years later, when I was about forty, I had the same pleasure, unexpectedly, on a smaller scale. Jeanne* and I had taken a trip by motor-boat from Tossa de Mar round several headlands to the neighbouring village of San Feliu de Guixols. I may have looked at the church of San Feliu – I probably did – but I remember nothing of it. What I do remember is that this was the terminus of a narrow-gauge line to Gerona, with little tank-engines, passenger-stock and everything originating from, I think, Munich some fifty or sixty years earlier, which were dealt with in a little works where all the machinery was driven by a vertical steam-engine in one corner, all in good going

* The author's second wife, who died in 1970.

order and busily at work. Well, fairly busily. The Spaniards were good mechanics in those days, the sort of good mechanics you always come across in a relatively underdeveloped country possessing high-grade equipment which it cannot afford to replace with new but has learnt to look after properly. We were, after all, not very far from the factory in which the Hispano-Suizas had been built and which was again in use making the Pegasos. A little later I was to sample the same Spanish husbandry in the loving care with which the fifty-year-old steamers in the Canaries were maintained. There were, to be sure, special circumstances. Wages were low in Franco's Spain, and the inter-insular schedules were such that they spent quite long periods in port during which their crews could do a lot of polishing and painting and treat them as the drivers on the old-style railways treated their engines. Furthermore, Mr Juan March, who owned the company, owned also the dockyard in which their annual overhauls were carried out, and because the ships were engaged on the postal service, the government paid a large proportion of the cost, so that there was every inducement not to skimp it.

As so often, a state of affairs which seemed delightful was sustained by a system for which no defence was possible. Even in real life this can be so, and in art it is even more so. Thus my abhorrence of whale-hunting does not prevent me from enjoying *Moby Dick* and especially the film made from it by John Huston. On the other hand, though I have made several unsuccessful efforts (to my shame) to read the *Iliad*, I have read the *Odyssey* right through with great pleasure at least once (both, I hasten to add, in translation). This, no doubt, brands me as less than fully adult, for the reason quite clearly is that the subject-matter of the *Odyssey* attracts me while that of the *Iliad* repels me.

VII

I remember hardly anything from my early childhood, at least so far as I can recall, though it is always possible that some stimulus could trigger off a recollection long dormant. One thing I do remember was the sound of goods trains being shunted at night in the marshalling yards of the Great Northern Railway a mile or two away: the characteristic clattering as each unbraked waggon bumped into the next and so on all down the line, like dominoes. The sound seemed to carry farther at night: at any rate this sound is one I associated with lying in bed, awake. I don't suppose I lay awake for long, being a perfectly normal boy in that respect at least.

We went for a summer holiday to Enniskerry a year before I went to school in Dalkey, when I was about seven. I remember the horseshoe forge (of a kind I now know to be a common type all round the Dublin area) which was, of course, in those days still an active forge, and the blacksmith's name was Byrne: not surprisingly as it is about the commonest name in Wicklow. That was my first visit to Dublin, but about Dublin itself I remember nothing at all from that time, and little enough from the five years I spent there at school in Dalkey. Small boys, it is clear, do not see architecture (and in that respect most of them never grow up). I do remember Baggot Street with the tram-standards down the middle of the street where the trees are now: this I saw on my visits to the dentist Mr Friel whose enormously bushy eyebrows I also remember, looming over me. He must have been in Fitzwilliam Square or Fitzwilliam Place, and so were the Pringles: surgeon Seton Pringle whose son was at school with me. I went there sometimes on the rather rare occasions when we were let out, and remember how enormous the Dublin houses were compared with ours in University Square, Belfast, and the great space behind them, backing on to the Grand Canal.

The most indelibly memorable experience of that period was the appearance of the R101 over Dublin in the year 1929. Though I had not the slightest interest in air travel, then or at any time since, as a ten-year-old schoolboy I could not but be fascinated by the idea of a vessel the size of the *Mauretania* floating overhead. Somehow we got wind of her approach, and in the very early morning of November 18 1929 a tiny speck

13

appeared over the Kish or the Bailey, well out to sea. There were wide seats under the window-sills of our dormitory, and we knelt on these in our pyjamas, oblivious of the chill, watching the speck grow bigger and bigger and rounder and rounder. She passed to the East and South of us, circling round Dalkey or Killiney Hill no doubt, so that we saw her at full length, at no great height, with her propellers whirring and the long strip of saloon window clearly visible, finally disappearing in the direction of Dublin.

This was one of the very few extended flights she made, before setting out on her fatal journey towards India, a disaster compounded of political meddling, moral cowardice and physical courage (all the necessary ingredients, I notice in passing, for war). In my memory it was only a matter of days or at most weeks before we heard that she had crashed in flames into a low hillock near Beauvais. But looking it up recently I found that there was in fact nearly a year between, during which she was lengthened in a vain attempt to improve her buoyancy. The force of the dramatic impact, covering both events, had moved them closer together.

An even more famous public disaster than that of the R101 left a small trace on my childhood memories. In about 1926 or 1927 when I was seven or eight, a man came to dinner with my parents, and at the time I remember being told that he was Mr Wilding and was a naval architect, by then, I think, living in Liverpool or it may have been Glasgow. I believe that it was not until many years later that I identified him as Edward Wilding the assistant chief designer, under Thomas Andrews, of the *Titanic*. It is, of course, possible that I remember his name because I was told at the time of the *Titanic* connexion: but I think not. My parents used to relate how my father saw her sail down Belfast Lough on her way to Southampton, and my mother saw her sail down Southampton Water on her way to Cherbourg, Queenstown and points West.

Nearly every maxim has a contrary which is equally true. Suppose, for instance, we wish to draw a moral from the loss of the *Titanic*. It is almost certain that had the ship met the iceberg head-on she would have survived. The first three or four compartments would have crumpled up (as later happened with the *Stockholm*) and many lives would have been lost: but she would have floated. As it was, she took avoiding action and as a result grazed the iceberg so that five compartments – one too many – were opened to the sea, and nothing thereafter could save her or most of those on board.

It would be rash to draw from this the conclusion that trouble should always be faced head-on and never evaded. There are times when avoidance – and even evasion, that subtly different manoeuvre – is the right course of action, and the trouble does, indeed, 'go away'. But no amount of proverbial wisdom avails to tell us which tactic will serve us best on any particular occasion. We have to decide for ourselves. Whatever we do, there will nearly always be some ready-made piece of proverbial wisdom to justify what we have done.

The disaster to the American *Challenger* bears a very close resemblance to that of the R101. In both cases the technical people expected a disaster and wondered only how long it would be in coming, and said so, but were ignored by those in charge, or their testimony suppressed. In both cases the programme was hurried forward against expert advice, for political reasons. Lord Thomson, the Air Minister, was on board the R101. Reagan, however, was not on board the *Challenger*.

It gives me little satisfaction to recall that about two years before the Zeebrugge ferry disaster I wrote a letter to *The Irish Times* drawing attention to the fact that this class of vessel is inherently unstable in the event of accident. This has of course always been known to naval architects and to anyone who has occasion to study the subject, such as a model-builder. I did not write out of the blue, but as a contribution to a correspondence about other aspects of safety at sea.

(As a small child, I showed reluctance to enter a rowing-boat on the grounds that it was 'an old boat with low walls'. I react today in exactly the contrary sense, greatly preferring a conventional vessel with adequate subdivision to one with a large free surface on the car-deck and too much top-hamper.)

The disaster was a paradigm of everything which is wrong with the current phase of capitalism. Not only was the vessel being operated in a criminally negligent fashion, gathering speed and going into a turn in the open sea with her bow doors open and her trim forrard adversely altered to speed up her turn-round in port, she was also one of the most strikingly ugly of a class noted for ugliness, and to compound all this she had been hubristically christened as provocatively as possible: *Herald of Free Enterprise*. Herald of free enterprise indeed. I have seldom seen a less convincing performance than that of the chairman of the company on the television a day or two later, blandly assuring us that nothing was amiss and that it was nobody's fault.

Some years ago Courtaulds (I think it was) held a solemn thanksgiving service for not having been taken over by Dupont (or some such), in St Vedast's Church, Foster Lane, which had been gutted during the war, but rebuilt and fitted out with hardwood joinery and plasterwork picked out with aluminium paint so that it looked, most appropriately, just like a boardroom.

VIII

Another of my few recollections from early childhood – it must have been in about 1924 or 1925 – is of my mother telling my father how her father (my grandfather) was experimenting with wireless and, with his crystal set and the aid of no doubt cumbrous aerials, could get this station and that station, and of my father's callous rejoinder, 'The old man is cracked.' My grandfather laboured under the disadvantage of being English, and my father, like others of his kind, did not suffer Englishmen gladly. I have often wondered how he came to marry an English wife. I expect it was to provide himself with an unlimited series of opportunities for sniping at her compatriots: opportunities which he did not neglect. In this I have neither taken after my father as I have in some things, nor reacted against him as I have in others. I have a dispassionate view of the English and, I hope and believe, a just appreciation of their better qualities, and of course I know them very much better than my father did.

Neither of my parents was much occupied with religion. My father appears to have been, like me, of a non-religious temperament. It probably helped that all or nearly all his sisters married clerics. My mother, on the other hand, was brought up as a devout atheist, which, in later life, gave her feelings of guilt. The moral of this I take to be that there is no use in giving people a present of freedom, because it goes bad and turns into bondage of some other kind. The only freedom worth having is the kind you have to work for. In this it is the exact opposite of money (though money can, in favourable circumstances, be converted into, i.e. exchanged for, freedom).

IX

When I want to startle a certain kind of person I remark casually that we once had a cook who was a cousin of the Empress Eugénie. This rather bizarre conjunction came about as follows. Eugénie de Montijo's mother was a Miss Kirkpatrick, the daughter of the American consul at Malaga. Exactly what the connection was between Kirkpatrick and Miss Brown of Co. Armagh I do not know, but I have no reason to suspect anything out of the ordinary. For a short period during the 1930s there was a fashion for having what was called a 'lady cook', meaning a lady who not only cooked your dinner but sat down with you to eat it as well and was your social equal. I remember Miss Brown dimly but lost sight of her completely afterwards. She, however, had clearly not lost sight of me, because when I was first married in 1945 she very kindly sent us a wedding present which I still have. In fact not so long ago I came across the card which accompanied it, but that I have since lost.

The game of remote connections can be quite enjoyable. When I first went into the English Office of Works in 1952, General Gordon's sister was still living in a grace and favour apartment in Hampton Court. General Gordon died in 1885.

(Before anyone objects and points out that by the time I went into it it was no longer the Office of Works but had become a 'Ministry', I reply that I am still the proud possessor of an Office of Works pass in which the word 'Office' has been cancelled by two ruled pen-lines and the word 'Ministry' substituted in a clerkly hand. I found that again the other day while clearing out old papers.) Everybody has heard of someone's aunt who in her young days danced with an old gentleman who had fought at the battle of Waterloo, or some variant of this pattern. I was once sitting with some English antiquarians in a pub in Northampton and the talk ran along those lines. I decided to startle them, and told them that in 1948 I had been living as tenant in the house of a man whose father had been condemned to death in 1848. This was not strictly true, as Charles Gavan Duffy was not actually condemned to death but merely tried for treason (the jury disagreed twice). But I was confident that nobody present knew enough Irish history to contradict me. Nor did they.

As a general rule I do not attach much importance to dates and places of birth. But I do take great pleasure in two things: one, that my birthday, October 25 1919, is the same date as that on which (by the Russian calendar) the storming of the Winter Palace took place in 1917; and two, that the great Wall Street Crash happened on my tenth birthday in the year 1929. As for my place of birth, it is a source of some satisfaction that the house later became the Senior Common Room of Queen's University and is now the Department of Modern History. I had difficulty in restraining myself from drawing attention in the caption to plate 259 in *The Architecture of Ireland* to the fact that the author's birthplace is just visible on the extreme left of the picture.

I share my birthday with Mícheál MacLiammóir who was born exactly twenty years earlier, and with Picasso.

When the backwash of the Wall Street Crash reached Belfast about two years later I was very well aware of it, because the linen tycoons were toppling like ninepins all around us.

I find it hard to believe that, at the age of ten or eleven, I was awarded a medal for dancing at Mr Leggatt Byrne's Académie de Danse. But I was. I found the medal thirty or forty years ago and have since lost it again. I have no recollection of winning it, or of taking any pleasure in dancing, then or at any other time. I can only suppose that, as all small children are full of potentiality in what seems to be every possible direction, I conformed to the general rule.

Soon after that I must have taken against dancing: against doing it and against watching it, presumably because it was done and enjoyed by people I disliked. Whatever the cause, the effect was permanent. Of all the major arts, the ballet is the one which has least meaning for me. I cannot see that those gestures and gyrations add anything to the music or convey any meaning which could not be better conveyed by other means.

The exception is certain kinds of comic dancing. Groucho's dance in the train in *Marx Bros at the Circus*, for example, is a delight to me, as are all of Groucho's dances, though they never go on long enough. Not merely is it very funny, but I can see that, in dancing terms, it is very well done. The same goes for the little dances occasionally done by Laurel and Hardy or by Morecambe and Wise.

Fred Astaire is another pair of shoes. When I was in my teens my contemporaries at school were besotted by the Astaire-Rogers films. That was enough for me. I faced firmly in the opposite direction and excluded all that sort of thing from my cosmos. If this sounds small-minded, as indeed it was, I can only plead that my contemporaries had already made clear to me their contempt for almost everything that I held dear. It was all very childish, no doubt, but we were, after all, still little more than children. By the time that I was free to make my own choices I was too preoccupied with other matters.

But long afterwards, indeed very recently, when Fred Austerlitz (to give him his original name) died full of years and honour, and was written and spoken of, seriously, as one of the great artists of the century, I had the opportunity of seeing those films of the 1930s on the television. And indeed they were captivating. The sheer accomplishment, inventiveness, wit and technical perfection is clear even to one as ignorant of the subject as I. But it is more than a mere conjuring trick or piece of sublime juggling, though it is that as well. However graceful and ethereal the performance, it has, nearly all the time, comic overtones; partly because in the plot Astaire is a put-upon figure in an essentially comic situation, but partly also because, until he begins to dance, he is so far from being a matinée idol. Not to put too fine a point on it, he is, facially speaking, downright ugly: a *joli laid*. And this is, of course, an enormous advantage. It means that people like me are automatically on his side.

XI

My grandfather died in 1876 when my father was only four. My grandmother continued to trade as 'James Craig Ballymoney' for many years afterwards. The business was the usual country mixture of ironmongery, hardware, clocks and watches, building materials and the like. I never heard that it included undertaking but it would not surprise me. My two uncles emigrated to North America and died, a great while since, and as my father was a doctor there was no one to carry on the business. I just faintly remember my grandmother who lived into her nineties.

My grandfather (or my grandmother) claimed to be a 'clock maker' as did every provincial shopkeeper who sold clocks, and grandfather clocks with 'James Craig Ballymoney' on their faces are still occasionally seen. I owe to William Stewart, who lives in Lucan but who came from Ballymoney, the information that my grandfather (or, of course, my grandmother) claimed to be a tuner of concertinas. Whether this, like the repairing of clocks, involved sending them to Belfast or some larger centre, or whether he kept a leprechaun in a back room tuning them, we will never know.

It is thanks to William Stewart that I know that my grandmother did her bit for the ruination of Ireland a hundred years ago. He has a bill furnished by my grandmother to his grandfather in 1886, for the supply of large quantities of cement. In due course cement, ousting lime-mortar, was to do more damage to our building stock than any other single cause. Ignorant owners were to be talked into believing that their damp gables could be cured by a coat of cement, and many square miles of wall were to be needlessly, carefully and hideously repointed in cement in the 'snail-track' style. This process, alas, still goes on.

It occurs to me that my lack of interest in my forebears may be a manifestation of extreme egotism. Some other people seem to regard their forebears with a kind of reverent wonderment, as though they felt humble at the idea that so many conjunctions were necessary to result in their own existence, which they see as a mere by-product.

I see my own existence as a by-product, indeed, but it is the only one of these existences which interests me. Unlike many other people, however, I am keenly interested in some former existences, as Gibbon, Schubert, Frederick II of Hohenstaufen, Peter the Great, Landor and so on: none of whom has any connection with me, but who were all choice spirits. Therein I show my egotism: or is it just intellectual snobbery?

I am interested in the life of, say, Einstein, though I could not have found anything to say to him had I met him. The perception of destiny which such a man had inspires great respect and even awe. But I am not awed by, for example, Napoleon.

Little pattern to be observed in this.

I would have welcomed the opportunity of meeting Sydney Smith: who would not? What an odd coincidence, by the way, that two of the greatest wits in the history of English letters should have inhabited the same village. One almost uniquely combined brilliant wit with goodness of heart and a complete absence of malice, while the other, just as witty, was one of the nastiest customers on record. The village was, of course, Combe Florey, and the other wit was Evelyn Waugh.

It is, when I come to think of it, very odd that throughout my childhood I never took the slightest interest in the natural world, so that now I cannot tell one bird from another, nor do I know the name of even the commonest flower. To be exact, I know all their names because I have met them in the pages of the poets, but have not any idea which flowers the names belong to. 'Nature study' was not then taught to children, though I recall that we had a book called *The Sea Shore Shown to the Children* and I picked up a little about fishes and seaweed in which I had rather more interest, reinforced by the experience of holidays. Presumably my elders sometimes said to me, 'Look, dear, that's a finch' or 'a tit', or whatever it might be; but if they did I took no notice and certainly I never asked.

I am told, on the other hand, that I was constantly making out what was written on the sides and the insides of the trams. We all have our own reality, and for me the written and printed word is more real than anything else. 'Spitting is a disgusting habit, offensive to fellow-passengers and stated by the medical profession to be the source of serious disease.' This literary gem, prominently displayed on an enamel tablet inside the trams, furthered my education in syntax, vocabulary and hygiene, as well as reminding me of what I was not in much danger of forgetting, the great respect accorded in North-East Ulster to the medical profession.

To this day, unless I am asleep, or swimming, or in my bath, I am probably reading, even when, for example, I am driving a car. I will tell elsewhere one of the odd results of this habit. If there is nothing else to read I will read the telephone directory or a seed catalogue or even the fashion page. But like most habitual readers I have more than one way of reading.

XII

Is English the only language in which the first person pronoun is given a capital letter? It has the result of making any author who chooses to write *in propria persona* look more

22

egotistical, in print, than he intends to be. An author writing in French can so much more easily slip by unobtrusively as 'je'. There are ways around this difficulty. Instead of saying 'I do not know' one can resort to 'we do not know' or 'it is unknown to me' (small 'm' you notice), or one can cast oneself as 'one'. Each has its drawback. 'The present author' is a cumbrous device, though still in use by some.

You can, of course, write a long narrative all about yourself in the third person, like Julius Caesar or Thomas Hardy or Sean O'Casey. Whatever about Caesar, Hardy did it with intent to deceive, and it stimulated O'Casey to tedious and embarrassing prolixity.

There is no satisfactory equivalent in English for 'man' in German or 'on' in French. In restricted contexts one can use 'one', as I have just done. But when the attempt is made to use 'one' as a substitute for 'I' out of some vulgar belief that to use the first person pronoun is not quite 'good form', the results are ineffably ridiculous, especially when 'one' is continually repeated. 'One's coat and hat are taken by a flunkey and put one doesn't know where. One is then kept waiting, afraid to take out one's watch lest one be caught consulting it . . .' and so forth.

The Americans had at one time, and may for all I know still have, though I am not aware of having seen it in anything written lately, a very sensible system whereby when 'one' has been introduced, correctly, as the impersonal pronoun, to denote an unspecified person, it is thereafter followed by 'he' or 'him' as the case may be. It sounds odd to our cisatlantic ears because we are not used to it, and like other American usages it has an archaic flavour; but there is no doubt that it is the right thing to do and I wish that we did it also.

I listen rather carefully, not so much to what people say as to the way in which they say it. For example, fairly early on in the present phase of the troubles in North-East Ulster, the BBC commentators had occasion to refer to Stormont, which they had clearly never heard of before. I caught them once or twice referring to it as 'The Stormont' on the analogy presumably of 'The Storting'* of Norway: for all the world as though it had a thousand-year history behind it, rather than being a trumpery affair cooked up (and abolished) within my lifetime.

Similarly when, in rather recent years, the Church of England took to following the example of the Church of Ireland and holding synods, the gentlemen of the BBC took to handling this strange word as though it were a piece of easily breakable china, pronouncing it 'syn-od' with a carefully enunciated short 'o' in the second syllable, rather than giving it the indeterminate short vowel which we give to, for example, the last syllable of 'stupid'.† English people, I fancy, do not use this indeterminate vowel as much as we do, for I remember an English author transcribing Yeats as having said 'wickud': presumably an Englishman would have said 'wickid' or 'wicked'. I know someone with an exaggeratedly (and clearly cultivated) 'English' accent who habitually pronounces 'provost' as 'provist'. By now, of course, she does it to annoy.

In the good old bad old days, when novels were full of laboriously transcribed attempts to indicate the pronunciation of Irish and other non-English speakers, they would habitually write 'shure'. But in fact the difference between the Irish and the English pronunciations of this word lies not in the initial consonant but in the vowel which follows it: English people pronounce it 'shaw': so that 'shaw', 'shore' and 'sure' all sound the same from their lips.

I note, however, that when I come across the American spelling of 'color' I want to pronounce it 'collar' rather than 'culler' which is how I pronounce it when I find it written 'colour'. But spelling is a funny business at the best of times. I sometimes ask people how would they feel about the Pazzi Chapel if it were spelt the Patsy Chapel.

* The syllable 'ting' in the Norwegian Storting means assembly or assembly-place, and crops up again in Tynwald in the Isle of Man, where the Manx parliament meets once a year, and in the Thingmote in Dublin where the Dublin Norse held their 'thing'. Storting is 'The Big Thing'.
† Gore Vidal says 'sigh-nod' (compare 'Dye-nasty').

24

To return to the BBC. As I write, two people both called Botha, South Africans, are in the news. As one man, and apparently simultaneously, the news-readers and commentators of the BBC have tortured their lips into something like 'Buöta': which for all I know may be correct. But why? Were they all instructed by the same person and at the same time? In the ordinary way, they would scorn to give the slightest attention to the pronunciation of Callaghan or Haughey. Not that RTE is without fault; far from it: not long ago I caught it pronouncing Ramelton with the stress accent on the first syllable instead of the second . . .

I have known for a long time that Parnell pronounced his name with the accent on the first syllable. I well remember his sister-in-law Mrs John Howard Parnell. It was the Irish people who displaced the accent and gave the great leader's name a resonance which has not yet altogether died away.

Parnell: the very word is like a knell. Though he has been dead for nearly a century, and died twenty-eight years before I was born, I can hardly hear the name without a shiver of the spine. It is the same with his portrait in the National Gallery. Though not a specially good painting and by an artist I have never heard of, it seems endowed with that air of cold command which makes it impossible for me to walk past it as though it were the portrait of nobody in particular. It is the same at the recumbent megalith in Glasnevin, or in the woods of Avondale. A very powerful ghost.

Even the ranks of Tuscany are not immune to the spell. A historian friend of mine, of Unionist sympathies, admitted to me that while he would speak of Sir John Párnell and Sir Henry Párnell and Thomas Párnell the poet, it would be an injustice to treat Charles Stewart so.

Vixere fortes ante Agamemnona . . . it is surely because of Yeats and Joyce that this magic still clings about the name. I had read *The Trembling of the Veil* at an impressionable age, and 'Ivy Day in the Committee Room' and the opening chapter of *Portrait of the Artist* when not much older. Yeats's later Parnell poems came out at about the same time:

Come, fix upon me that accusing eye.
I thirst for accusation. . . .

Such is the power of the spell that it is only now that I notice
that in those poems the scansion demands that the name be
pronounced in the historically correct, and not the mytho-
logical, way:

And Párnell loved his country,
And Párnell loved his lass

though, in another poem of the group, he makes him rhyme
with 'fell'. But Yeats, being a genius, could do as he damn well
liked.

Most anglicisms provoke me to, at most, contemptuous
amusement. One provokes me to rage, and that is the intru-
sive 'r': 'the Inca Rempire', for example, heard recently. If
Beethoven had been a modern Englishman, his last words would
have been

Comedia Finita Rest.

It is not even as though they cannot sound two such vowels
without putting a consonant between them. I have a test sentence which I lay before suitable subjects, asking them to read
it aloud:

I saw a copy of *War and Peace.*

Unbelievably, it always comes out as

I sor a copy of Waugh and Peace.

I heard an English weatherlady on the wireless carefully
saying 'faw aw five degrees'. But of course, what between the
wireless and the television and 'improved' communications
generally, it will not be long before Ireland goes the way of
England. By then, all being well, I will be dead.

Hosanna Rin Excelsis

XIII

The little I now know about Nature, which I have learnt
mostly from the television and from my son Michael, does not
seem much to resemble the beneficent power invoked and celebrated by Wordsworth. Nevertheless I believe that Wordsworth
was right. It will not do to explain him and the other nature
poets simply as being in reaction against the industrial revolution. After all, when Wordsworth declared that Earth hath not
anything to show more fair he was looking not at the countryside
but at an unusually large town, which, even more surprisingly, he
saw as 'All bright and glittering in the *smokeless* air' (my italics).

The truth is what was going on inside Wordsworth's head
is much more interesting to us than what was going on around
him, whether he was in London or among the Lakes.

At the age of twelve or thirteen I read avidly a number of
authors whom I should now find quite unreadable: Harrison
Ainsworth, Fenimore Cooper, Bulwer-Lytton, Dumas *père* and
Victor Hugo, the last two of course in translation. Revisiting,
for example, *The Last Days of Pompeii* I have been astonished
at the badness of the prose style, and wondered how I could
ever have ploughed through such stuff. But a child is mercifully
uncritical. He is so impatient to get on with it and see what is
going to happen next that he does not notice the great banks of
verbiage which lie in his way; he thrusts them impatiently aside
and plunges on regardless.

Most writers (and many who are not writers) have had the
same experience. Hardy certainly did, and some flavour of Harrison Ainsworth clung to him to the end. Time itself cured me of
tolerance for such prose, but the quantity of erroneous history
which I absorbed from such books was more difficult to get rid
of. To this day I have some difficulty in purging Pompeii of the
Grand Guignol characters with which Bulwer peopled its streets.

XIV

It surprises me now to recall that at the age of fifteen I
developed a bad stammer – obviously a symptom of the turmoil

27

of adolescence. My father was not noticeably sympathetic to this misfortune, which he met with impatience shading into ridicule. But a kindly clergyman called Mr Whitfield, who taught the form I was in, had suffered from the same affliction when young, and gave up his evenings to instructing me in ways of outwitting it. Certain vowels and consonants were to be avoided. I was taught to identify these and always to avoid beginning a sentence with any of them. Having jumped off from the secure ground of a pronounceable phoneme, I could nearly always get the momentum to carry me over the 'enemy' sound before it had time to trap me. As a result, I formed the habit of examining and discarding several alternative openings very quickly before opening my mouth, and turning the sentence around so that it became manageable. This became second nature so that in time I almost forgot about the stammer and it gave up trying and went away.

Some older people were unbelievably kind to me. Richard Rowley, for example, lent me his copy of the first edition of *Ulysses* when I was seventeen: something I cannot, alas, imagine myself doing in similar circumstances. In its original, wrappered, state, it was peculiarly vulnerable to damage, being large and heavy, but I hope and believe that I took proper care of it.

Mrs Kathleen McCloy and her sister Fay Kyle did much to brighten the intellectual horizon of my youth. They were both early graduates of Trinity to which they were much attached. They were well travelled and well read in both English and French. They lived in a house full of books, off the Malone Road. They took me seriously and expected much of me; more, I fear, than I ever delivered during their lifetimes.

Two sayings of Kathleen McCloy remain in my memory. 'There are only two opinions which matter about anything you have written: your own and the Holy Ghost's.' The practical value of this saying may seem problematical, but I have found it comforting even if the Holy Ghost has mostly held his peace.

'The best service a parent can do for a child is a healthy dose of neglect.' I could well have done with more neglect than my parents ever gave me, so my appreciation of this aphorism was at the time heartfelt and I took it to heart so that my own children have had plenty of neglect from me of which I think they are reasonably appreciative, to judge by results. When I was a child I had a poorish grasp of medium-scale topography. I could hold in my head the relationship between the streets immediately round where I lived, and a few radial routes in familiar directions, but did not connect these latter with each other at all clearly. Places to which I went by tram or train occupied a different kind of space. I never quite grasped the topography of the town of Shrewsbury though it is not very big, and the routes out of it on which we were allowed to go by bicycle were learnt by pure rule of thumb and never put in relationship to one another. The first city which I made real sense of was Paris, and after that Dublin. I learnt quite quickly to get about Cambridge, though having two principal and parallel streets which ultimately meet at right angles it gave me some trouble. I learnt, as a bicyclist and later as a motorist, a good many practical (and ofte⸗ original) ways of getting about London, but never fitted them together to make a coherent whole and quickly forgot them all as soon as I stopped living there.

I visit sometimes in my dreams a town or city which has a rather coherent and consistent topography. I could not draw a map of it, but when I arrive in it I can usually find my way about. I think it is a rather tidied-up version of Liverpool which I used to explore three or more times a year on my way to and from boarding-school.

I have never, so far as I can recall, read anyone else's attempt to give an account of this aspect of their experience. I am not capable, as many people are, I gather, of summoning up visual images comparable in clarity to the aural 'play-backs' which I can summon at will. The only times when such images appear briefly before my 'mind's eye' is during the few seconds between sleeping and waking, while on my way out of sleep into the waking world. At these times the sensual paradise may float like a mirage, across still water, the invitation to the voyage, the embarkation for Cythera.

I have not much use for the kind of narrative in which the author tells the world how miserable he was at school. I was not more miserable than an unathletic bookish boy might reasonably be expected to be. The one really unforgivable feature of school life was the total want of privacy. No matter how old you were nor how high you rose in the school, you were compelled to share space with at least three other boys. This, I now know, was not the case in other comparable schools, and considering the scale of the fees I can find no excuse whatever for it.

In other respects we got our parents' money's worth. The teaching, at least in the Upper School, was very good. People like me started at the bottom of the Upper School and in due course arrived at the top of it. The majority of boys started somewhere near the bottom of the Lower School and never reached the Upper School at all, especially if they left at seventeen which many of them did. In the Lower School they were herded into large classes presided over by amiable drunks little, if at all, more academically minded than their charges. The money thus saved was lavished on us, who were taught in small classes by specialists. Even at the time I recognized that this was an entirely proper use of resources. As Harold Nicolson said of his schooldays: 'They had their fun then: we have been having ours ever since.'

One thing it did cure me of. I have never been able to take seriously the Tory pretence of being interested in freedom. It was only too clear to me that to them conformity was the supreme value: dissent or divagation from the norm was not to be tolerated. The only kind of freedom they understood or valued was the freedom to make money. And this is now clearer than ever. What is not clear to them (though it is to me) is the difference between making money and creating wealth.

One of the more attractive traits of the English is their unwillingness to get worked up about religion. I do not of course mean private or personal beliefs: there are plenty of zealots in England, as everywhere else. But the country at large is resolutely Laodicean, and, it seems, always has been, even in the Middle Ages. People were indeed burnt at the stake, but not so many as in other countries.

Their incuriosity about religion is very conspicuous. My late friend Tom Rolt wrote his admirable biography of Brunel without once mentioning his (Brunel's) religion or his father's, which is odd considering that the father was a refugee from revolutionary France. It does not seem to have occurred to Tom to ask the question, and during his lifetime I never thought of asking him why he had not asked it.

The younger Brunel, at least, conformed to the Church of England and so, it seems, did the elder Pugin who, like the elder Brunel, was a refugee from France. Old Brunel, presumably on landing in England from America in 1799, took the protective coloration of the Church of England, and his friend old Pugin must have done the same, because it was his son, Augustus Welby Pugin, who in 1834 became a conspicuous convert to Catholicism. The older pair had, perhaps, no very strong religious convictions but merely wanted to avoid being guillotined, a motive which would appeal to your common-sensical Englishman.

What little religion I have sits lightly on me, I am glad to say. I was not very deeply imprinted. From time to time we sat in our rented mahogany horse-box, with our name on it, in Rosemary Street Church, to see the minister emerge from a mysterious door behind his high, wide and solid pulpit, where he sat, like God, in his gown and bands, rising at intervals to preach and, at even greater length, pray. My father joined us very rarely in the horse-box. On one occasion when he did, I remember the minister expressing satisfaction, from the pulpit, at seeing him there. Sunday mornings were consecrated by my father to doing the rounds of his nursing homes, where the private patients formed, no doubt, the most lucrative part of his practice. My brother and I sometimes went sampling the rich variety of religious fare which Belfast had to offer: the Moravians who shook hands with you (which nowadays the

Catholics do), or the half-built cathedral of the Episcopalians, or May Street, where the Reverend Wylie Blue, a large man with a large voice and a great deal of white hair, had a line in histrionic pulpitry with which, when not bombinating in Belfast, he used to stump the circuits of North America or Australia.

My father did not parade his unbelief. His unbelief, if he had any, was not very strong. It was like mine. Two of his brothers-in-law were ministers, which may have had something to do with it.

At the English public school to which I was sent it was customary to process boys through confirmation. In the Church of England, naturally. I announced that I was a Presbyterian. I do not, even now, accuse myself of hypocrisy, nor did I then. I was perfectly well aware that my motives were primarily political though, like all motives, mixed. The Anglican elasticity was equal to the challenge. Letters passed between the school chaplain and the minister and it was providentially discovered that the Anglican preparation would be perfectly valid for Presbyterian purposes. (I suspect, now, that their motives were just as political as mine.)

I kept my side of the bargain faithfully. I tried to mesmerize myself into thinking that I was experiencing religious feelings, with no success whatever, like someone leaning forward in a bus to make it go faster. This, I believe, is quite a common adolescent experience. I recall the chaplain telling me that it was just as well that I was a Presbyterian and not a Methodist, because by no stretch could a Methodist be admitted to the Anglican communion. This strikes me as odd, in view of the fact that John Wesley lived and died in the Church of England. After all, in no territory is the king of England head of the Methodist Church.

What enraged me was the arrogant complacency of their assumption that I would, without question, agree to be matriculated into their institutions and thus acquire protective coloration. If they had thought about the matter at all (which of course they had not) they would have supposed that I would be more comfortable that way. By this kind of insensitivity they have undone themselves in many places and at many times.

We may not have been very sure of being Christians, but at least we knew for certain that we were Protestants. To be more precise, we knew that we were not Catholics. Not that we were bigoted: dear me no. My father had one Catholic friend, Dr McLornan, with whom he played bridge and golf just as he did with the Protestant doctors. We knew two Catholic boys, the McGonigals, who went to some, at least, of the same children's parties as we did. It was the same in Dublin. At Castle Park, out of the fifty-odd boys, two, the Gills, were Catholics. But for political purposes all those mentioned counted, of course, as honorary Protestants. In the same way, I was being invited to become an honorary Englishman, and I was not having it. For the time being the only form of protest open to me was a 'religious' protest.

It is wrong to persecute religion, just as it would be wrong to persecute irreligion. But besides being wrong, it is also unwise, since persecution causes religion to flourish. Religion may be best understood as analogous to a disease such as measles, which nearly everybody gets in youth and recovers from, but which if contracted in later life may have serious effects. Some parents nowadays try too zealously to protect their children against the contagion. This often has the same effect as over-protection against bacterial infection, which is widely blamed for the prevalence of polio-myelitis in excessively hygiene-conscious societies such as the richer strata of the United States. The children of devout atheists are apt, sometimes, to veer violently in the opposite direction.

I am now inclined to the view that the best way to deal with religion is as they do in Switzerland and parts of Germany: for the state to levy a small tax on everyone for the support of a Church specified by him. This helps to keep religion mildly unpopular while depriving it of a grievance.

It is obviously desirable that children should grow up with a knowledge of the Bible, because of its linguistic value and because, if not taken too seriously, it is fun. The old prep-school and public-school system of forcing you to listen to, or at least to hear, bits of it every day for ten years, has much to be said for it. It is not such an intolerable imposition as to provoke a violent reaction, while to a child who is receptive on the literary plane it amounts to a kind of half-conscious drip-feed which is wholly beneficial.

Bacon says somewhere that reflexion at first leads men towards atheism, but that further reflexion inclines them again to belief. I think that this is largely beside the point, and that the key is to be sought not in ratiocination but in temperament. It is not to the purpose to tell me – what is certainly true – that more powerful minds than mine have been convinced of the truth of religion. Minds of equal or greater power have been unconvinced. At any given moment in history, the temper of a society will incline towards belief of some kind. But there will always be people whose attitude towards the matter is: 'That is as it may be, and of course I will conform, but it has little to do with real life, at least until I come to be married or buried.'

It gives me pleasure to reflect that the words 'spiritual' and 'animal', so often thought of as opposed in meaning, do in fact express the same root idea: the idea of breath. Let everything that hath breath: praise the Lord: *anemos* as in anemometer: spirit as in respiratory diseases. Insofar as Soviet Communism is, or was, a religion I hold it in no higher regard than any other religion. Some have denied it the name of a religion, but it has all the marks of one. Sacred scriptures, holy ikons, saints and martyrs, a thriving exegetical industry, persecution of heretics – all these it has had. Nor is it less ready to tamper with the evidence and muddy up the wells of truth than any other religion.

It does not hold out to its devotees the hope of a life beyond the grave. But not all religions do this. Judaism lays, or laid in the past, little stress on personal survival. It gave its adherents better reasons for behaving well. Personal survival is, I gather, without meaning for the Buddhist, as it is for me.

Even among the adherents of Christianity I seem to notice less hunger for the prolongation of personal existence than there used to be, and a closer approach to the notion that eternity is not like time only longer, but altogether different in kind. I have never been able to understand why the thought that I will not exist twenty years hence should disturb me any more than the thought that I did not exist eighty years ago.

> Leaf after leaf drops off, flower after flower,
> Some in the chill, some in the warmer hour:
> Alike they flourish and alike they fall,
> And earth who nourished them receives them all.
> Should we, her wiser sons, be less content
> To sink into her lap when life is spent?

I recognize, of course, the instinctive animal struggle against extinction. On the more typically human plane, I recognize, and share, the reluctance to see the last of anything, the melancholy that attends the end of an old song, the moment when someone puts up the shutters for the last time: on the Venetian Republic, for example, or the Irish College in Salamanca, or the Bentley motor company. So powerful is this emotion that few can resist the temptation to hang on to or revive the name and insist that nothing has changed in the restaurant/publishing house/theatre company, even though the person on whom it all depended is dead.

'Having done most of the things I had wanted to do and having seen most of the places I wanted to see, I saw no particular point in living to a much older age.' This observation by Lord Gardiner the Lord Chancellor shocked Victor Gollancz who presumably thought it impious to be resigned to laying down the burden of life. It does not shock me, except to the extent that I deplore the slovenliness of the expression, the conversational cliché of 'no particular point' and the pleonasm of 'a much older age'. If this was indeed the style in which he, by then, was giving his judgments, it was well time for him to fade away.

Curiosity, I must admit, is a powerful incentive, not to sample the delights of the next world, but to wait and see what will happen next in this one. The crucial difference between the time before my birth and the time after it is that one is open to enquiry and the other not. Curiosity may have killed the cat, but it certainly helps to keep me alive.

Nevertheless, there are strong aesthetic objections to the tacking on of a draggle-tailed coda to a life which has already a satisfactory shape. Sequels are seldom very successful, and the wise man knows when to recognize that the party is over.

> Is it not better at an early hour
> In its calm cell to rest the weary head,
> While birds are singing and while blooms the bower
> Than sit the fire out and go starved to bed?

Landor was particularly good in this vein of stoical resignation. He had had a lot of practice. He had begun rather early in life, like T. S. Eliot who wrote of himself as an 'aged eagle' at the age of forty-nine. Landor's best-known expression of it, the 'Dying Speech of an Old Philosopher', was written on his seventy-fourth birthday, and there is no reason to doubt that, as he said, he was 'ready to depart'. But fate kept him hanging about for another fifteen years and he did not die till he was nearly ninety.

Among the poems written in his last fifteen years are at least thirty which are among the most moving that he ever wrote. Embedded in a poem entitled, less than invitingly, 'Appendix', we come upon this:

> This breathes o'er me a cool serenity,
> O'er me divided from old friends, in lands
> Pleasant, if aught without old friends can please,
> Where round their lowly turf-built terraces
> Grey olives twinkle in this wintery sun,
> And crimson light invests yon quarried cliff,
> And central towers from distant villas peer
> Until Arezzo's ridges intervene.

For those lines, and others of equal quality, the years of deafness, poverty and loneliness were, for us at least, not wasted.

Landor is buried, not on the carefully prepared Fiesolan terrace as he had hoped, nor in Widcombe churchyard outside Bath as he later expected, but in Florence to which in old age he had returned, in the cemetery surrounded by swirling traffic to which I came, at last, in 1951. Two years earlier I had the good fortune to attend the second funeral of William Butler Yeats, a remarkable occasion which has, perhaps, not been written about as much as might have been expected.

Yeats died at Roquebrune near the Italian border in January 1939, and was buried there. Ten years later, after the war, it was decided to repatriate the body and bury it in Drumcliff churchyard in Co. Sligo, where he had wished to be buried and for which he had written the epitaph. An Irish frigate, one of the three units of our small navy, was despatched to France for the task: *Banba, Fodhla, Cliodna* or some such name. The quay at Sligo, from which the merchant ships of Yeats's mother's family, the Pollexfens, had traded, was now silted up and unable to take a vessel of any size: so the journey would be by motor-hearse.

Frank MacManus, the director of talks on Radio Éireann, had appointed me to do a talk on the wireless for the occasion, and for that, or for some other reason, I found myself bound for Sligo. Not many people in Dublin had cars in those days, but Bob Collis, a doctor and dramatist, had one, and would take Louis MacNeice and myself. We were both to present ourselves at 7 a.m. at Fitzwilliam Square.

I was on time, as I usually am, but there was no sign of Louis. We knew that he was staying with Tom and Ellie Agnew at Monkstown.

At that time some occupants of whole houses in Fitzwilliam Square still had their garages in the mews. So we went out at the back and were soon at Montpelier Terrace. No sign of life. Perhaps, we thought, they had gone out fishing in Dunleary Harbour. Tom Agnew's Alsatian dogs were baying from behind the door. Perhaps, after all, the occupants were still asleep? Beside the front door, over the area, I noticed a sash-window partly open. By working along the railing and on to the sill I was able to open it and get inside.

37

Nothing to be seen in the front room. I opened the door into the hall, and there, between me and the front door, were the three Alsatians which I had completely forgotten.

I have never been so frightened in my life.

The dogs, however, were in no way perturbed and merely stood placidly regarding me. I had not even, I notice, the presence of mind to realize that if I had quickly shut the door and retreated by the way I had come in, they could not have done me any harm. Instead, I went upstairs followed by the dogs, waving their tails and sniffing. (I have since discovered that barking dogs are quite useless against intruders: once an intruder is inside he is 'all right', and, besides, dogs are cravenly class-conscious.) The bedrooms yielded nothing but teacups half-full of tea or stout. We went back to Fitzwilliam Square to find that, predictably, Louis had come in at the front door as we were going out of the back.

The journey to Sligo was uneventful. We looked in at the Great Southern Hotel and saw only Lennox Robinson sitting at the bar. We went straight on to the Imperial Hotel and there was Lennox Robinson sitting at the bar. (Lennox Robinson, it should be said, was not a man who could have been mistaken for any other man.) By now the expected time of arrival of the cortège was at hand, so we joined the crowd in front of the Town Hall, where a space in the middle was being precariously kept clear by the Gardaí. On the Town Hall steps stood all the notabilities, Lennox Robinson at the back, towering conspicuously over the rest.

When the hearse arrived the coffin looked unnaturally large. I reflected that there were probably three or four coffins altogether, inside each other.

I pass over the commonest topic of discussion for that week, which was the rumour that the French authorities had dug up the wrong man. It was inevitable that the Irish deflationary genius should come up with this one: it was kicked about for a while and then forgotten. It may, of course, be true . . . but, if so, what then? (It has surfaced again since I wrote these lines.)

Outnumbered and outflanked, the Gardaí could not prevent a crowd of shrieking children (who had been given the day off from school) from breaking into the square and swarming around the hearse. I heard afterwards that this gave particular pleasure to Jack Yeats, the poet's brother.

We decided that if we were to have any hope of getting anywhere near the graveyard on those narrow Co. Sligo by-roads we had better leave the official party to get on with their ceremonies and start at once. As a result we were able to park close by and walk to the churchyard. Standing by the grave was Lennox Robinson.

I remember three things about the actual burial. One was seeing Mrs Yeats, Anne and Michael standing there while the Anglican burial service was read: so beautiful and effectual, but, speaking as it does of present grief, in places so incongruous on this particular occasion. Another was seeing Mr de Valera standing motionless under a tree, a little apart from everyone else, in his long black overcoat. The third was being greeted by name by Mícheál MacLiammóir who had met me only fleetingly several years earlier, when I was even more insignificant than I was by now. I was most impressed by this most useful gift and have often wondered whether it betokens a real interest in other people, or is merely a knack.

The following week *Picture Post* (London) carried a full coverage of the funeral, including a photograph of me captioned 'son of Lennox Robinson'.

The rest of the expedition was inevitably anti–climax, though pleasant and in its way memorable, as when Louis suggested we should call on a friend of his, a sister of the actress Joyce Redman, who was living on an island near Killala in the estuary of the Moy. The state of the tide when we got there was such that we made the journey over the sand through the water on a horse-drawn cart. I remember the sister's voice as being exactly like that of the actress: just such a family resemblance as there was between Tyrone Guthrie (at whose desk I am writing this) and his sister Peggy Butler.

I cannot help wondering at the reason for my lack of the competitive spirit. If I see anything in the shape of a competition looming up, my instinct is to withdraw and abandon the position. I cannot believe that I am without my share of ordinary human envy and jealousy, but I am seldom aware of it. It is true that fate has been kind to me in this respect: with one or two exceptions I have had a clear run towards my goals, with no competition in sight. As to the exceptions, I have recognized defeat at the earliest possible moment, and given up. I am not a fighter.

Perhaps the explanation (as with my lack of interest in genealogy) is vanity. Rather than be a loser I prefer not to be a competitor. It is no more than a coincidence that it was Landor who wrote 'I strove with none, for none was worth my strife': my admiration for Landor is founded on other writings which I knew before ever reading that epigram.

Too proud to engage in any contest which I might not win, I have perhaps some temperamental affinity with Landor. The bulk of his work is in a form which nobody else used: the 'imaginary conversation'. It is true that he also wrote verse-drama; but so did everyone during the whole of the nineteenth century, and in this he had no more success than anybody else. I have usually found myself heading for territory which nobody else was cultivating. I suppose that if I gave it any conscious thought, the thought would be not that I would do it better than anyone else, but that nobody else would be doing it.

I have not been much troubled by reviews. If a reviewer seems not to have understood what I was trying to do, I am irritated. But if he does not like my work that is his affair. If he says I am wrong about something he may be in the right: if so, I am grateful to have it pointed out. If not, I can feel superior with a good conscience. On a more philosophical plane I am reminded that neither immediate neglect nor wide acclaim is any guide to what may happen in the fullness of time.

Good manners forbids us, in general, to tinker with or groom ourselves in public. Scratching, picking the nose, exploring the outer ear, are not to be done when in company. Even running a comb through one's hair is to be resorted to only surreptitiously and in an emergency. But there is an exception to this rule. When, as a child, I was taken to expensive hotels, toothpicks were always provided on the dining-table. They were not there for ornament. My father carried his own toothpick, of gold or at least in a gold case, and had, like other diners, no hesitation in using it *coram populo*.

For many years after that, toothpicks seemed to have disappeared from the scene, but now, I am glad to say, they seem to have returned.

We are not the only species to grant a special indulgence to the picking of teeth. Does not the crocodile extend a licence and a safe conduct to a certain bird whose duty and pleasure it is to perform this office?

In the libretto of Purcell's *Dido and Aeneas*, which was written by Nahum Tate, occurs the couplet

> Thus, on the fatal banks of Nile,
> Weeps the deceitful crocodile.

Those who know the opera will remember how the first seven syllables are all on one note, the next up a semitone, down a third for the next five, and up a semitone again for the crocodile himself. This makes it extremely difficult to judge it as poetry. Poor Tate, a Trinity man, is almost the archetypal 'bad poet', slighted (like many others) by Pope, and entered in the DNB as a poetaster.

But is it really such bad poetry? It certainly sticks in the memory, but not, surely, for quite the same reasons as do the classically bad lines of poetry, such as

> Spade! with which Wilkinson has tilled his ground.

There is nothing lame about it. We no longer believe that crocodiles weep, but we do not believe the stuff about phoenixes and unicorns either, and that has not done the poetry any harm. 'Fatal' is a conventional epithet, but not unfitting. 'Deceitful' is appropriate, nor is it otiose. The consonantal and vocalic harmonies of the couplet strike pleasantly on the ear. I am obliged to the conclusion that it is in fact rather good poetry. Its only fault, as far as I can see, is that considering its function in the tragic story, there is a faint overtone of the comic about the crocodile himself. Not for nothing, perhaps, is the famous Russian journal called *Krokodil*. And there is Lewis Carroll's saurian friend, welcoming little fishes in with gently smiling jaws. None of this, of course, will have been in Purcell's mind when he set the words to music. Though there is a weeping crocodile in Spenser, and in Bacon and in Burton, Antony's crocodile in Shakespeare is not to be taken altogether seriously. Today, if a lady, spurned by her gentleman-friend, calls him a rat, that is what we expect to hear. If, ranging further into the animal kingdom, she calls him a crocodile, she is suspected of jocularity.

XVIII

When I hear or read Sam McAughtry's accounts of his boyhood in Belfast I feel deprived: deprived because sheltered. I cannot believe that even the children of the professional classes, even in Belfast, are now protected as we were protected, from the contagion of what for want of a better term I must call 'real life'. I doubt whether I should much have enjoyed the life lived by so many people only a mile or two away; but it is impossible to tell, because I am what my experiences have made me. That life was incomparably richer and more tumultuous than mine. Working-class children grew up much more quickly than we were allowed to do. Our existence was circumscribed, cloistered and colourless by comparison. Yet we were supposed to be the privileged ones. Every effort was being made to give us a better start in life than our fellow-citizens were getting.

How much of what Sam McAughtry recounts really happened to him, and how much of it is an imaginative re-combination of things seen and heard about, I can only guess. But even if we suppose that one-quarter of what he tells is first-hand experience, it is still ten times more than what happened to me. It seems, also, that the rough-and-tumble of working-class street life, whether in Belfast or in Naples, stimulates the mythopoeic faculty, provided, of course, it is there to be stimulated. I repeat, it is impossible to tell. Perhaps I am naturally an unimaginative fellow.

Nothing in our house was ever done on the spur of the moment. Anything which was embarked upon had to be care-fully prepared in advance, precautions taken, contingencies provided for. We never visited anyone else's house except by prior arrangement, and nobody ever came to ours. Present-day children stay overnight in the homes of their friends, and ring up their parents if they remember to do so. We never stayed overnight in anyone else's house, not even by arrangement, nor anyone else in ours. My brother and I were given one bicycle between the pair of us, which, even at the time, struck me as less than lavish. Yet it would not have occurred to us to question this dispensation.

There were not, even, many books in the house. There were two copies of Lord Macaulay's essays; one had been won as a school prize by my father, and the other had been won as a school prize by my mother. There was no copy of the works of Shakespeare. The copy I still possess was bought by me in 1934 at the age of fourteen.

Yet benefits were lavished upon us. We were packed off for three months at a time to expensive boarding-schools. There was no going home at weekends, not even at half-term as happens nowadays. We spent, once, a part of the holidays with a school-friend in Dublin, and the same friend spent, once, part of the holidays with us. We were led to believe ourselves privileged, as indeed we were. We had the best of everything, handmade boots and shoes, dancing-lessons and other such benefits. We hardly ever went to the cinema. If my memory were good enough I could still enumerate the three or four films I saw between the ages of ten and fifteen. We never went round the corner to buy sweets. We had not much taste for sweets. I am grateful for this: I still have quite a few teeth of my own.

I am grateful, too, for the fact that when I was eleven we went by the Pacific Steam Navigation Company from Liverpool to La Rochelle for a summer's holiday at Les Sables d'Olonne where I had, to my own great satisfaction at the time and since, French lessons three or four times a week from a M. Brodu. When I was fifteen my mother, my brother and myself went to Germany. My mother and my brother (who was a year younger than I) went to stay in a hotel at Bad Ems, while I stayed with a family in a village some twenty miles away, so that I was totally immersed in German and spoke no English at all for about six weeks. I am deeply grateful for that. I had prepared for this by doing a year's German at school, and thereby hangs a tale.

At the end of the previous school year I, in common with the rest of the class, was asked whether I wished to do science or German in the next school year. Naturally I opted to do German.

When my father heard about this he was hurt and angry. Why had I not consulted him? Why, I replied, should I have consulted him? I did not need to be told what my own preferences were. Then it all came out. It had, it now appeared, never entered my father's head that I would do anything other than follow in his footsteps and become a doctor. It had, of course, never entered my head that I would do any such thing. Mutual incomprehension was total, and arrogance symmetrically shared.

It says a lot for my parents that when I was eighteen they packed me off to Paris to live with an old couple in St Germain-en-Laye to learn French and get up to whatever wickedness I might have a mind to. Admittedly, I had by then won a scholarship to Cambridge, and so had some right to be taken seriously.

44

My father was very distrustful of my intention to follow a literary career. I do not blame him for this. In his position I should have felt the same. But I am glad to know that in his later years he used to do a little covert boasting when my first three books came out.

In one of Trollope's less well-known novels, *The Vicar of Bullhampton*, he commiserates with the working-class father whose son can get a job and go his own way even before being legally of age, contrasting him with the more fortunate middle-class counterpart who can keep his son in subjection by promising or threatening to give or withhold economic support. It is clear from the context that Trollope is speaking entirely without ironic intent. It obviously never occurred to him that this nexus could be demoralizing to both parties. Our modern ears are shocked to hear the naked realities of power expressed without reserve or apology. The exercise of such power was in Trollope's eyes clearly a duty, though it was no doubt also a pleasure. Yet Trollope valued self-reliance and the determination to stand on one's own feet, not only in young men but even in young women. Part of his merit as a novelist comes from his recognition that the conflict between two goods is as interesting as, and more lifelike than, the conflict between good and evil.

My father had set up a small trust from which I got an income of about £300 a year. It would not, of course, he explained to me when I was about eighteen, be enough to live on, but it would serve as a kind of safety net. Needless to say, I used it to live on. It was not princely, but it could just about be done. Without comparing small things with great, I may borrow the words of Gibbon and say,

> in circumstances more indigent or more wealthy, I should never have accomplished the task or acquired the fame of an historian. . . . Few works of merit and importance have been executed either in a garret or a palace. [I cannot resist quoting the continuation.] A gentleman possessed of leisure and independence, of books and

talents, may be encouraged to write by the distant prospect of honour and reward; but wretched is the author, and wretched will be the work, where daily diligence is stimulated by daily hunger.

In plain English, but for my small private income I would never have been heard of. I would have found some reasonably congenial job which would have absorbed all my energies and I would have written no books but would probably be richer than I am now. The distant prospect of honour has always been more interesting to me than that of reward. Vanity, in other words, is the most powerful of motives. Gibbon again:

In old age, the consolation of hope is reserved for the tenderness of parents, who commence a new life in their children; the faith of enthusiasts who sing hallelujas above the clouds; and the vanity of authors who presume the immortality of their name and writings.

The beauty of this approach is that if, by any chance, somebody does open your book and reads you when you have been dead a hundred years, you are proved right, whereas if nobody does, there is nobody to prove you wrong.

XIX

I was a buyer of books from the age of fourteen onwards, nor would it have been easy by the expenditure of the same sum to have procured so large and lasting a fund of rational amusement. I bought books in Belfast, in Paris, in Cambridge and in Dublin, and began to leave off doing so only when I was in my early thirties. By then I had acquired most of the books I needed: those which I still desired were for the most part beyond my means or were so unlikely to come my way that it was not worth looking for them. Space was now short and it had begun to dawn on me that there were other things in the world besides book-collecting. During the past thirty years more books have come to me in the way of trade than I have actually gone out to buy.

Foolish people sometimes ask me whether I have read all my books. They have all been of use to me in one way or another, and may be of use again, otherwise I would not keep them. I have never bought a book with a view to reselling it at a profit, though I have in fact done so a good many times. During my collecting days there was a wealth of eighteenth- and early nineteenth-century books to be had in Dublin and Belfast, and one could pick and choose. I bought books because I wanted to read them, or as source-material, or for their typographical or bibliographical interest, or for their illustrations, or their beauty, or their bindings or out of sheer caprice as in the case of *Dodd on Death* (see p. 213).

This sometimes turned out very happily. There came my way, as a reviewer, a book of George Moore's letters to John Eglinton, published in Bournemouth, in which Moore told Eglinton, with characteristic hyperbole, that the best English prose ever to come out of Ireland had been written by the Reverend Edward Berwick, and went on to say that he (Moore) had caused the printers to model the Ebury edition of his books on the style in which Berwick's *Apollonius of Tyana* (1809) had been printed. Not long afterwards I came across a copy not only of the *Apollonius* but also one of the same author's *Messala Corvinus and Pomponius Atticus*, and a book which had belonged to Berwick: a late eighteenth-century compendium of contemporary biography with MS notes not only by Berwick himself but also by Francis Hardy, the biographer of Lord Charlemont whose life I myself had also written. These, like all the other books I bought at the time, were to be had for shillings rather than pounds.

There were disappointments and opportunities missed, as well. I dislike buying odd volumes and will not do so except under extreme provocation. However, when I saw the first two volumes of William Hickey's *Memoirs* (of which there are four volumes) I bought them, on the grounds that the first two cannot be described as 'odd'. A day or two later I saw volume

IV in another shop, but refused to buy it on the grounds that it would be 'odd'. Almost immediately I found volume III in yet a third shop, bought it and rushed back to get volume IV but it had gone. Similarly I once failed through hesitation to buy the splendid two-volume edition of Stephens and Catherwood's *Travels in Central America, Chiapas and Yucatan* and later had to make do with an inferior single-volume edition.

Though governed by a very proper distaste for inferior copies I learnt that there were some books that should be bought regardless of condition. Thus I had the sense to buy Shaw's *Pictorial Directory of Dublin* (1850), of which all known copies are scruffy and unattractive, when I had the chance. No second chance was ever offered.

None of this could have been done without plenty of time, of which I then had much more than I had money. The bookshops on the Dublin quays were a rich hunting-ground: Bachelor's Walk, Massey's, Morisy's, Webb's and Fenning's. Before my time, as I know from old photographs, there had been bookstalls along the front of the Four Courts, as in Paris. Edward Massey, who had bookselling brothers and a nephew in Cork and London, would hardly let you into his shop on Crampton Quay and harried you while you were inside, even when you had got up on to a ladder out of his reach. Old Mr Fenning, on Wood Quay diagonally opposite the Four Courts, father and grandfather of booksellers, had a sporting attitude. He worked at night in Cahill's the printers, and was consequently sometimes asleep in bed, but you could look through his stock in the upstairs front room. If you took a fancy to a book which he had not yet looked up and priced, he would toss you for it. You supplied the half-crown and he tossed it. If you won you got the book and he kept the half-crown. If you lost he looked up the book and priced it correctly. In this way I acquired a minute 1713 Dublin-printed *Select Collection of Modern Poems* in contemporary panelled mulberry morocco which I had vamped into good order by Owens the binder in Warwick Terrace. The book had an inscription 'G. N. Plunkett 1876' beneath which I wrote 'M. J. Craig 1946'. A few days

48

later I saw G. N. Plunkett (Count Plunkett) in Greene's of Clare Street, still buying books at the age of ninety-plus. He had filled several flats with books and it was said that his relatives went round clearing out the flats and selling the contents. This kind of story is current about other book-collectors also. On another occasion Fenning had a magnificent Tonson quarto two-volume Milton which I coveted, in exchange for which he accepted a first edition of Coleridge's *Table Talk*. This transaction was probably in Fenning's favour: at least I hope so. I was and am satisfied with my side of the bargain.

On a visit to Birr I bought, for fifty shillings, from old Pennefather, a large album containing, besides eight splendid Piranesis, the whole of Nolli's enormous map of Rome in first-rate condition. After enjoying this for several years I sold it in London, which I regret though I was glad of the money at the time and put it to good use.

The books which abounded in those days have disappeared or become very expensive for a combination of reasons.

The sources have dried up. Fewer country houses are being broken up and their libraries have nearly all been dispersed. The number of books of the period is finite and cannot get larger.

The buying public is larger and better informed than it was. Eighteenth-century books in good condition and available for a few shillings were then cheaper than they ought to have been, even when those prices have been translated into present-day values. If they could have been pushed under the noses of the right customers in London thirty-five or forty years ago they would have commanded four or five times what I paid for them. An obvious instance is that of Irish bookbindings which could be bought cheaply (though not often) before my book about them came out in 1954. At about that time *all* book-bindings, not just Irish ones, started to climb very steeply, because they were being put on the map by Nixon, Hobson, Mitchell and others.

Institutional buyers, such as the newly founded universities and many in America, were setting out to equip themselves with the kind of stock which older libraries already had.

XX

How much of a misfortune is it, I wonder, to be born without talents? The sad fate of many talented people is only too well known: endowed with a facility for drawing or playing an instrument or mimicry, they are tempted to regard themselves as artists or musicians or actors (or indeed all three) and not to work very hard at any of them. Some of these people, especially perhaps in Dublin, become bywords for the great works they were going to do and have never done.

But how I envy them! As a child, I obstinately refused to believe what must have been obvious to everyone else, that I could not draw. I worked hard at it, like a monkey mother suckling a dead baby, till even I, at the age of about fourteen, realized that there was nothing doing. I could, it is true, draw ships and locomotives, though even these not very well, but any attempt to draw a living thing produced a result which looked as though it was made of plasticine. I turned to music. I would be a composer.

Even I knew in my bones that I had no gift for this either. I could not play a bass and a treble at the same time. I attributed this to some neurological defect and transferred from the piano to the violin where, for most of the time at least, there is only one line to worry about. I had little more success: my fingers were not nimble enough. I noticed that the viola, being larger than the violin, was usually not required to do so many things so quickly, often playing only one note to the violin's two, three or even four. That suited me better.

All this time I was taking lessons in harmony and counterpoint, sonata form and fugue and the rest of it. I could understand about this, but I could not actually do it. Looking back, I am reminded of the sentence in Beckett: 'Watt had never smiled, but he had seen other people do it and thought he knew how it was done.'

At the age of eighteen I finally gave up and became a writer. Does that mean that I believed then, or believe now, that since everybody can write, in a sense and after a fashion, writing is easier than other arts? It does not.

Like every other writer, I started with verse. I was to be a poet. I had some gift for this, provided the language was English. In Latin verses, at which my stupider classmates excelled, I was a duffer. Unfortunately I cannot extrapolate this into a theory that those who can write Latin verses have, *ipso facto*, nothing to say, because Landor, a poet whom I revere, devoted a lot of time and energy to writing Latin verse at which he excelled. I wrote verse in English successfully enough to be published in literary magazines for some years, until a well-known London publisher wrote and proposed publishing a book of them, which he did. By this time I was twenty-eight, but the springs of Helicon had run dry for me. I was left with prose, and I have been stuck with prose ever since.

In prose I have little facility: less than I once had with verse. It is true that sometimes, when writing a letter to a friend, I find my fingers running away and I go clattering on for page after page and the result has sometimes a certain vivacity, and I am so well educated that the grammar is generally sound enough.

I attribute any success I have had in prose to the excellent education I was given. Though I disliked my ten years of school, I was taught by a succession of masters who had a real feeling for English and who loved and understood grammar. As a result I love grammar and have a pretty good under-standing of it and can practise it, and by dint of having read and reread a rather small number of really great writers, I have acquired a feeling for sentence structure, balance and euphony. But as a general rule the process of writing is slow and painful because of the difficulty of finding out what it is that I really want to say, and in what order it would be most effective to say it.

One of the results of having very little talent is that you must put everything you have into whatever you do. If you do manage to accomplish anything, there are no reserves left by the time it is done. The sensation is like that of starting out to swim across a rather wide estuary of which you cannot see the farther bank, especially as your head is only just above water.

You seriously doubt whether you will ever reach the other side, and when at last you do, you crawl exhausted up the beach. Had it been a few yards wider, you feel, you would not have reached land. The nightmare of such a misfortune as befell Carlyle or Pirenne, the loss or theft of the manuscript, so that it had all to be done again *ab initio*, is intolerable.

It may be that all this effort, verging on desperation, gives the work some quality absent from that of those whose fluency carries them, or seems to carry them, along, unburdened by care or panic. If so, this will be apparent only to the consumer, never to the contriver.

John Amis says of someone: 'His technique was fabulous . . . and he could get away with practically anything. The result was that he did not work hard enough at knowing his music from the inside.'

I take comfort from that thought.

I sometimes speculate on what it would have been like to have been born to the intellectual purple: to have been a Huxley or a Strachey or a Trevelyan. Would one have looked around and said, 'It will be difficult to shine among that lot!'? And if so, would one have said, 'I may as well not try'? Or would one's situation rather have seemed to be a kind of intellectual springboard from which it would seem natural to try to jump higher still?

There is, or was until lately, a tendency amongst the intelligentsia to affect incompetence in practical matters, and in particular to be unable to do anything with their hands. Some writers, e.g. T. H. White, cultivated the opposite affectation: that of being master of practically all trades, especially the manual. As a result he did some of them very badly, which is perhaps marginally better than not doing them at all.

I myself suffered, especially in my late teens and twenties, from the first of these affectations. Perhaps this was nature's way of concentrating my mind on the task of honing to a fine edge the few mental talents I did in fact possess. It was not till my mid-thirties that I took up doing things with my hands, and turned out to have some talents in those directions and to be able to do things which were and are a source of pleasure: such things as model-making which, being free from all taint of being 'work', give unalloyed enjoyment.

Sixty or seventy years ago, at the time of the Arts and Crafts movement, an attempt was made among architects to re-establish the Greek principle of equality of esteem between hand, eye and brain. When I was young I knew one or two old architects who went back to those times. But now it seems a rule, with few exceptions, that whenever architects put pen to paper they write poppycock of an awesome vacuity unparalleled by any other category of professionals with which I am acquainted. In part this is the result of the disease through which, in the sour words of a wit, the architects for a while produced more manifestoes than buildings.

Of the 'movements' which make the chapter headings in histories of art and architecture, and indeed music, very few were so labelled by those who participated in them in the past. From about 1880 onwards the degree of self-consciousness increases sharply. It is true that in the days of Boileau, Pope and Lord Burlington there was a good deal of theorizing preparatory to, and concomitant with, the production of actual works of art. But there was still some kind of a balance between doing and talking.

For some people, of course, talking is the only kind of 'doing' open to them: orators, salesmen, diplomats and the like. And insofar as writing is a form of 'talking', a writer's characteristic action is to 'talk': i.e. to write.

(In parenthesis, I remember old Joe Hone's indignation when one of the top Nazis was executed or otherwise punished: I think it was Rosenberg. 'All he did was write books,' Joe complained. As a book-writer himself, he should have known better.)

There are several ways of dividing up the arts, from Lessing's *Laokoön* onwards. One favourite division is that between the arts of space, e.g. painting, and those of time, e.g. narrative poetry and music. Efforts have been made, as by the French Parnassians, to smuggle, for example, a poem from one of these categories into the other. A fairly obvious division is

53

between those arts which are mimetic and those which are not. Most painting has usually been mimetic: most music has usually not. This is connected with the distinction between those arts which have subject-matter and those which have not. Neither architecture nor music needs to have any subject-matter: from a distance it is not immediately obvious whether a cupola is over a church or a town hall, and both Bach and Handel, as we know, made the same pieces of music serve both secular and sacred purposes.

A distinction which appeals to me is that between the art which requires large quantities of money – usually someone else's money – and the art which can be brought into being without much expenditure. Obvious examples of the first are architecture, the film, the drama and to some extent the longer forms of literature. The capital outlay in publishing the *Decline and Fall of the Roman Empire* must at all times have been considerable. But you can write sonnets and even novels without spending much money, provided you can in the meantime eat. Most of the prime cost in the manufacture of the *Iliad* must have been food, drink and lodging for the poet/s.

This distinction is cognate with, but not I think quite the same as, a distinction which preoccupies me quite a lot: that between writing a programme and actually making the thing yourself. Musical composition and designing a building are clear examples of writing a programme: until the programme is actually carried out the work itself cannot quite be said to exist. There is, I suppose, a perfectly valid sense in which the sonnet or the novel are merely marks on paper until a reader recreates them by reading them, supplying the scenery, as we all know, himself. But in common sense this is surely a different matter from the realization of a set of drawings and specifications or a musical score. (I know that there are people who can sit down and read a musical score so that the work re-enacts itself in their head as fully as the novel does in that of the ordinary reader; and I know also that, being practised in the matter, I can understand the three-dimensional implications of a set of plans, elevations and sections better than most people, and that some people cannot understand them at all. But these seem to me to be extreme cases.) I learn only today that J. S. Bach's 'B minor Mass' was not performed in his lifetime.

The painting which is physically carried out from beginning to end by the painter himself and by nobody else is perhaps not now a rarity, but it was certainly a rarity during the classic ages. Some paintings, such as those Allan Ramsays of George III and Queen Charlotte, were carried out in batches almost like a small edition of a book. So also with Van Dyck's equestrian Charles I. These are examples of series-produced if not of conveyor-belt art, and the master is half-way between the maker and the director of makers.

It is ironical that William Morris, who was a printer, should have been so hostile to mass production, because printing is the archetypal form of mass production. The good influence of Morris, Cobden-Sanderson, Emery Walker and the like, has been felt, in the end, much more in true mass production than in the somewhat precious productions of the private presses, which, I think on the whole deservedly, died of an excess of self-importance.

There is only a limited value in fixing our eyes on the original purpose of a work of art, because if the work has quality it is almost certain to outlive its original purpose. This applies to town houses, masses by Haydn, pamphlets by Swift, as well as to countless objects now used as, for example, cigarette-boxes, flower-vases, doorstops or umbrella-stands. To understand them it is usually necessary to know something of their original circumstances. To enjoy and value them it is not. We must not allow ourselves to be made to feel guilty because we no longer dance to the minuet.

There are always plenty of people trying to make us feel guilty for enjoying or consuming the art of some previous time in preference to that of our own, on the grounds that the art of our day is more 'relevant' – blessed word! – to our situation than that of the past. This fallacy overlooks the fact, noted long ago by W. G. Collingwood, that any given present always contains a large deposit of the past. The difference between educated and uneducated people is perhaps largely that the educated can sometimes identify and allow for the inherited elements in their ways of thinking and feeling, whereas to the less educated they appear to be part of the order of nature and hence unquestionable.

XXI

In 1938 I was eighteen years of age, spending the spring and summer in Paris – or to be exact in St Germain-en-Laye and later in Versailles – between leaving school and going up to Cambridge.

The most vividly recollected experience I had during that time was a performance of Berlioz's *Grande Messe des Morts* in the great court of the Invalides on the hundredth anniversary of its first performance there. I did not know the work already, which was a pity because one always gets more out of a musical work which one has heard at least once. If I were to hear it now in the circumstances in which I heard it then . . .

The whole of the great court was filled with seating except where the choir and orchestra were at the South end, under the statue of Napoleon which stands, in his characteristic attitude, in the central niche of the upper arcade. Berlioz provided for divided choirs and for brass sections to be dispersed in various quarters. On this occasion, and in this place, all this was done.

As the great Mass proceeded, it got darker and darker, though some discreet lighting had been provided so that Napoleon was still in view. Behind and above his niche some distance away rose J. H-Mansart's dome. At the moment in the 'Tuba Mirum' when the brass all speaks together, a switch was thrown and the golden dome was instantly illuminated. Never was a theatrical effect better justified or more successful.

Four years earlier, in 1934, with a group from school, I had seen *Comus* performed in Ludlow Castle on the three-hundredth anniversary of its first performance in that place. As a result, my schoolfellows had nicknamed me 'Comus' which I resented, foolishly as I now think. I ought to have been pleased to be equated with the sinister magician . . . but back to Paris.

Travelling one day in the suburban train from St Germain to St Lazare, I found myself sharing a compartment with an elderly man in a light grey suit, with flowing white hair, obviously very distinguished and obviously English. We fell into conversation and he asked me my name. When I told him it was Craig, he replied that he also was called Craig. This was no less a person than the great theatrical designer, theorist and graphic artist, Gordon Craig. He had lodgings just round the corner from mine, and there I visited him several times. He gave me a copy of his life of Henry Irving which had just been reprinted, and an introduction to W.B. Yeats. Yeats's daughter Anne kindly arranged a meeting in the foyer of the (old) Abbey Theatre. I cannot claim that it was a very memorable conversation: half of it was taken up with explaining that I was not related to his old friend Gordon Craig, and for years afterwards I kept a matchbox out of which I had taken a match to light the great man's cigarette. I am not ashamed of this pathetic little piece of *pietas*, nor of having deliberately contrived the meeting. I wanted to meet certain great men just because they were great men and, young as I was, I would have those meetings 'under my belt', as it were, for a long time to come. In this spirit I had called on Henry Nevinson, a writer whom I admired, and on James Joyce. A few years later I would not have had the nerve. James Boswell, also as a very young man, went round collecting the scalps, so to speak, of literary lions; and we all know what that led to . . .

On another occasion I was at the first performance of Yeats's play *Purgatory* (the last time, I believe, he ever made a public appearance). After the curtain he came out, very slowly, from the steps on the right, up on to the stage, and made a short speech in which he spoke of his symbolical intention in the play. Then he moved slowly off to the left and disappeared from sight. I heard afterwards that Larry Morrow, a notably irreverent wit of the time, had been heard to say, from his seat in the stalls, 'Symbolical Bill the Playwright'.

Geoffrey Taylor, under whose influence I and several other young writers (and some not so young such as Bertie Rodgers) were for several years, had a somewhat depreciatory attitude towards Yeats. This was not jealousy: he was not, for example, so close to Yeats in age and aspiration as was Austin Clarke, who felt his career to be blighted by Yeats's mere existence. It was more that Geoffrey tended to stand back at a certain angle from sacred cows in general and from Irish sacred cows in particular. Also, Geoffrey came from Sligo – Phibbs of Lisheen he really was – while Yeats's connexion with Sligo was a good deal more tenuous and intermittent in real life than it suited him that the world should think. He was aware of a streak of falsity and pretence in Yeats which there undoubtedly was; but whereas I think (still) that this falsity operated only on one level and was unimportant, Geoffrey thought it pervaded and vitiated the whole of Yeats. He always insisted that Yeats was a minor poet: the way he put it was that the coinage, though not gold, was well graven and would be seen to be such. He did not put the case so well made against Yeats by Yvor Winters: that he had really no subject-matter and consisted of nothing but style.

I must confess that I am surprised that Yeats seems to have escaped the operation of the general rule that writers suffer a slump after their death. Yeats seems to have gone, and still to be going, from strength to strength. It seems to me morally certain that there will, sooner or later, be a slump, though it may coincide with the final bursting of the absurdly inflated balloon of the whole industry of literary commentary.

Ireland seems to have suffered from (or benefited by) this disease out of due proportion. The Yeats, Joyce and Beckett industries are hardly paralleled in England, unless perhaps by the scraping of the Bloomsbury barrel which must now, we can only hope, be nearly at an end.

XXII

The only formal qualifications which I hold are in English literature, but some instinct guided me away from that field, almost from the beginning. It was as though I foresaw the dismal plight of literature dons who are constantly looking for ever more recondite subjects with which to keep their brighter students employed. A very unhealthy state of affairs.

By contrast, Irish architectural history hardly existed when I came sliding sideways into it. There was no shortage of genuine questions which really needed to be investigated, and in recent years my colleagues and I have had to look for suitable people to do jobs which identify themselves very clearly. There is a great deal to be said for arriving on the scene at or soon after the birth of an academic discipline. To put it at its lowest, one is in a position, in large part, to help in framing the rules by which the game is thereafter played. Also there is, to a large degree, a definable body of material to be studied: there cannot be any serious argument whether it exists or not.

This disquisition began with Yeats's funeral, so I return to funerals. Like most of my countrymen, I like a good funeral. I enjoy funerals, to be truthful, more than I enjoy weddings. With funerals you know where you are, and also where, before long, you yourself will be. A funeral closes a chapter, gracefully or otherwise, according to the nature of the case. A wedding, on the other hand, opens up, as Landor long ago observed, a train of awesome possibilities. At a funeral you meet people you know and may not have seen for a long time and are glad to see. At a wedding it is quite otherwise.

XXIII

By far the most widely known of any thing I have written, much better known than any of my books, is a ballad I wrote in about 1940, to a refrain which I then thought to be traditional. It is sung in pubs by people who think it is a piece of folk-poetry and who have never heard of me, which gives me great pleasure. Was it Ennius, the early Roman poet all of whose works have been lost, who wrote

volito vivu' per ore virum?

It has been reprinted countless times, and even quoted in the House of Commons. The genesis of this little poem is worth recording.

In 1938 I went to see James Joyce in Paris, and afterwards had some correspondence with him. Among other things he asked me whether I could track down for him the text of a poem containing the line

May the Lord in His Mercy be kind to Belfast.

I did in the end trace it. It is a very indifferent poem, and the line in question is the first half of a rather lame couplet. It continues

For the poor Irish exile she cheered as he passed.

I have forgotten who the author was, nor can I remember where I found it. The 'poor Irish exile' was Thomas Russell and the line refers to his departure from Ireland after the 1798 Rising. I think I can flatter myself that I have made better use of the line than its original author did.

By the time I did find out the origin of the line it was too late to tell Joyce about it because he was dead. But in the meantime it had worked on my mind and stimulated me to writing my four stanzas.

The most recent of its many reprintings has been in an anthology of Irish religious poetry edited by a priest. It qualifies presumably because the Lord is mentioned in it. I cannot think of any other reason. Another irony of the poem's fortunes is that those people who do know that I wrote it commonly attribute its best-known line to me, whereas it is the one part of the poem for which I can take no credit.

XXIV

There are some things which are not funny stories, which are not even stories at all, which my memory keeps at the ready to be brought out and fired when occasion serves. They are usually quotations from other people, who have put some fundamental truth in a form more forcible than I could hope to do.

For example, when Commander Bill King was a submarine commander in the Second World War, his enemies were: the sea, the Admiralty and the Germans, *in that order*. This is not just a witticism: it is profoundly true and of much wider application than may at first appear.

Thus: as a writer my enemies are: the language, my publishers and the reading public, each of whom plays a part very closely analogous to the terms in Bill King's triad. The language is the medium in which I work, as the sailor works in the sea. It is full of hidden dangers, and it has a will of its own. Like the sailor, I must try to work with it and persuade it to work for me.

It is mostly not their fault that my publishers are my enemies. They are the middlemen who control the logistics of my profession. They embody the constraints and limitations, technical, financial and commercial, within which I have to work if I am to have any effect at all. It is only to be expected that they will want me to do things which I do not want to do, and hinder me from doing what I should, ideally, like to. They furnish my *matériel de guerre*. Like the Admiralty, they are there to help me: but I would not be human if I did not sometimes think the contrary.

As for the reading public, I must identify those few of them whom I can reach, and pick them off or overcome them, separately, one by one, knowing that by far the most important factor in the process will be pure chance.

I have no doubt that there are many other professions in which the analogy holds equally good.

When a writer speaks of his books as his 'children' there is a good deal more to the metaphor than is commonly noticed. As they grow away from him they acquire an independent life. They move in circles in which he has never moved nor will ever move. To other people they appear quite different from how they appear to him. With any luck they may survive him and make alliances of which he has never dreamt.

XXV

Denis Johnston used to say that when asked to give his nationality he was tempted to reply 'Dublin'. I find myself tempted in the same way. Denis Johnston was born in Dublin and I was not; but I do not think that this is in itself of much importance. I am a Dubliner of many years' standing by adoption and by my own choice, and if I belong anywhere Dublin is where I belong. I have as good a right to identify myself with Dublin as Samuel Johnson had with respect to London.

When I left Belfast, where I was born, to come to live in Dublin, at the age of twenty-two, the only part of my Ulster heritage which I was repudiating was the political part. My having been at school in Dublin for five years, less than a decade earlier, had little if anything to do with it. My education, on the other hand, in the wider sense of that term, had everything to do with it.

> A man's education [says Ernst Gellner] is by far his most precious investment, and in effect confers his identity on him. Modern man is not loyal to a monarch or a land or a faith, whatever he may say, but to a culture.

My formal and informal education, till that time, had been Belfast, Dublin, Shrewsbury, Paris, Cambridge, in that order. (It should be remembered, in passing, that children who are sent away to boarding-school spend little more than a quarter of their time between seven and nineteen in the place where they ostensibly 'live'; and, if their parents take or send them away for holidays, commonly a good deal less.) My attitude towards the culture offered to me by educators had been increasingly selective, especially at Shrewsbury, until in Paris and at Cambridge, intoxicated by freedom, I had swallowed everything in great hungry gulps. Or so it seemed at the time. In retrospect I can see that at the unconscious level I was, like everyone else, taking in only what I wanted.

An outside observer, whose ideas of Belfast and of Dublin had been formed by the stereotypes current in journalism and some kinds of literature, might suppose that in moving from one to the other I was going from an industrial town dominated by Orange politics, philistinism and golf, to another town, little, if any, less provincial, inward-looking, decaying, devoted to nationalist ideology and saturated in an atmosphere of oppressive Roman Catholicism and Gaelic linguistic fervour.

The fact was that we lived in the most civilized quarter of Belfast, on the doorstep of the university, not far from the museum, some of whose staff had befriended me. I had taken part, on two consecutive seasons, in an excavation at a crannog in Co. Tyrone which spanned from the Bronze Age to the seventeenth century; I knew a few writers, poets and painters, some my seniors and a few my own age, and the town was not without good libraries, theatrical and musical life and even the occasional literary venture. But the literary magazines of Belfast were precarious and short-lived, much of the cultural endeavour had a provisional and makeshift quality, and those of the not very numerous intelligentsia who did not huddle together for comfort as though beleaguered, held themselves aloof. The things I wanted, and was by now accustomed to, were rather thin on the ground.

In Dublin, by contrast, there was more of everything. The institutions were longer established and more deeply rooted and there was much greater breadth of choice. Dublin, in short, was the capital and had the amenities which only a capital city can offer. It was also, as I thought then and in spite of everything still think, very much more beautiful. It was richer in nearly everything which mattered to me.

In the forty-five years since then there has grown up a cult of the centrifugal. For a hundred years or so there have been people who have fled from the contaminations of Baggot Street, Bloomsbury or the Rive Gauche to wild and remote places such as Connemara, Harrar or Tahiti; but the flight to the provinces is something different and more recent. I have never been tempted by either.

As for the religious complexion of society in the capital, this did not obtrude itself. The great difference from Belfast was in precisely that point. The people I met were of all religions and of none, nor was their affiliation usually at all obvious. If I had needed reassurance as to the Protestant presence, I had only to look around me. Trinity College was still largely Anglican and had a large segment of Northerners both undergraduates and dons. *The Irish Times*, the only paper in Ireland which, in my opinion at the time, printed anything but fairytales, was largely Protestant in tone and has only recently acquired its first Catholic editor. The complexion of the Bank of Ireland, the Rotunda Hospital, Guinness's Brewery, the Royal Dublin Society and many of the more prominent businesses was predominantly, though in no case exclusively, Protestant. There were the two cathedrals and a large number of old parish churches. I had friends, a Protestant doctor and his family, who had a whole house in Merrion Square (one of the last two survivors) and I later came to know a civil servant, also a Protestant, who had a whole house in Mountjoy Square: the only house in which I have ever been formally asked to take a lady down to dinner. The National Monuments Service was, or seemed to be, a Protestant enclave. Much of this is still partly true, forty-five years later.

The reassurance which, if I had felt the want of it, I could have got from all this was neither political nor religious: it was cultural. It went hand in hand with daily association with Catholics in a way which simply did not happen in Belfast.

Among the poets, I already knew Don MacDonagh as a friend of Louis MacNeice's, and before long I got to know Austin Clarke, of the older generation. Lynn Doyle (whose real name was Leslie Montgomery) was an old friend of my father's and had come, of course, from Belfast. The Belfast painter William Conor came often to the Palace Bar, where R. M. Smyllie held his court.

Among my close contemporaries my schoolfellow Bruce Williamson was at Trinity and soon to go on the staff of *The Irish Times* from which he retired as deputy editor.

One who did not go to the Palace Bar was Geoffrey Taylor, the poetry editor of *The Bell*. He was a Sligo Protestant, and so was Smyllie; but there was no love lost between them.

All this, it must be remembered, was a bare twenty years after Independence, and I was, as I still am, two years older than the state. Since then there has of course been gradual quantitative change, most obviously in the virtual disappearance of the Protestant working class. I now know personally only one member of that class. The world of Sean O'Casey is gone for ever. The Protestant working-class families have either died out, or emigrated, or risen into the middle class, or intermarried with Catholics so that their children are, inevitably, no longer Protestant. This is most obvious in central Dublin where most of the city churches have closed or are hanging on by a thread. It is not so obvious in the suburbs where there have even been new churches opened.

In the countryside the picture is different again. Take, for example, a country funeral in the midlands.

The church is small, standing by itself on top of a small hill. It is a plain building, a simple oblong with a shallow sanctuary at one end of it and a tower with four pinnacles at the other. Around and in front of it are a few trees. There is not much room to park cars, but the roads leading up to it, narrow roads, one from each point of the compass, are beginning to fill up. Fearing to be too early, I find that I have to park rather a long way from the church gates, and the church is already full. There is standing-room just inside the tower-lobby.

The name of the parish is Tickmacreevan or Moylisker or Tattykeeran or Almoritia or Drumclamph or Sallaghy or Magheradroll or Termoneeny or Moybologue, and the church is dedicated to St Crumnathy or St Tida or St Gedanus or St Lugadius. The parish name is almost certainly not in daily use for any other purpose and the dedication would be hard to match anywhere else. Both the parish name and that of the saint are corruptions of ancient names in the Irish language. By these signs we know that it is a Protestant church. Catholic churches are called after the present-day names of their localities and have post-Tridentine dedications such as the Sacred Heart or the Holy Family or St Mary of the Angels, and a dedication to an Irish saint is a rarity.

By this time seventy or eighty cars have arrived and the late-comers are clustered round the outside door of the West tower. A few years ago most of them would not have been allowed to come at all, for it is only since the Second Vatican Council that Catholics have been allowed to come to Protestant services. At a guess, two-thirds or more of those present are Catholics, come to show respect to someone well liked, even well loved. I divert myself by speculating on which are the Catholics and which the Protestants. This is more difficult to tell now than it would have been thirty or forty years ago. In many cases it is impossible. It used to be possible to distinguish between us by the fact that Protestants said 'Our Father which art . . .' whereas Catholics said 'Our Father who art . . .' but nowadays everybody says 'who' except me. How long will it be, I wonder, before 'art' goes out of the window too?

The church is like several hundred others, all built by the Board of First Fruits. The South side is lit by three pointed windows. There are no windows in the North wall, so that there is plenty of room for plaques commemorating members of three or four local families: here a JP or DL, there an officer who fell at Inkerman or Balaclava or Spion Kop, a bygone rector or two and perhaps a Mr Jiggins of Jigginstown or a Sir Marmaduke Crosbie of Castle Crosbie: all, by now, extinct. The usual attendance, every third or fourth Sunday, is of twelve or fifteen souls; but there are perhaps two hundred people here today.

Few of them, not surprisingly, seem to know the responses, or where to find them in the Prayer Book, or the tunes of the hymns. But they do their best. They are stiffened not so much by the tiny sprinkling of regulars as by a gramophone which is, rather audibly, set in motion for each hymn. It was playing organ music while we waited for the service to start. At one point it developed a recurrent crack. But at least it did not get stuck in a groove.

Nor, so far, had they adopted the modern fashion of addressing the Almighty as 'you', as though he were a bank-manager.

As every user of the old Ordnance Maps knows, only the churches of the (formerly established) Church of Ireland are marked 'Church' (Ch.). Those of the Catholics are marked 'Cha.' for 'Chapel' and those of the Presbyterians are marked 'Mtg Ho.' (Meeting House). This went on till at least 1910 even though the Church of Ireland had by then been disestablished for forty years.

The Catholics felt, rightly, that their church was being slighted and consequently made a point of calling their churches churches. To be exact, it was the upper bourgeoisie who made a point of this, especially in the towns. The ordinary people went on saying 'chapel' and in the countryside even now, in the 1980s, 'chapel' is in everyday use.

All this, it need hardly be said, is quite without reference to the technical meanings of the two words, where a 'church' is the church of a parish and a 'chapel' is any non-parochial place of worship.

As usual, once it had been resolved that 'church' was the word to use, it was used both in and out of season. In particular the domestic chapels of institutions such as colleges and hospitals were called 'churches' because it was felt that to call them chapels was to downgrade them. The final absurdity came when the whole business was turned on its head. I have heard, and even seen, the chapel of Trinity College, Dublin, referred to as the 'church' because the speaker did not want to slight it by calling it a chapel, especially as, though exclusively Anglican in origin, it is now used for services of three or four denominations including the Catholic.

In much the same way, very large churches such as that at Athlone are popularly christened 'cathedrals' even when they are no such thing. Perhaps in time the word cathedral will acquire the secondary meaning of 'any very large church'.

I lament, in vain, the wholesale destruction of the beautiful Catholic barn-churches of the early nineteenth century in

Ireland. Nobody takes the slightest notice, and they are disappearing or being gutted at an accelerating rate.

I can identify five reasons for this. One is that the parish priest, being celibate and having no posterity, wishes to be remembered, and the easiest way to ensure this is to erect a monument to himself. This is a very natural human motive and I am prepared to believe that it is often unconscious.

The second reason is that it is always easy to get an architect to say that the existing structure is unsafe or has become too expensive to repair or maintain. Most modern architects are afraid of old buildings and often very ignorant of how to treat them. I have seen in Co. Clare a fine church, with a noble Corinthian reredos, which was declared unsafe years ago and is still perfectly sound, sheltering tractors. When the old building is suffering from neglect, whether deliberate or only half-deliberate, this story is readily believed.

There is generally a contractor or builder at hand who may expect to get the job. He is often an influential parishioner.

The fourth cause is perhaps the most difficult to identify. The national feeling of inferiority prevents people from feeling that anything made locally by their own great-grandfathers can be any good, and it goes with the belief that everything new is better than everything old, a superstition no more helpful than its counterpart which asserts the contrary and is frequently held by the same people. The new and shiny is preferred to what is perceived as shabby and redolent of hard times and tightened belts.

Finally, and at present most persuasively, there is the plea of liturgical reform. No matter that in Italy it has not been found necessary to bundle away the altar-pieces, let alone abandon the churches, in pursuance of the directives of Vatican Two. In Ireland, apparently, nothing less will serve, and so the Gadarene rush gathers momentum and soon there will be nothing left.

The want of piety shown by the devout is to me quite shocking. Once a church has been deconsecrated (if there is such a process – or do they simply unlock the tabernacle and walk out with its contents?) they seem not to care what indignities the remains may be subjected to. The behaviour of the Protestant churches, I may say, is little if any better.

I have to confess that in dealing with these buildings in my book on Irish architecture I did not play entirely fair. I told no untruths, nor did I distort any facts. What I did do was to make much of them at the expense of the hard-Gothic churches of the latter half of the nineteenth century. If I gave the impression that they were more numerous than those, this was not altogether misleading given my terminal date-line of 1880. But I went further: I mixed them, both in the illustrations and to some extent in the text, with the Presbyterian churches of the same period, pointing up their similar origins and character. I had of course a political motive in doing so, and I wanted to celebrate buildings which were essentially folk-art, not done out of books nor prescribed by central boards but unselfconscious achievements by the self-denial and devotion of local people.

All in vain. Two of the best were destroyed even as the book in which they were illustrated was going through the press. Not, of course, that I expected to arrest the process by such rarified means. Pamphleteering is one thing: writing history is another.

A historian is not bound to allocate his space in proportion to the quantity of the material which offers itself: quality and significance must be allowed to override mere abundance. It is more difficult to know how much attention should be given to buildings which no longer exist. In Ireland, as a general rule, when a building has gone it is very hard to find out what it was like. If it was of transcendent quality or very influential, I have not resisted the temptation to take it in.

To return to the churches. It is noteworthy that the more liberal and 'progressive' the bishop, the more destructive he is apt to be. The late Bishop Birch of Ossory, a most admirable man, wrought terrible havoc in his diocese and, had he been spared, would doubtless have made a clean sweep of it. Some of the traditionalist old ruffians, by contrast, were content to leave well alone in this sphere and turned their energies in other directions. Virtue is, unfortunately, not indivisible.

XXVI

I do not know whether after-hours drinking is as much of a compulsion as it was during my student days. I suspect not. In those days the pubs shut at 10 p.m., winter and summer. A certain class of person went 'bonafiding' to the licensed premises which were five miles or more from O'Connell Bridge, from which point travellers were deemed to have started their journey. We preferred to drink in the inner city.

Phelan's was on the corner of Werburgh Street and Hoey's Court where Swift was born. There was a bust of Swift in a niche in the pub wall. At 11 p.m. we would knock on the back door and, after a conspiratorial exchange, be admitted. We were served with long black pints and sat in darkness or near-darkness. We were not encouraged to talk. From time to time there would be an alert: the little remaining light would be extinguished and we would hear the sounds of whispered consultation in the hall. We always understood that this was the Guard, whose duty it was to detect and suppress illegal drinking, getting his pay-off.

If we were foolish or careless enough to let our voices rise, or, worse still, laugh, Mr Phelan, who looked rather like Khrushchev with an apron, would come in and say angrily, 'Yiz are not here to enjoy yerselves, yiz are here to drink!' Such was my riotous youth.

XXVII

Cecil ffrench Salkeld was the very epitome of the gifted Dubliner of promise. He was a talented painter, I believe he could write well and play the piano nearly as well as his cousin Douglas Ffrench-Mullen, and he knew about philosophy and could speak several languages. By the time I knew him he spent most of his time in bed, attended by his German wife Irma and largely supported by his mother, Blanaid, with her British officer's widow's pension. They lived in Morehampton Road. Old Mrs Salkeld grew contraband tobacco and, as the Gayfield Press, published my first separate publication when I was twenty-one.

Cecil spent much time in philosophical discussion with his friend (and mine) Arland Ussher, but left little behind him. A few paintings, and most notably a set of murals in Davy Byrne's (done before the pub was gentilified out of all recognition) which took him a long time to do because he was being paid in drinks. Legends about him were numerous. The one I like best is that during the post-war inflation in Germany the local value of his share of his mother's meagre pension was such that he was able to hire a brass band to march in front of him through the streets of Berlin. I am so attached to this story that I have been at some pains not to verify it.

In due course Cecil became the father-in-law of Brendan Behan, which is probably how he is now best remembered, like his contemporary Francis MacNamara, the father-in-law of Dylan Thomas. MacNamara was another great man of promise. He appointed Arland Ussher his literary executor and left behind a MS diary in many volumes. Arland opened one at random and read, 'called on Arland Ussher who talked his usual piffle'. Arland, who used to tell this anecdote with relish, did no further literary execution.

Elpis is the Greek word for hope, and it was also the name of a once well-known nursing home in Lower Mount Street. When I was about twenty-two or twenty-three, I fell ill, in my little top-floor flat on the corner of Merrion Square and Upper Mount Street. I thought it was only flu, but an old family friend Florence Irwin, who had nursing experience, immediately realized that I had jaundice and put me into Elpis. (Jaundice is a very convenient illness because it exempts you from being a blood-donor for ever afterwards: I recommend it.)

John Betjeman's office was just round the corner and he came to see me bearing half a dozen books to alleviate the boredom of illness. One of them was a novel by W.B. Maxwell called *In Cotton Wool*. At that time, and indeed later, John was inclined to overvalue anything which for the time being was out of fashion, so *In Cotton Wool* came very highly recommended. I read this novel and it made a great impression on me. Whether because of the depression which accompanies

71

jaundice or not, I found myself identifying with the by no means attractive or enviable hero of the book, and it took me quite a long time to shake off the self-depreciation induced by this. Maxwell was a run-of-the-mill commercial novelist of the Edwardian period, now quite forgotten. Many years later I came across a book of his short stories, and most of them had not worn at all well.

It was also some years later that I learnt that Synge had been in Elpis during his last illness and had died there, quite possibly in the very room I had occupied. It was a room at the back from which, if you were raised up in bed as Synge was in his last moments, you could see the Dublin mountains.

In such bizarre ways do life and literature sometimes meet.

XXVIII

The climate of Ireland is mild, genial and salubrious, but characterized by excessive humidity.

My father was fond of repeating, with relish, this sentence which he had learnt, parrot-wise, at the age of six or seven, at the National School in Ballymoney in the 1870s. It comes, no doubt, from whatever book was prescribed for universal use by the authorities in Tyrone House, Marlborough Street.

I am all in favour of this. In learning this sentence my father learnt a good deal more than a single rather banal climatic fact which he did not, in any case, need to be told. The vocabulary and the rhythm were what really mattered.

I derive pleasure from the thought that, as I have been told, the Minister for Education in Paris can look at his watch and know, for certain, which book lies open before each French schoolchild of each grade at that particular moment. The centralizing tradition of Richelieu, Colbert and Napoleon seems to me very valuable: to put it at its lowest, it ensures some kind of shared culture. I am glad that so many institutions in Ireland are centralized and not left to local option as they are in Britain, even if the centralization was imposed on us by the British as suitable for subject races but not for home consumption.

When I was a civil servant in Britain I would cheerfully have assented to the proposition Central Government Good, Local Government Bad, because in the sphere of my activity it was so obviously true. Local government was in the hands of publicans, car-dealers and building contractors and reflected sectional interests and prejudices, whereas we in our Olympian detachment dispensed impartial decisions in the best long-term interest of the public. Of course I am caricaturing myself, but that, on balance, is what I thought and still think. It depends, of course, on the subject-matter: with respect to a subject other than historic buildings and ancient monuments I might take a different view. But I would still be, by temperament, a centralizer.

Perhaps it does not matter as much as I think it does. The number of those who have a firm grasp on the core of the inheritance has perhaps always been small, and may be no smaller today than in the past. My son Michael is a good example. He seems to have learnt little at school, but as an adult he is at least as well educated as I am, and in a more balanced way. He is an autodidact, widely read both in the humanities and the natural sciences, on whom an allusion is seldom lost. Though his family background was chequered he was always in an environment in which the things of the mind were respected and books were always available and it was thought natural to read them.

I have sometimes said, partly to shock, that I do not believe in education and regard it as a fraud. This is not altogether true. I think there are two important parts to education. One is to make sure that you learn what you need to know whether you like it or not. About this there can really be no argument. The other is to teach you how to organize knowledge and how to follow up any line of enquiry which happens to take your fancy. The rest can safely be left to the osmotic properties of obsession which makes little boys (in particular) absorb and retain information apparently through the pores of their skin and at an astonishing speed. There is also the occasional phenomenon of the outstanding teacher who can inspire and influence whole generations.

73

Such a one was Frank McEachran who taught at Shrewsbury. He has been modestly celebrated by Richard Cobb and perhaps others, and he wrote half a dozen books which have mostly been forgotten. He never actually taught me in the formal sense, but that did not matter. He used to hold voluntary evening classes in Dante, at which we read the *Divina Commedia* using the bilingual Temple Classics edition.

He had a distinctive gait, walking apparently rather flat-footedly on the balls of his heels, hitching his gown up around him in a much-parodied gesture. How he managed to walk round the whole of Greece, which he did in 1934, I cannot imagine. He had a very distinctive laugh or cackle, not unlike mine. This also was much copied, and it occurs to me now that perhaps that is where mine came from.

He fired countless boys with the love of poetry, by reciting it and inviting us to recite it with him: all the way from

> Bricks and straw, bricks and straw
> A man may not marry his mother-in-law

through

> No doubt but ye are the people,
> and wisdom shall die with you.

The seraphim in Isaiah:

> Each
>   one
>   had
>   six
>   WINGS
> With twain he covered his feet
> And with twain he covered his face
> And
>   with
>   twain
>   he
>   did
>   FLY!

and

> Diuturnity is a dream and folly of expectation

to

> *E la sua volontate è nostra pace.*

Very sensibly, he began at the right end, with the incantatory mode which lies at the very origin of poetry. Learn and enjoy the sound first, and afterwards the meaning will unfold itself. Eliot, Auden, Rimbaud, Calderon, Victor Hugo, Ezra Pound, Lucretius, Homer, Christopher Smart, Racine – from all these he extracted gobbets some of which he later published under the title *Spells* (1954).

He called himself a liberal but was in fact an anarchist, and he adhered steadfastly to the economic doctrines of Henry George, 'Single-Tax' George, who advocated the taxation of land values. To this day I more than half believe in this gospel.

It certainly seems to me axiomatic that nobody can 'own' land in the sense that we own a book or a motor-car or a toothbrush. We are so obviously only temporary tenants or trustees that the point would not be worth labouring but for the fact that some people think, or at least feel, otherwise. There was recent corroboration of this from Neal Ascherson, who relates how he pointed to a mountain in Scotland and remarked to the Israeli journalist who was travelling with him that it belonged to the Duke of —. The Israeli was baffled. 'How can a mountain possibly *belong* to anyone?' How indeed? Presumably, though, the journalist would assent to the proposition that the land of Israel 'belonged' to the Israeli people. Not everybody would agree with him.

Kek (as he sometimes signed himself), like many other great and good men, was implacably opposed to the power of the state. I think he believed that if land values were properly taxed the state would, as the Marxists used to say, 'wither away'. In one of his books he alludes slightingly to Hobbes. Having been a servant of the state I take a different view. I don't think that Kek gave the state enough credit for what, to me, is its most important function: to defend the weak against the strong. How much of the voluminous legislation passed from 1850 onwards is for the purpose of protecting us from businessmen, and how necessary it was and is.

I notice, reading one of his books which I had never seen at the time when I knew him, that he is suspicious of music and of architecture, and denies them both the full status of art. It is easy to see why. Both arts, having no necessarily explicit and translatable content, lend themselves easily to the emotional exploitation of the uneducated masses. In *The Civilized Man* (1930) he has a strangely prophetic sentence:

> What is characteristic of music is the absorption of the intellectual and rational element in a man into the emotional, and a consequent stress on emotion which is dangerous to the mental calibre of any but the strongest character. It is, moreover, this stress on emotion which increases as we descend from the highest to the lowest forms of music, from the sublime to the purely sentimental, which has given rise very probably to the conception of the artistic temperament, a conception quite alien to any culture epoch which we know of in the past.

Surprisingly (at least to me), he couples sculpture with tragedy as 'the highest manifestations of the human spirit'. I suspect that when he did classics at school he swallowed too uncritically the three Sacred Ps of public-school classicism as it was presented at the time: Pericles, Phidias and Plato. All three have been exposed to a good deal of destructive criticism since then, and none of them survives undamaged in my pantheon nor, I suspect, in that of anyone of my generation. Fifth-century sculpture and fifth-century statesmanship no longer attract the adulation which was once thought to be their due.

XXIX

I am a great taker of sides. Not in sport, but in practically everything else. I have to admit that even I prefer Cambridge to win the boat-race, but this is because I went to Cambridge and have a strong attachment to Cambridge as opposed to Oxford: politically, theologically, architecturally and in every way. And why wouldn't I prefer the home of poetry and common sense to that of lost causes and screaming tyres? Yet it all came about by accident. I went to Cambridge only because I happened to get a scholarship and that was only because of the way in which the scholarship examinations were then arranged. None of my family had ever been to Oxford or to Cambridge so they were all the same to me. As far as I remember you got two, or perhaps three, chances of getting a scholarship. The colleges were arranged in groups: about three groups to each university. All the Cambridge groups and one of the Oxford groups held their exams in, say, November, and later in the academic year the remaining Oxford groups held theirs. It therefore made sense to try first for Cambridge so that if you failed you had one or two more chances to try for Oxford. Then there was the question of which college to put first in my order of preference: as I knew nothing about any of them this could only be done on the blindfold-and-pin principle. The sound and shape of the name of Clare appealed to me, so I put it down first.

Clare, as it happens, did not particularly like the look of me, but Magdalene awarded me a major scholarship; so that was that.

I remember well my first arrival in Cambridge to sit for scholarship examination. It was a foggy winter's evening and the taxi deposited two or three of us at the corner of the lane between Caius and the Senate House. The air was thick with the clangour of bells, and all the time I was in Cambridge I have a recollection of the church and college bells tolling out over the Fens.

I was lodged in somebody's rooms in Memorial Court. Nothing was locked – nothing was ever locked in Cambridge in those days. There was a large box of Turkish cigarettes to which I helped myself. Every day for a week I went to the Great Hall of Trinity and sat under the portrait of Henry VIII and not far from that of Charles Villiers Stanford, and did my papers. In the evenings, I think, we dined in hall in Clare. The contrast with school existence was unimaginable. Everyone, from dons to porters, called me 'Mr Craig'.

I cannot imagine how I would have felt if I had failed to get a scholarship. As it was, though my school usually got twelve or fifteen classical scholarships, mine was a dull year and they got practically nothing. Except mine which was in history. *Schadenfreude* is a most intoxicating emotion and I indulged it. When next year, I went up to Magdalene I was given the rooms Parnell had occupied. This was the doing of my tutor, Frank Salter, a history don and a lifelong liberal, for whom I retain an abiding affection.

My father could not conscientiously sign the paper saying that he could not afford to send me to Cambridge without my scholarship, so that by the regulations I was credited with rather less than one-third of the value of it. My father could therefore still make noises from time to time about how much my education was costing him, but the noises were rather more subdued than before.

He was, increasingly, in the position in which many successful men find themselves: faced with a son whose education favoured tastes and aptitudes progressively divergent from his own. There is a poem by Kipling about a dying shipbuilder, 'The *Mary Gloster*', in which this situation is very powerfully expressed. It was aggravated in my father's case by the fact that he was forty-seven years older than I, so that the 'generation gap', which has perhaps been more conspicuous in our time than before, was for us more intractable still.

My scholarship was mostly the result of good teaching: officially by Murray Senior who managed the rather small History Side, unofficially by Frank McEachran who rallied all the avant-garde elements around him. The masters were rather bitterly divided into the Left Book Club types and the Old Guard. A year or two before me, Murray Senior had had two pupils more distinguished than I, Richard Cobb and Richard Wainwright, who went on to be respectively a Professor of French at Oxford and a Liberal MP: but my little triumph helped as well.

At the end of my first year the college authorities suggested that I should transfer myself and my scholarship intact to the English School, which I did and was glad to do. I have now, as it happens, come round very nearly to the view that English should not be a subject with a Tripos all to itself. Just what, with hindsight, I think I ought to have read at Cambridge I cannot readily say. Probably a combination not very unlike the English Tripos of my day, but more rigorous and with more scientific content.

Some time during 1939 I ate some pâté de foie gras which had been intended not for me but for Sigmund Freud, who was by then too ill to eat it. This took place at the table of the G. E. Moores in Cambridge. How the consignment, which someone had sent to Freud as a present, found its way from Maresfield Gardens to Chesterton Road, I do not know: but so it was. Even as my teeth closed over it I was aware of its intended destination, and I remember feeling greatly awed by the experience.

(Awe is an emotion which I have not felt very often. I remember most vividly feeling it when I first set eyes on the triple serpent in the At Meidan at Constantinople, knowing that this was the identical bronze serpent which had supported the tripod dedicated by the thirty-one cities of Greece after the defeat of the Persians at the battle of Platea in 479 B.C. Shortly afterwards, in the Topkapi Museum, I saw the actual head of one of the serpents, the only one which survives. Goethe's waistcoat, Napoleon's inkstand and other such memorabilia, have no comparable power, at least not over me. But the Stony-hurst Gospel, as I will tell, has.)

Forty-odd years ago degree-conferrings or Commencements in the Senate House at Cambridge or in the Theatre of Trinity College, Dublin, were unruly occasions. The Chancellors and other bearers of office stuck doggedly to their lines, while rabbits, pigeons, white mice, balloons, raspberries and even fire-crackers enlivened the proceedings, to the accompaniment of ironical cheers and catcalls.

Nowadays, in Trinity at least (I cannot answer for Cambridge), all this is at an end. The ceremonies are enacted with a solemnity formerly found only in provincial universities. The young men and women, dressed up as at no other time in the year, gowned, mortar-boarded and clutching their scrolls, are watched by their admiring parents in a reverent hush and afterwards photographed.

What has happened to cause this depressing transformation? The answer lies, I think, in the presence of parents. They have not, for the most part, themselves been to university. This, for them, is a 'Great Occasion' and they would think themselves defrauded if they did not get their money's worth. But their money is not worth what it was, and nor are the degrees. The paradox is that in proportion as the substance is devalued, the outward and visible forms become more solemn and portentous.

The same, or a similar, law may be observed at work in other contexts. I used to be puzzled by the fact that, whereas the manuscript Journals of the Irish Parliament were bound in volumes of unparalleled splendour and richness, those of the – much more important – British Parliament were treated much more modestly. The clue was suggested by a friend who pointed out that the patents of Irish peerages were much more grandly engrossed than those of British peerages. An English or British peerage was something worth having. An Irish peerage was decidedly second-best: a cheap way of paying off time-servers, and everybody knew it. The Irish Parliament was relatively impotent, but till 1800 it sat in a much grander building than the ramshackle and higgledy-piggledy palace of Westminster.

One of Parkinson's laws says, if I remember right, that an institution is fitly housed only at the point of death, or words to that effect. *Post hoc* is sometimes also *propter hoc*: there have been some recent instances of organisms spending millions on housing themselves and then promptly folding. But not always. Sometimes the writing is already on the wall while the wall is being built. New Delhi is perhaps the most spectacular example. This is the converse of the law which says that most of the best work is done with extemporized equipment in makeshift premises.

David Cannadine in *The Invention of Tradition* (1983) has demonstrated how the much-vaunted British skill in managing great ceremonies of state, supposedly the fruit of many centuries of monarchy, is in fact a thing of yesterday, but recently perfected and in large part recently invented. Down to late

Victorian times this side of their public life was haphazard and perfunctory, and they were perversely rather proud of this.

In one of his essays Aldous Huxley notes that public religious ceremonies in Southern Italy are ramshackle and ill-organized: Latin Catholics, he says, are like the 'Old Man of Thermopylae/Who could never do anything properly'. He draws the moral, I recall, that they were so totally believing, so whole-heartedly immersed in their religion, that such details were of small account: the inward substance mattered so much more than the outward show. When the English really had an empire on which the sun never set, they had no need of televised coronations. In those days they were content to call their country 'England': now, forsooth, it has become 'the mainland'; and the royal soap-opera has become a staple of the tourist industry.

XXX

The biological fallacy is now out of fashion in art history. In identifying it, naming it, and attacking it, seventy-odd years ago, Geoffrey Scott no doubt performed a useful service. He came at the right time. Today we tend to see the totality of things that happen as a complex wave-pattern with intersecting cross-currents, so that ·when one thing is rising another is falling, and the unexpected is constantly happening. We think more of change than of decay. What used to be called decay we now call change. Where Baedeker (for instance) saw only the end of the Renaissance, the end, indeed, of Italian art, after which everything is labelled 'debased' or not mentioned at all, we see the emergence of Mannerism, then of Baroque, then of Neo-Classicism, and so forth. It is a gain in understanding, and has brought a great increase in enjoyment.

Yet it is surely undeniable that in many fields of human activity there is a primitive and experimental phase, followed by one of assured maturity, followed by a silver age which may be characterized by carelessness, or commercialism, or by being overblown, or diluted, or repetitious, or plagued with any one of a dozen 'vices' as (invoking the 'ethical fallacy') we are apt to call them. Yet this third phase may itself, if looked at from another angle, be the chrysalis-phase of something quite different.

This is very clear in, for example, the evolution of the steamship. Down to about 1890 steamships were still sailing-ships with engines. They were square-rigged, their deck-houses had a tentative character, they often had clipper-bows and bow-sprits, and in other ways they had not yet gained their aesthetic independence. But for the next seventy years or so they changed very little. This period, from about 1890 to about 1960, was also the period during which they most explicitly embodied the aspirations of the societies which had created them: more so, even, than contemporary public buildings, and certainly with a far surer touch.

There were, of course, changes, which were mostly for the better. Some were internal, such as the change from the recipro-cating engine to the turbine, and from coal fuel to oil. Both of these affected, in the main, the larger and faster ships, and the mass of smaller workaday vessels, which were very beautiful, were not touched by them. Subdivision for safety was improved, and so was the provision for passengers and even for the crew. All through the period the diesel engine was encroaching pro-gressively on the domain of steam, gaining ground first in the smaller sizes, but with setbacks and false starts among the larger.

There were some externally visible changes as well, such as the supersession of the counter stern by the – to me much less graceful – cruiser stern. Funnels became less numerous, for good reason, and fatter, for no good reason other than mere fashion. Lifeboats in gravity davits may not look quite so nice as boats stowed under radial davits, but that was a great gain in safety and efficiency. The 'soft nose', graceful enough in its way, took the place of the bar stem, and there were good practical reasons for this. But, taken all in all, it was a 'classic' period in which one knew what a ship ought to look like.

After the middle of the present century the rot set in and spread with increasing rapidity. No freakish shape was too bizarre to be tried out, and there was hardly ever any rational pretext for what was done. The original aesthetic crumbled away under the impact of a capricious and arbitrary futurism. The latest manifestation is the covering of the sides of ships with legends a hundred feet long or more, in letters twelve feet high, turning the ship into a floating hoarding. A new aesthetic is no doubt struggling to be born, but it will have no connexion with the old one.

The same thing happened with motor-cars, but a good deal more rapidly. From the beginning till shortly before the First World War not only was the motor-car visibly a 'horseless carriage' but it was also to a large degree experimental. Different makes were genuinely different because their makers were pursuing rival systems and nobody yet knew which option would come out on top. The Model T Ford, for instance, of which fifteen million were sold, used a system which had, in the event, no future. But by the beginning of the vintage period, in effect by the eve of the world war, the motor-car had settled into the form which the French call *classique*: the engine is in front, the driver sits behind it, it is water-cooled, he steers by a wheel and not a tiller, the drive is through the back wheels, the electrics are largely standardized, the petrol tank in all but the smallest cars is at the back, and so on. There is a good deal of brass and aluminium to be seen, and the various organs are separated by enough space for owner-maintenance to be an inviting and agreeable operation. A good deal of the machine is made or at least finished by hand, and the standards of design and finish approximate to those to be found on the railways or at sea.

With all this went an appropriate aesthetic, so that even now, when a child draws a motor-car, it may well have a 'radiator', a 'bonnet', mudguards and even perhaps a visible spare wheel. It was quite clear where one element ended and another began.

This lasted for about fifteen years. Then everything changed with great rapidity. The great Wall Street Crash of October 1929 accelerated technical changes which were already on the way. Most of the changes were for the convenience of the manufacturers or to reduce costs, but of course they were all presented as 'improvements', which some of them, inevitably, were. Pressed steel took the place of cast aluminium and elektron, chromium plating was substituted for nickel-silver, the separate chassis soon disappeared in favour of monocoque construction, as repairable components yielded to bolt-on replacements, and instead of the laborious coach-painted finish the vehicle was sprayed with cellulose.

In aesthetic terms the effect, which was not immediate, was for the separate parts to coalesce into a single whole. The headlamps sank into the wings, the petrol tank and the spare wheel disappeared from view. The bonnet ceased to have any sides, sometimes with disastrous and dramatic results, as when a front-opening bonnet, inadequately shut, flew open and upwards at speed. The radiator was first encased in a separate chromium-plated casing and was later replaced by a dummy perched out in front of the wheels, which in turn, save with Mercedes-Benz and Rolls-Royce, was superseded by a grille.

The most persistent skeuomorph is that of the mudguards which faded away very gradually and have even now not entirely vanished, reappearing from time to time as though 'drawn' on the sides of the doors, or as a dip or 'hiccup' in the sill line just forward of the rear wheels. The grin of the Cheshire Cat.

Those cars in which this process was still incomplete look very unhappy indeed: as well they might, being neither one thing nor the other.

One paradoxical and unwelcome result followed from technical change. Whereas during the vintage period the open car cost less and went better than the saloon version, this was very soon the other way round. When the car was basically a chassis, light open bodywork kept the weight down and the performance up, and saloon coachwork was heavier and dearer. But when some of the stress was taken through the roof structure, as it now is in nearly all cars, the only way to make an open car was to saw the upper half off a saloon, strengthen the underbody to restore rigidity, and spend even more money on a 'soft top' by which time the whole thing was heavier than the original and therefore did not go so well. This suited the ordinary customer but did not suit those who drove for pleasure: a race now almost extinct.

XXXI

I wish I had taken a photograph of Quaritch's window in Grafton Street, London, during the week or so in 1954 when it contained nothing but three copies of my bookbindings book: one in the centre and one on each side of it. Never before or since have I been made so much of.

There are some people for whom civilization is typified by a room rather under-furnished than over-furnished, in which a very few pictures are carefully hung on spaces otherwise blank, and a small number of bookshelves, if admitted at all, are rigidly subordinated to the whole austere scheme. There are others for whom civilization means having books in every room and in the passages as well. I was about to say that I belong to the second school of thought, when it occurred to me that the distinction is of another kind altogether. Both concepts are perfectly valid in their way, but one of them represents art and is ordered and static, while the other represents real life which is the world of becoming, in which all the work is done. One is for looking at, the other for living in.

The arrangement in Quaritch's window was very beautiful, especially to my eyes, but evanescent. That is why I wish I had photographed it.

XXXII

Why do I get so much pleasure from the thought that Yeats could not spell? Certainly not from any desire to see the great man taken down a peg. From the age of twelve to that of forty-five or more, I believe I never made a spelling mistake: so I know just how little it means to be a naturally good speller. It comes from quickness of perception, a retentive memory and a desire to conform (in this respect if not in others).

Also, I think, a sense of history. The spelling of English, like that of French but unlike that of, say, Italian, is 'historic': that is to say it is littered with clues to the origins and previous forms and sounds of the words in use. For people like me, a word is not fully apprehended until it is spelt. Even when listening to a foreign language I find myself mentally making the effort to spell the words as I hear them. Though it is no doubt theoretically true that 'all speech is spoken speech', the history and spelt form of words colour the way in which they are apprehended in a long-literate society such as ours. Remember the Patsy Chapel.

Does this mean that Yeats lacked a sense of history? Certainly not. His sense of history was very powerful but different in kind from that of ordinary people. I remember once defending, rather feebly, to David Greene, the value of a classical education, and putting forward the argument that it helped one to write better in one's own language. Nonsense, said David, and pointed out that Yeats, who wrote superbly both in prose and verse, was ill-educated and virtually illiterate. I was annihilated and had not the presence of mind to make the obvious retort (which occurred to me on my way down stairs) that Yeats, unlike the rest of us, was a genius.

So what is the source of the pleasure to be had from Yeats's misspellings? In part, doubtless, the enjoyment of incongruity, as in the Patsy Chapel. In part also a certain benevolent amusement such as we get when watching the mistakes made by small children, but inverted: we are looking not down from above, but upwards from below, and reassured by evidence of his fallible humanity. More than that, there is an inventive and fantastic quality about some of his misspellings lacking in those of lesser writers. He would have been at home in the seventeenth century.

This reminds me that I once passed over an opportunity which many would envy. Not very long after Yeats's death I saw in Greene's bookshop a copy of *Coryat's Crudities* which had belonged to Yeats. It was the Glasgow edition of 1905. It was not expensive and I could have afforded it. But I do not much care for early twentieth-century 'press-books' and I let it go. I now know that books from Yeats's library are so rare as to be virtually unfindable.

This, in turn, reminds me of an acquisition which I did make. In a bookseller's shop in Cecil Court, London, I made what was then my routine enquiry, whether he had any Landor. Not exactly, he replied, but if I was interested, there was something else. To go back a little: Stephen Wheeler had in 1897 produced a book of letters and miscellaneous writings by Landor which represented the contents of a desk. My bookseller-friend had, in a mahogany cigar-box, those of the contents of that desk which Wheeler had not been able to publish: to wit, two pairs of Landor's spectacles – his reading-glasses and his sun-glasses – a few curls of the hair of Pomero his dog, and the tail of the same dog. These he gave me, and I have them still. The tail is very feathery and not at all repellent.

Some time later there was some correspondence in *The Times Literary Supplement* concerning the whereabouts of the grave of Pomero in the garden of a house in Queen's Square, Bath. For some unknown reason I was too lazy to write and tell them that wherever the rest of the dog's body might be I knew where the tail was. I also missed the opportunity of lending these mementoes to the Warwick County Museum for their Landor Centenary Exhibition in 1964. But in my will I have left them the box and its contents.

XXXIII

There is a phrase near the beginning of *The Trembling of the Veil* about 'artists who considered religion at best an unimportant accessory to good architecture'. I would feel myself at home among those artists but for a nagging doubt about the word 'unimportant'. The word catalyst is, like other words drawn from the physical sciences, much bandied about today, not always in its precise sense. A substance, the presence of which is necessary for a given reaction, but which itself undergoes no permanent change, is a catalyst. The analogy is not exact – analogies seldom are – but as an accessory before the fact of much great art, especially in architecture and music, religion can hardly be called unimportant.

If we were to subtract from architecture and music all those works which have, at least ostensibly, a religious content, the ranks of the masterpieces would be perceptibly thinned. It is, of course, essential to make the distinction between works produced at a time and in a place when the Church was in effect the only available patron, and works produced in a freer environment in which the religious content is chosen rather than imposed.

I think that most good judges hold, as I do, that the Mass in D (*Missa Solemnis*) is a more satisfactory work than the Ninth Symphony. It does not of course follow that the superiority of the Mass comes from its religious content, except, I suppose, in so far as the canon of the mass was already familiar to all composers and had its own in-built drama, whereas in the symphony Beethoven was inventing a hybrid form and trying to extend the frontiers of the possible. There remains, even to the sceptic like myself, a residual feeling that the brotherhood of man, for all its nobility, is, as an idea, banal and coarse by comparison with the awe and reverence evoked by the Sanctus or the Agnus Dei. But perhaps the difference is really that which comes from having a ready-made programme? Or is it perhaps that the verbal formulae are ancient and beautiful and not fully understood, as Coleridge hinted; more moving, and a better starting-point for music loaded with emotion?

We all know that both Bach and Handel, who were genuinely devout, were quite prepared to transplant whole movements and not always solemn movements at that, out of operas into their oratorios and even their masses, endowing with a fresh set of devotional associations something which started life quite otherwise. And there is a moment in Haydn's jaunty setting of 'Qui Tollis' in the 'Creation Mass' where he suddenly brings himself up all standing, as though remembering that he is in church. It was precisely because these composers were personally devout that they were able to do this. We cannot conceive

Verdi or Berlioz or Fauré doing so. Yet, paradoxically, Verdi used to be reproached by those who did not know better for writing operatic music under a religious guise. By the same token, Pugin and Ruskin and Co. complained that the churches of the Renaissance were deficient in the numinous. They went so far as to deny them the name of Christian architecture. Milton, a great classical artist, gave the requirements most succinctly:

> . . . the high-embowèd roof,
> With antique pillars massy proof,
> And storied windows richly dight,
> Casting a dim religious light . . .

We are apt to forget that Milton, for all his republicanism, had one foot in the Middle Ages.

Fergusson argued that all solemnity in architecture derived from the architecture of the temple and that when such solemnity, as for example the orders or the dome, was borrowed for secular purposes, whether personal or municipal, it was simple appropriation and could never amount to more than that. Thinking of Louis XIV, one is inclined to agree. It seems inevitable that the mausoleum at Castle Howard should be a better building than the house itself.

If the questions raised by religion are real, they are of transcendent importance. But we do not know whether they are real or not. Perhaps this automatically makes them important. A. W. Kinglake was of this opinion. All churches, he said, should display, like a 'government health warning', the inscription IMPORTANT IF TRUE. The topic was more profoundly treated by Pascal.

My dislike of religion springs not so much from disbelief in its tenets (though I have plenty of that) as from having observed that, generally speaking, religion makes people behave badly. Some of the grosser forms of this are only too well known, especially in Ireland. I cannot now recall who it was who said that there is nothing like the conviction of possessing the truth to make people misbehave. That is obvious, and in a way excusable. But the all-pervading dishonesty of mind which religion engenders infects the dealings of the religious in other spheres: for example, in the matter of undertakings given with respect to the use and treatment of buildings and, indeed, funds. I have found some clerics to be quite unscrupulous in such matters. And indeed one can see why.

If I had the ordering of Hell I would assign a special place in the seventh circle for the Reverend J. W. Cunningham, who refused to allow Byron's daughter Allegra to be commemorated in the parish church at Harrow.

When I hear the truths of religion (whatever they may be) enunciated from a pulpit or over the wireless I instinctively disbelieve them. There is a religious voice, and an advertising voice, and a political voice, all of which are instantly recognizable even before you have heard what they are going to say, and which immediately compel disbelief.

If I am subjected to the presentation of the same 'truths' by, let us say, Poussin or Brunelleschi or Beethoven, I am receptive to them, and even my 'beliefs' (such as they are) are modified. Many years ago T. S. Eliot noticed this and denounced it. For him the 'ordination' of the artist to fill a vacuum of unbelief was an aberration. I suppose he would have said that the parsonical voice was a stumbling-block put in the way of the path towards faith. All I can say is: it's a mighty funny way of going about things. But God, we are assured, moves in a mysterious way.

Fortunately there are works of art such as the last two piano sonatas of Beethoven, or Haydn's opus 76 no. 5 quartet, which deliver a message of equal profundity to which no religious tag is attached. And after all, perhaps the Hawksmoor mausoleum is really 'about' solids and voids rather than about death?

The claim of being rational, even the exclusive claim of being uniquely rational, has been made, at one time or another, for almost every kind of architecture you care to mention: for the Gothic, for the Classic, and most obviously for the 'Modern Movement' of recent memory. The claim is in each case perfectly justifiable. Why, then, the layman wants to know, is there no agreement on what is rational architecture?

The answer is, of course, that the question is improperly formulated, as so many questions are. The questioner has forgotten, or never knew, the dictum of Hume, the arch-rationalist, that 'Reason is and ever must be the slave of the passions.' Reason, in other words, can tell you neither what you want nor what you ought to want; but once you have decided what you want, reason can tell you how to get it.

It is, of course, not quite so simple as that. When people speak of 'rationality' they have usually something more in mind than the mere adaptation of means to ends. Regularity and symmetry seem, to some temperaments, to speak the very language of reason: much as the interlocking clock-like mechanism of a play by Racine seems more 'rational' than the diversions and loose ends which so abound in Shakespeare.

The 'Modern Movement' borrowed, from the classical mode, the cleanness of outline, the repeated module, the horizontality, while from the practice of the nineteenth-century Gothic revivalists it borrowed the informal groupings of mass which were – or so it was proclaimed – dictated by the programme.

The 'reasonable man', that abstraction beloved of lawyers, is not a logician but an *homme moyen*, and this is the sense in which many people understand the idea of rationality in architecture: something, for example, neither extravagant nor mean but moderate, like a 'reasonable' price. On this count eighteenth-century street architecture scores very well: hence the gibe that so many 'Modern' architects prefer to live in 'Georgian' houses.

XXXIV

Considering how many other ways there are in which a man may spend his life creatively and usefully, it may seem surprising that I should hold book collectors in high esteem: but I do. I have known three or four great collectors in my time, and been proud to do so, as well as several people more like myself who were, incidentally and inevitably, collectors of a kind, such as John Carter and John Hayward. One of the most agreeable of the first category was Henry Davis, who spent his working hours making, I think, electric cables at Leytonstone. Contemplation of his collection, which he kept in his house in Regent's Park, was a great joy and he was generous in sharing it with visitors. He left the bulk of his library to the new University at Coleraine, not because of any personal connexion but simply because the university was newly founded and would therefore be without old books.

Beyond a certain point collecting cannot be practised without wealth, and some of the great collectors I have met, such as Albert Ehrman, Benjamin Iveagh and Chester Beatty, have been very well-to-do. But it is nice to see great wealth being rightly used: I get no satisfaction from seeing a rich man make a fool of himself.

Beautiful as a collection may be when fully formed – if that phrase has any meaning – I hold the view that nine times out of ten, or even more, the right thing to do with a collection at the owner's death is to disperse it. And on the whole I hope that, at the auction, some at least of the choicest items will be bought by collectors rather than by public institutions.

I met Chester Beatty only once, when my friend Walter Armytage took me to lunch with him in Shrewsbury Road. It is still not well known that the Chester Beatty Library is not confined to Oriental and Islamic material. It has a very strong section of Western bindings. One day the Librarian, Paddy Henchy, turned me loose to browse in the roomful of Western books. Two of them, an Irish binding of about 1740 and an English one of about twenty-five years later, seemed strangely familiar. I had bought two such books in my impecunious days: one in Dublin and the other in London. For one I had paid £3 10s, for the other perhaps a little more (that was the Dublin one). A few years later, when the price of bindings had risen tenfold, partly as a result of the publication of books such as my own, I had sold them to Quaritch. I checked the dates through the Library's accessions records. Sure enough, Chester Beatty had snapped them up from Quaritch's very soon afterwards. By now they will have appreciated by at least another factor of ten.

Some of my learned colleagues, who should know better, are prey to the vulgar heresy of despising collectors and connoisseurship and regretting the high prices commanded by rare books. I like to tease such people by telling them that this is nature's way of protecting that which intrinsically deserves to be protected and cherished, because something for which a lot of money has been paid will stand thereafter a better chance of being properly looked after.

A deal of nonsense is talked about the money values of such things. You will hear it said that such-and-such an item is not 'really' worth the high price which is being paid for it. But money is nothing more than a notation by which people express the value which they set on what they are buying. Of course there are freak prices, and booms which burst like bubbles (and usually harm only those who deserve to be let down with a bump); but in the aggregate, such values are as real as any other values.

The collectors I admire most are those who collect in categories which are not, at the time, very highly esteemed. To begin with they buy cheaply, and what they buy is almost never to be found in institutional libraries. But as their collections gather shape, history is reconstructed, fugitive items are rescued from the bonfire and the pulping-mill, and bit by bit the materials are assembled for a serious study of a kind which would not previously have been possible. A good and often quoted example is Michael Sadleir's collection of nineteenth-century fiction which made possible an analysis of the reading habits and composition of the Victorian travelling public. The point is that institutional libraries cannot be expected to collect in these fields until they have been explored by the private collector. Academic involvement is always secondary.

An interesting problem arises with early nineteenth-century illustrated topographical books, which may contain anything from one to two hundred steel-engravings or lithographs. Such books could be bought for five or ten shillings forty years ago. Today they cost £150 or so. The reason is obvious. Besides the fall in the value of money, the increase in the number of people interested, and the fact that they cannot in the nature of things become any commoner, there is the special consideration that if the book is 'broken' each of the plates can be sold for between £5 and £10 depending on the market in which they are sold. So, not only has the price gone up by something like sixty thousand per cent, but there is a strong inducement to dealers to break even the best copies of the book. Breaking imperfect copies has always been a respectable activity: I have myself sold imperfect though attractive books, knowing that I was sending them to the knackers.

Logically, the price of a perfect copy in good state ought to rise till it is safely above the level at which there is still a temptation to break it. But I do not think that this is what actually happens. Antiquarian booksellers are, as a class, fond of books and do not like murdering them. Nor do they like pushing the price of a book far above the price to which they think it ought to go. Still, the price, for the book I have in mind,* is high and, paradoxically, so far from protecting it, it constitutes a threat to the continued existence of every copy that comes on the open market. I know someone, a print-dealer by profession, who has seventeen copies of this particular book, none of which he has broken. Perhaps he is keeping them as an insurance for his old age.

Photofacsimiles of these steel-engravings are now of such good quality as to deceive most people; to some extent this must be taking the pressure off the real thing, which can stay between its original covers while the substitute does duty as a table-mat.

XXXV

It must be well over thirty years since George MacCann remarked to me that he was giving up the *Observer* 'because it was so full of tycoonery', by which he meant that an increasing amount of its space was devoted to the movements of the money market and the manoeuvres of big business. Since then this tendency has become ever more obtrusive, crowding out the literary

* G.N. Wright's *Ireland Illustrated* (1831).

and allied departments, including the wireless and the television, not only in the 'posh Sundays' but everywhere else.

Faced as we are today with the cutthroat commercialism of the fine art market and the trade in antiques, rare books and the like, we are tempted to look back to a golden age of patronage and connoisseurship, before these matters were taken over by the smart operators and the wide boys. But the sad truth, I fear, is that most patronage and collecting has always been, as it is now, ruled by snobbery, ignorance and greed and catered to by charlatanism and skulduggery. The difference is that the conspiracy involved quite a small number of people, whereas now nearly everybody is in it.

XXXVI

It is customary, as old age approaches, to speculate on what would have happened had circumstances been other than they were. One of the rules of the game is that only one circumstance at a time may be changed, because each single circumstance draws in its train so many other variables that in no time at all the enquiry leads into uncharted waters. Life appears to us as a series of open forks, but for all we know it may also be a series of convergences, as in O. Henry's *Roads of Destiny* or Wilder's *Bridge of San Luis Rey*, or the Arabian folk-tale about the appointment in Samarra. At school we used to be invited to speculate on how much difference Metternich, for all his efforts, made to the course of European history. The suggestion was: not very much.

I am sure that had I remained in London after the end of 1969 I would now be a good deal richer than I am, but the last third of my life would have been more or less wasted. The rising salary and cumulative pension benefits of my London job would have enabled me, for example, to travel much more, especially as, starting from London, I would already have been well on my way to wherever I might want to go. I would also, very possibly, have lived a more varied sexual life than I have. But unless I had returned to Dublin neither of the books which have been the principal justification of my existence would have been written; nor, I am sure, any others.

It is not, however, at all probable that I would have remained in London, or at least not for long. Already I was beset by the feeling that if I had any goods to deliver I had better start delivering them soon. The immediate cause of my return to Dublin was the unexpected offer of the job in An Taisce, just at the earliest moment when I could leave the London job without forfeiting my right to a pension. But nearly a year earlier we had bought the little house in Dalkey because it had become available and I happened to have the money. We certainly never thought of it as just a retirement home to be resorted to ten years later. I knew by then that Jeanne had not long to live, and so, I believe, did she. Increasingly we had taken to talking about the prospect of living in or near Dublin on what little we had, and hoping for the best. It was clear that a good many things were likely to come to an end at much the same time: and so it was. It is quite possible that a little later I would have lacked the energy/strength of character (call it what you will) to make the necessary break without the stimulus of external force. It was, perhaps, just as well to get several different kinds of suffering over simultaneously, and at the same time as a change which held hope for the future.

So perhaps the part of chance at this juncture was after all not so very great. Eighteen years earlier it was much more crucial. Is it axiomatic that choices made, or made for one, earlier in life are that much more critical? The odds against my walking straight into a job as an Inspector of Ancient Monuments in 1952 were very long indeed. There were very few such jobs to be had and they turned up very rarely. I might so easily not have had a proof copy of my *Dublin* (not yet out) to take with me into the interview. I had left Dublin for a combination of emotional and economic reasons and it was much more likely that I would have ended up in the world of publishing, bookselling, broadcasting or curatorship. But they happened, at that moment, to want someone not in his first youth and with special experience of the eighteenth century: so

I got the job which above all others was the most suitable for one who would go on to write more architectural history, because it gave me practical experience of buildings which I would not otherwise have had.

It also supported me in gradually increasing comfort as well as being congenial and agreeably diversified as between indoor and outdoor work. In time it became the equivalent of an additional post-graduate degree, because I had not, and still lack, any formal qualifications in the subject in which I have earned my living. (This is, of course, not uncommon, and I hope it will never become so.)

I do not reproach myself with the books which I did not write during those eighteen years. There are other things in life besides writing books, and I cannot think of any book which I ought to have written and did not. One book, written during my first years in London, had already had all its groundwork done in Dublin.

The one real regret of my life is that I have spent so little time in Italy. I know, and envy, people who have spent months and years there. But once I had taken a civil service job this was out of the question, at least until it would have been too late to be worth while. It was a fair bargain, but in that respect a hard one. I exploited the fact of being in London to go to France, Italy, Spain, Holland, Russia and Scandinavia, but not so much as I might have done. My colleagues in the Inspectorate reproached me, tacitly, with giving up about half my annual leave to go to Las Palmas every January or February. As, in the ordinary way, I never go anywhere except for the purpose of experiencing its architecture, they had some reason on their side.

There is in fact more architecture in the various islands of the Canary group than might be supposed, but that was not our reason for going there. We had friends who live in Las Palmas, and to break the back of the winter by spending a fortnight in the sun, lazing and swimming, exploring the harbour with its constant comings and goings, drinking cheap brandy and playing *vingt-et-un* in the evenings, for a fortnight or three

97

weeks, was a great relief. We would take occasional trips to the interior or the North and West periphery of the island, where no tourists ever went, and from time to time go by steamer to the other islands, all seven of which we visited at one time or another. Even Las Palmas itself was in those days not so greatly infested with tourists: Puerto de la Luz, where we always stayed, was very much a working town and with the great harbour and Las Canteras beach back to back, completely insulated from one another yet only a few yards apart, it offered an ideal combination of attractions.

There was a special appeal, too, in the idea of going year after year to the same place, as other people do, to return to familiar sights, sounds and smells, and to know and be known in the way which comes only from repetition. Above all, perhaps, there was the pleasure of going by sea, which was already becoming rare and has since become virtually impossible, of feeling that one's holiday had begun the minute one stepped aboard in the West India Docks, knowing that for the next five days or so one would be, for the time being, 'at home', till the climate outside the cabin had gradually become warm and bland and almost that of the tropics.

It was a good bargain and I do not regret it. All the same, had I saved the time and money I could have gone to Umbria or Dalmatia in the spring or autumn, or been twice to Apulia and Sicily instead of only once, and had more time in Turin, and been to Milan which is full of things I would like to have seen. I would have liked to follow in the footsteps of Norman Douglas in Calabria, and could have done with much more time in and around Naples. It would have been nice to have seen Cordoba and Granada, Würzburg and Vierzehnheiligen, Prague and Mannheim and Stuttgart, Bruchsal and Stift Melk and Schönbrunn. But already the list of places that I have been to and enjoyed is rather longer than the list of desiderata, unless I add the majestic roll-call of the place-names of Upper Egypt and of the Isles of Greece. On the whole I have no cause for complaint. Travel, as it used to be understood and as I still understand it, is in any case now virtually impossible.

XXXVII

In the matter of books I have been extraordinarily fortunate. All my books, except the first, have been written to order. Any book which I have been capable of writing, someone has, sooner or later, asked me to write. When they have asked me too soon, when I did not feel able to write it, they, or someone else, have in the end asked me when I was ready and could deliver the goods. As a result there is a kind of logic in their progression: the Charlemont biography, the Dublin book, the *Bookbindings*, the Roxburghe book with Howard Colvin, the smaller houses and the *Architecture of Ireland*. It is difficult to imagine them being written in any other order. It is true that in theory I might have liked to write a book on Gandon: but I had my chance, for about twenty years, and it is just as well that I did not take it, because the book which Eddie McParland did in fact write is very much better than anything I could have done. I take great satisfaction in having helped to form the climate of interest and even the level of scholarship represented by that book. It is much more satisfying to be excelled by one's followers than to have no followers at all.

It was a great piece of luck for me that my publishers Allen Figgis had the wit to reissue my Dublin book in paperback in 1969 and again in a much superior production in 1980, so that it has been kept almost constantly in print for thirty-six years. The indirect benefit to me from having a 'live' and longevitous book is incalculable, even though it is not my favourite among my books and it irks me to be so closely and exclusively identified with it, as with an anthology poem or poor old Raff and his 'Cavatina'.

I have found it to be a rule of fairly general application that the more valuable the work, the worse it is paid, and vice versa. The Knight* and I were employed by the Berkeley Square book-factory, which was run by the Reader's Digest Co. for the

---

* Desmond Fitz-Gerald, Knight of Glin, an old friend and collaborator of the author's: architectural historian and expert on furniture and pictures.

Automobile Association, to write a gazetteer of notable buildings and monuments in Ireland. This we did, and were, by our standards and those of the time, handsomely paid for it. It was then put through a process of tinkering and untinkering and retinkering. Above the man with whom we dealt there was a hierarchy of editorial staff, each of whom needed to show that he or she was earning his or her salary by doing something to it, so that it went all the way up and all the way down again and returned much the same.

Then came an order from on high – probably all the way from America – that everything had to be reduced in length by twenty per cent. So we went through it taking out one word in five and were paid for that. Some time passed, and out came an edict that the original length or something like it was, after all, to be restored. Editorial scrutiny *da capo*, of course. For putting back all or most of what we had taken out we were paid again.

I have long thought that businessmen were incompetent footlers, at least by contrast with artists and writers. But the book, of which our labours were quite a substantial part, sold the best part of a quarter of a million copies.

My best work has brought me in, directly, very little money and sometimes no money at all. On the other hand I was once paid £100 for giving an opinion about a place-name, over the telephone, to the developers of a projected office building, presumably for no better reason than that they had, for the moment, a superfluity of money to fling about. Better, of course, that some of it should have been flung my way than none at all. But it serves only to re-emphasize the complete separation of value from 'value'.

Anyone interested enough to enquire would notice that there is a void of twenty-two years in the middle of my writing career. Between 1948 and 1954 I published a book every two years. The next full-sized book of which I was the sole author did not appear until 1976.

It would be easy to account for this by saying that for nineteen out of those twenty-two years I had a nine-to-five job. Plenty of other people have had such jobs and written books as well. In my case I can identify three reasons: the Occam principle, the Heracleitus principle and the Antaeus principle. These were reinforced by simple laziness. I had no desire to burden the world with any books which were not strictly necessary. I had a strong objection to covering the same ground ('stepping into the same river') twice. And, broadly speaking, I wanted to write only on Irish subjects, and both the desire and the ability to do this were weakened when I was not actually living in Ireland. Besides, I devoted most of my leisure to enjoyable pursuits such as playing with motor-cars and building and playing with ship-models. Nevertheless, it was during these years that fate, helped by my own curiosity and the alertness and generosity of my friends, put me in the way of making rather important discoveries about the career and personality of Pearce, which I had the good fortune to be able to embody in a book of joint authorship with Howard Colvin which was sumptuously produced by the Roxburghe Club. My job involved my having to produce a quantity of writing to a deadline, for a known readership, once a month, so that I kept my hand in. I do not, generally speaking, write for fun, and this discipline was exactly what suited me best.

There can be few things more satisfying than when a hypothesis, laboriously and perhaps shakily constructed from three or four kinds of circumstantial evidence, is resoundingly confirmed from a totally unexpected quarter. Among the rather modest achievements of my life, one of the most satisfying has been the reconstruction of Sir Edward Lovett Pearce. The means by which providence enabled me to do this were so elegant that the story is worth retailing.

I have told, in the preface to the Roxburghe volume, the first part of it: of how Pearce's relationship to Vanbrugh began to emerge bit by bit from a study of the drawings, of the contribution made by Susi Lang's identification of the notes in the RIBA Palladio as being in the hand of 'someone called Pearce' (who meant nothing whatever to her) and of the moment of blinding revelation when I suddenly realized the implications of the matrimonial fortunes of Sir Dudley Carleton's daughters.

By these means, and by the identification of three or four houses, notably Bellamont Forest, Cashel Palace, Drumcondra House and No. 9 Henrietta Street, Pearce had been transformed from a mere name to a figure with a life history and a corpus of known works.

There remained the problem of Castletown: the greatest house of its time in Ireland, a key building in search of an architect or architects. In essence, what happened was that I was enabled to construct a kind of cat's cradle connecting, by different kinds of link, four people: the architects Pearce and Galilei, and the patrons William Conolly and Marmaduke Coghill. Coghill is, in a sense, peripheral to the argument but nevertheless of crucial importance, since it was the connexions established through Coghill which triangulated the finished structure and made it capable of bearing the desired load.

The object of the exercise was to establish what we had begun to suspect to be the case: that the basic design of Castletown was, in outline, by Galilei, and the execution of the interior and the design and execution of the wings by Pearce.

I had already ascertained that there were two more drawings of Castletown in the Elton Hall collection in addition to the one already noted by Sadleir and Curran (because it had 'Castletown' written on it). One of these was a plan of the house and the other a dimensioned plan of the entrance-hall. Correspondence still extant in Florence and investigated by the Knight of Glin had established a connexion between Pearce and Galilei in respect of services to be rendered to Conolly (a much older man than either) while both Pearce and Galilei were in Italy: services of an architectural and/or art-patronage and collecting kind. From a drawing and letter in the Elton Hall collection we knew that Pearce had designed, for Coghill, Drumcondra House which was still there.

Beside that house, and in its grounds, there stands a kind of folly of extremely Italian character: just a frontispiece, like the top half of an Italian church façade. In design and detailing it is closely similar to the front door and flanking windows of Castletown. How nice it would be, I thought, if there were some evidence of a closer connexion between Marmaduke Coghill and William Conolly than the mere fact that they both belonged to the same rather small ruling clique. Putting it diagrammatically, the position was:

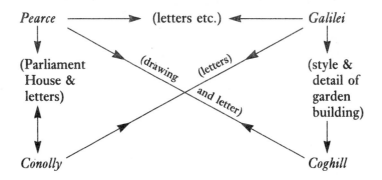

What was wanted was a horizontal link across the bottom to complete the cradle.

And, one afternoon, idly browsing as I had been when the momentous kinship between Pearce and Vanbrugh had suddenly dawned on me, I found it. Conolly had, by his will, provided for the foundation of what later became Celbridge School. As trustees he had named his widow, his nephew and successor, the rector of the parish and – Marmaduke Coghill. The cat was well out of the bag and safe in its cradle.*

There was one more trick to come. John Cornforth, working through the diaries of the Duchess of Northumberland for the mid eighteenth century, found her visiting Castletown and recording that it was designed by 'Signior Gallini the Pope's architect who afterwards designed the Pope's palace on Mount Palatine'. The Duchess has got it slightly wrong all along the line. His name was not Gallini, nor was it the Pope's palace, nor was it on Mount Palatine: it was the West front of St John Lateran which Galilei did indeed design before dying as prematurely as Pearce himself.

* I tend to think in engineering terms, and so I like to see a structure properly triangulated. This is of a piece with my attitude towards drains: see p. 145.

How much less satisfactory it would have been if John Cornforth had found this entry before we did our detective work rather than after it.

I have never written about any other country but Ireland with one small exception. In the mid-sixties, after a couple of visits to Leningrad, I was persuaded by Mark Girouard, who was then at *Country Life*, to write them some articles on Leningrad architecture. Only the fact that at that time there was virtually nothing on the subject in print in English allowed me to override the obvious caution that one does not set up as an authority on a country's architecture on the strength of a few days' acquaintance. By assiduous plagiarism from sources in French and German, and even in Russian, obligingly translated for me by a colleague at my office, I managed to cobble up a reasonable outline of the subject. Even without knowing Russian I could recognize pictures and read dates and decipher proper names, and I am, even now, not altogether ashamed of the result.

Some of the illustrations were from my own photographs, some from those of other travellers, and some supplied by the Anglo-Soviet Friendship Agency in the Tottenham Court Road. These took a long time to arrive, and were not always exactly what was wanted. For the article on Tsarskoe Selo (Pushkin) they were particularly dilatory, and the magazine was becoming impatient as the weeks went by. I had brought back from Russia an obviously well-researched and authoritative book on the palaces and their gardens, with good photographs well reproduced. The art department of *Country Life* were confident that they could make satisfactory blocks from them, which would not look like copies of plates from a book. So they did so, for two or three of them, and the article came out.

Within forty-eight hours the Soviet embassy was on the blower, breathing fire and fury. *Country Life* got on to me. What were they to reply? they wanted to know. Tell them three things, I said. Point out to them that the USSR is not yet a signatory to the Berne Convention; offer them three guineas a frame (which was then the going rate); and tell them to go jump in the Caspian Sea.

They followed the first two pieces of my advice, though not, I think, the third. No more was heard from them.

I get great pleasure from thinking that somewhere in the Kremlin there are armies of readers with nothing better to do than to read *Country Life*, and probably also *The Field*, and *Horse and Hound*, *Fur and Feather*, *Field and Stream* and, for all I know, the news-letter of the Country Landowners' Association to boot.

XXXVIII

All Irish people get used to the fact that nobody else remembers where Ireland is or indeed that there is such a country. This is hurtful to our self-esteem, but we would do well to remind ourselves that there is a great deal to be said for not being noticed. It is exasperating to find that other Europeans know of us, if they know of us at all, only through Britain, with the inevitable resultant distortion. I have, quite recently, had, in Castelvetrano in Southern Sicily, the experience of using an international telephone directory in which every European and some non-European countries were to be found, except Ireland. This was some eight years after our accession to the EEC. I could multiply instances of the general law that ignorance of Ireland begins much nearer home. The reporter who stood on the shore at Windscale and looked out to sea, watching the rollers of what she fondly supposed to be the Atlantic. The day an Irishman tossed a canister of CS gas into the House of Commons, giving them a taste of their own medicine, after which the English papers published a list of the various legislative chambers in Europe with details of how the members were protected from the spectators, omitting of course Leinster House. Or the map recently published in another English paper, showing which countries had proportional representation – except, it goes without saying, Ireland, on which the British themselves imposed PR, which, in the Twenty-Six Counties, we have had the good sense to retain. (It is very noticeable how certain the British have always been that PR is good for the subject races but unsuitable for themselves.)

As for the business of explaining to continentals that we do not mean Holland nor yet Iceland but Ireland: of that there is no end and it is, to be sure, very irritating. But it is almost entirely the result of our being right out at the edge of Europe (some would say beyond the edge) and not on the way to anywhere. Would we really prefer to have two powerful neighbours to deal with, one on each side, rather than only one? It would, of course, be easier all round if, instead of two islands, there were three islands or even four, of approximately similar size and power, with a name common to them all that did not mean 'British' or 'Irish' but stood in the same relation to each as 'Scandinavian' does to 'Danish', 'Norwegian' and the rest. But, alas, it is not so.

If we were in the middle of Europe, it is unlikely that our population-density would be as low as it is, and it is precisely this low density which more than anything else makes Ireland an agreeable country to live in. It also tends to make us and keep us poor, and it would do us no harm to be a bit richer. We are already a little richer than we were, and I hope this improvement continues, up to a point.

Since England is so hideously overcrowded and Ireland so empty, I have from time to time wondered why they do not simply pour into Ireland. They have, after all, done so in the past. The reason why they do not is not that, if they came in appreciable numbers, they would not be welcome. The reason is much simpler than that. It is that it simply does not occur to them. *There is no such country as Ireland.* It does not exist.

We may be very thankful that it is so. For the blessing of being ignored we should be prepared to put up with all the slights and inconveniences it entails, however galling they may be. Very recently I opened a new book by the former Director of an institute of advanced architectural studies, if you please, and found the Dublin Custom House described as an example of the Greek Revival. . . . Over forty years of hammering away has made no impression on such invincible ignorance.

The writer has a special problem to face. Until very recently and perhaps still, any Irish writer who expected to be taken seriously had to be published in London. Some of the reasons for this (such as access to the English-language market) were good, and others bad. But good or bad, it necessarily affected what was written. The moment you are aware that a substantial proportion of your readers will be English, that is to say people who cannot be presumed to know this, or who may be expected to think that, the character of your writing begins to change, and you go out of your way to enlighten the reader on this point, or to combat that preconceived idea. Or it may be no more than a change of tone, imperceptible even to the writer, yet cumulative in its effect. The ideal, which would be to write it in a resolutely take-it-or-leave-it manner, is much more difficult than it appears to be.

What can outsiders be expected to make of a country in which, to the naïve observer and at first sight, the Protestants appear to be royalists and the Catholics appear to be republicans, thus reversing the order of nature?

XXXIX

I have been watching a television programme relating how a group of people from the Baltic provinces, Lithuanians, Letts and Estonians, living now in England or America, went with their children and grandchildren on a cruise from Stockholm across to the coast of Courland and so North and round the corner towards the waters off Reval or Tallinn and so to Helsingfors, shadowed by Russian warships and straining their eyes to catch a glimpse of the low-lying coast.

I ought to have been feeling more sympathetic towards them than I was. The younger members of the party were so very English or so very American, except when they switched on their Lettishness or Estonianism. No doubt it is theoretically desirable that these people should be able to go to and from these places and that they should be governed by a liberal democratic regime. But there seems not to be the slightest prospect of this happening, and there are compelling reasons for this.

I cannot help remembering that these three provinces were detached from Russia and erected into separate states after the First World War, when Russia was weak, and that during most of the twenty years of their separate existence they were governed by authoritarian regimes, and that if they had at present an independent existence under American protection they would doubtless be governed by the usual unsavoury characters whom the Americans always favour. I cannot blame the Russians for taking them over after the war. They had every reason to be frightened and to secure their own borders by a *cordon sanitaire*.

Arnold Bax is credited with the saying that one should try everything once except incest and folk-dancing. I have no reasons to suppose that these ethnic Estonians were incestuous except in the metaphorical sense, but they certainly kept their spirits up by singing their lugubrious ethnic songs, their national anthems which sounded as other peoples' (except for the Austrian, French and old Russian) national anthems always do – that is to say even worse than our own – and above all by folk-dancing. Such exhibitions, whether their origins be Estonian, Aymara, Cretan, Kalmuk or just plain Irish, have the same effect on me: one of stupefying boredom. As someone else said, folk-dancing is not for watching, it is for doing. And these Baltic people went out of their way to tell us, in their very mundane English and American accents, what deep satisfaction they got from doing it: satisfaction, clearly, of a political and quasi-religious kind. How shall we sing the Lord's song in a strange land?

Why am I labouring this point? Do the activities of these unfortunate people do any harm?

Unfortunately I think that they do. They nourish in some quarters the belief that, given the chance, these peoples and others within the present Soviet empire would rise up and throw off the Communist yoke. I do not believe that this is true. But the belief that it is, is an encouragement to mischief.

How, it may be asked, do I square this attitude with my attitude towards nationalism in my own country, which is about the same size as Estonia and Livonia together, and itself hideously divided? The Baltic provinces are ground between Russia and Germany, Sweden and Poland, and have for centuries been the plaything of one or other of these larger entities. We, on the other hand, have only one neighbour, and on the other side of us is empty space. We were not given our political independence by some third party for the purpose of annoying the British. For what it is worth, we got it partly because of our own efforts and partly because the British wanted to be rid of a nuisance. The Baltic provinces have nuisance value too, but that is precisely why their political independence is unlikely to be permitted in any future that I can foresee. In any case, the nationalism to which I subscribe has little to do with folk-dancing. It is a luxury which, in different circumstances, we could very probably not afford. But, as things are, it is vastly preferable to the alternative. And, make no mistake, if you do without nationalism you must make do with something else.

XL

I suppose it is inevitable that men should begin by thinking of women as tyrannical naysayers. The earliest experiences of all of us are of being taken up and put down at someone else's will, of being told not to go there, not to do that – always by a woman. Don't leave your toys there, don't put your feet on that, don't bring that into the house. Later it becomes 'Surely you don't want to keep this?' or 'That? surely it wasn't important? I threw it out.' As for the confusion and destruction brought about by the unremitting activity of 'cleaning' the less said the better.

'Cleaning' consists of using a damp cloth to spread a fine emulsion of dust, grease and water distributed uniformly over *everything*; not just over wherever the dust happened to be in the first place, and regardless of whether it was doing any harm there or not. Books are taken up and banged about, filling the air with dust which, as an embittered bibliophile (Harry Aldis in *The Printed Book*) long ago observed, immediately shows its intelligence by heading straight for the open window, while the poor books nurse their bruises.

With 'cleaning' goes 'tidying'. Tidying is of two kinds: tidying *mitis*, making things difficult to find by putting them back in different places, and tidying *gravis* which is hiding things in drawers so that they are virtually impossible to find. In its extreme form it forces the possessor to go out and buy a replacement, at which point the original miraculously reappears. It is of no use for him to enquire after it by name, since women never know the name of anything (the odious C. S. Lewis did say, to his credit, that 'women speak a language without nouns') and in the end it will turn out to have been hidden, in all innocence and of course meaning no harm, under something or behind something.

'Cleaning' and 'tidying' between them are responsible for a great deal of damage and delay, since before he can get back to work the victim must do his best to put everything in order once again, bind up the wounds and restore the *status quo*.

I think it very improbable that there will ever come a time when the masculine and feminine view of these matters will coincide, or even be brought very closely together. When all the dust about Women's Liberation has settled we may be a little nearer knowing what are the real differences between men and women, as distinct from those which custom and culture have engendered, but I shall not be alive to see it.

The difference between the masculine and feminine attitudes to oil is instructive. To a man, oil is something which makes things work more smoothly, and, for example, stops things squeaking. Women do not seem to mind things squeaking, nor to interpret it as evidence of malfunction. To women, oil is something which is liable to make things dirty, and is itself a form of dirt.

There is, of course, truth in both views.

I am surely not the only person for whom there is something wrong about tidiness? I have been in houses where nothing whatever was out of place, to the point where one

wonders how life of any recognizable kind could possibly be
lived in them. An official with a 'clean' desk is an intimidating
sight. One cannot help asking oneself at what cost such
unnatural bareness may have been achieved.

It is, I suppose, no more than common good manners to
clear away or straighten out the worst evidences of disorder
when visitors are expected. But when they are *not* expected . . . ?

Tidiness is, in any case, not the opposite of disorder. A
building-site, when observed *in medias res*, is a very untidy
spectacle. Yet, as a general rule, everything has a reason for
being where it is. It is unreasonable to demand that a process
should look like a finished article.

I have to remind myself that most of human activity is not
concerned with finished articles. As a maker of finished articles
I am in a rather small minority. Most people knock off at half
past five leaving everything *in medias res*. But we, the minority,
try to leave some things in a state where nothing need ever be
done to them again: not even routine maintenance. When
Shakespeare wrote the line for Caliban

A plague upon the tyrant that I serve

he must have known that no amount of further tinkering would
be needed: the utterance was in its final and perfect form.
Whether he had any inkling of the uncountable number of people who would find it springing to their lips unbidden from the
heart, is another matter altogether: probably not.

The tyrant of tidiness demands some service even from such
as me. When I was a civil servant my desk was notoriously
overcrowded and untidy: yet I could always find anything I
needed, and nearly always quickly. My work-room at home is
dauntingly over-full and at first sight chaotic. Yet it contains
files, card-indexes, boxes, catalogues in which I can find things
very quickly indeed, as well as heaps of material which I dare
not throw away, and in which I sometimes have to rummage
for quite a long time before finding what I want.

Every once in a while, usually between once a fortnight and
once a month, I make an attack on the room, reduce to order

such things as are capable of being so reduced, and, with luck, find some things which can be destroyed. But, either for reasons of size and shape, or because no classification fits them, there remain many things which cannot be put into even metaphorical pigeon-holes. Even so, when I have done this, the room looks marginally tidier than before. It is an activity which I find on the whole pleasurable, largely because it represents a respectable form of work-shirking.

I once drew up a list of activities which look like 'work' but are in fact forms of work-avoidance. It ran to thirty-two items, not counting such obvious forms of work-avoidance as washing shirts or dishes, clearing ash out of the fireplace, or hoovering the library carpet. Several of these have the merit of engaging the lower centres of the brain, thus releasing the higher centres for metaphysical speculation or even for turning over problems connected with my real 'work'.

Mowing the lawn, or hoovering, are too noisy to permit of any kind of thought. (The two noises which most exasperate me are someone else hoovering, and someone else using a typewriter.) Mowing the lawn is like weeding, among the most futile of human efforts, because nature always wins in the end. Music is a useful accompaniment to thought. I am quite shameless about having it pour out of the wireless without giving it attention: even the best music. But if I have it on at night in bed I tend to listen to it which keeps me from going to sleep; so for insomnia I tune in to the virtually ubiquitous political propaganda from Radio Tirana, the Voice of America, Moscow, Prague, London, it really doesn't matter which: they all work equally well.

XLI

Raymond Mortimer says, 'Most men, as they grow old, see the decay of their own powers reflected in their environment, and are convinced that the country is going to the dogs because they themselves are going to the grave.' This is unquestionably true: yet I cannot help suspecting that, this time round, there is an objective component, and that things really are getting worse. I think also that by the end of his life Raymond Mortimer came to see that this was so.

Not everything, of course. There is always something on the up-grade while other things are on the down-grade. But just at present it does seem that, from the planet's point of view, man is a disease, possibly a fatal disease, and that this has been the case, with increasing momentum, for perhaps 150 years. Many people's attention is on this matter, which is far too large to be the direct concern of someone like myself. Better for a single person to concentrate his attention on a few small things about which he may know something worth knowing. Such as, for example, book production or the shape of ships.

So often the agent of deterioration is something which is put forward as an 'improvement'. From about the mid-twenties till about 1960 the standard of book production rose steadily, largely under the influence of Stanley Morison and the Monotype Corporation. But since 1960 it has become increasingly rare to find a well-designed book, well carried out. The reason is of course the introduction of film-setting and offset lithography. No presswork now has the 'bite' of real raised type on paper, and the precision in the relationship of line with line which was ensured by the leading and the forme, has gone, it seems, for ever. Black is no longer black, nor white white. Worse still, from the author's point of view, corrections, after a certain point, have become virtually impossible. I do not quite understand how this has come about, because what technical knowledge I once had of the processes of printing is now quite out of date. The reduction in cost which these innovations brought about has of course been concealed from us by inflation, but I am prepared to accept that there has been a reduction.

But it is heartbreaking to see the very real gains of the thirties and forties wiped out at a blow. And of course, when one thing slides, other things slide as well. So there has been an ill-advised revival of Art Nouveau display faces which could better have been left in obscurity.

The fact that there are some authors who neither notice, care about, nor understand any of these matters, is no consolation to those of us who do. The comparison of my later books with my earlier is a melancholy exercise.

All my life I have taken delight in the shape of ships. For centuries they have been the most unfailingly pleasing of the works of man, and largely for reasons which are identifiable and, one would have thought, the product of necessity. But modern progress has contrived to circumvent necessity itself.

Up to a few years ago I used to watch keenly for the appearance of a Blue Funnel liner in Dublin Bay, knowing that they were gradually being withdrawn from service and that at any time I might see the last of them. They were uncommonly handsome ships, with great flaring bows, plenty of sheer and a single almost vertical funnel. (For the benefit of those who do not know, sheer is the concave curve which normally extends from stem to stern, so that the bow and stern are – disregarding deck-erections – higher than the middle. A ship with negative sheer is said to be 'hogged'. Some small vessels such as cabin-cruisers have this characteristic.) Apart from their beauty, the knowledge that they were built to their owners' special standard which was more exacting than the highest Lloyds' class, and that Alfred Holt & Co. did not insure but carried their own risks, added to their attraction.

I have said that they had pronounced sheer. This is a paradox, because rather a long time ago Holts discovered that a ship, being a beam, should be at least as deep in the centre as at the ends. So they adopted this system and made the decks flat, in the longitudinal plane, from end to end. But since the result of doing so is to make a very ugly ship, they re-introduced the sheer in the form of a continuous curve of the upper edge of the bulwarks and in the paintwork. And since a raised fo'c'sle is of great advantage for seaworthiness, they used that to reinforce the aesthetic effect. So much for the cherished heresy of form following function . . .

I remember once studying, in Las Palmas harbour, a ship – I think it was the *Rhodesia Castle* – where three different and discrepant kinds of sheer could all be seen together: one formed by the lines of the hull plating, one indicated by the lines of portholes and therefore presumably corresponding to the decks inside, and a third which was the paintwork.

I have never seen any serious attempt made to account for the origin of sheer, not even in David Pye's book on the aesthetic of ships and boats.* One account of the matter which seems to me to be at least a partial explanation is that which arises from the technique of making a hull by planking over frames. If the section of the vessel at her widest part, amidships, approximates to a semicircle, let us call the circumferential distance x. This distance will be distributed among a given number of planks. But towards the ends of the vessel, where the section is no longer round but approximates more nearly to a V shape, the same number of planks will necessarily rise higher, thus automatically generating sheer. (In practice it is usually necessary to mitigate this effect by tapering the planks somewhat towards the ends.)

Note that none of this applies to hulls such as dug-out canoes or vessels such as currachs made by stretching skins over a framework. If these display sheer, it has been introduced for other reasons. What are these reasons? One, I think, must be aesthetic. All over the world, and at all times, it has been felt to be fitting that the ends of a ship or boat, and especially the forward end, should rise higher than the middle. We know that this is of advantage both in an oncoming sea and a following sea.

But, if we express this another way round, can there be any advantage in the gunwale being very low amidships? The effect may be seen in extreme form in the caiques of the Eastern Mediterranean, where, when the vessel is fully loaded, the gunwale amidships is actually under water and effective freeboard is provided only by an inboard upstand round the hatch. One imagines that in a beam sea such a vessel would be very wet. Yet there always seems to be some good reason for the peculiarities of local and traditional craft.

Two causes have almost banished sheer from the ships of today. The vast majority are either container ships or vehicle ferries or a combination of these types, completely flat on top

* David Pye, *Ships* (1950).

and sometimes furnished with rails for a mobile gantry. In such a ship we sailed from Genoa to Palermo and Palermo to Livorno, and, some years earlier, from Dublin to Rotterdam via Le Havre and back via Belfast. In both cases all the accommodation was in a tall tower perched over the stern. Below the waterline these ships may well have been as beautiful as any, but there was scant inducement to buy a postcard of the ship as a memento of the voyage.

Even the pure passenger ship, where it survives, has been infected by the mania for straight lines. This is no doubt because it is cheaper to cut rectangular plates than rhomboids, because when a ship has continuous sheer, there are no right angles anywhere. Thus the *Queen Elizabeth 2*, in spite of being held up as being in the lineal succession of the great liners of the past, is in various ways no such thing: for several hundred feet she has no sheer whatever.

It is commonly assumed, and said, that in the days gone by there was money and time to spare. But this cannot be true: economic competition was as relentless then as now, if not more so, and society as a whole was poorer. The one thing that was relatively cheaper was labour; and that, no doubt, accounts for the difference.

All these matters are superficial trivialities to the naval architect. What exercises me is that they should be of so little apparent interest to people who claim to concern themselves with design and its place in the scheme of things at large. They keep this kind of thing in a different box, which they never open.

XLII

I have what I take to be a normal and healthy interest in the macabre. If it is abnormal, as the attitude of some of my friends seems to imply, the abnormality is shared by practically all children and a great many adults.

There was, in the Belfast Museum, within walking distance of my home, an Egyptian mummy which was a great favourite of mine. I was fascinated, as who cannot be?, by the extraordinary difference between a human being and a corpse. In the National Museum in Dublin there was a bog-corpse which I used also to frequent whenever I could. Both these ex-persons have now vanished from view.

I remember, when I was about ten, playing funerals with a girl called Margaret Cotton (who was later killed in a motor accident in Galway). I do not recall playing with her the games that so many others recall as being played between the sexes at about that age. We did a little of that, my brother and I, but communally, in the box-room at home, with the daughter of a history professor.

Neither necrophily nor necrology: the Greeks, for once, do not seem to have had a word for my reasonable and measured interest in cadavers. The famous corpses of St Michan's in Dublin naturally claimed my attention early on: but I do not recall them as specially impressive and the last time I went to see them was in 1948 when Henry Wheeler and I were writing our booklet on the Dublin city churches and took in the vaults as a matter of duty. They continue, I believe, to pull in the tourists.

According to the Youngs in their book on *Old London Churches*, 'A mummied person with a pleasant smile is kept in a cupboard in the vestry' of St James Garlickhithe. I reproach myself that during my years in London I neglected to make this person's acquaintance. I see by a pencil note which I made in the margin that the church was under restoration in 1961: I do hope that the mummied person was not banished. It is all too probable, in our degenerate times. I have been with grown persons of unimpeachable sanity who have refused to accompany me to such sites.

Skeletons and mere bones hardly count. In sheer quantity of these I suppose I scored highest in a visit to the catacombs under the Place Denfert-Rochereau: 'Ici le Royaume des Morts'. But for rarity value I put forward a visit at the age of fifteen to the church of the 11,000 virgins in Cologne, the whole interior of which was made of bones and skulls, all blown to smithereens in the Second World War.

117

Jeremy Bentham's mummy, so called, is not really a mummy. It sits on a chair, fully clothed, with the skull between the feet and a waxwork head in its place, in University College, Gower Street. There used to be a game played by members of the *New Statesman* staff who gave lifts to other intellectuals from Hampstead towards Holborn and the City. The game consisted in nursing and nudging the conversation, without mentioning utilitarianism or penal reform, towards the point at which your passenger would mention the name 'Bentham', if possible just as you were passing the mummy. I, as it happens, have neither played the game nor seen the mummy: but I like the story.*

In some ways the high point in this genre was seeing the corpse of Bothwell, the husband of Mary Stuart, at the little town of Faareveile near Kalundborg in North-West Sjaelland. He is displayed in a glass-topped coffin, and is in pretty good preservation, including his privy member which got him into so much trouble. The DNB churlishly casts some doubt on the identity of the corpse; but I will have none of that.

(At Kalundborg, till then known to me only as the name of a wireless station like Hilversum or Daventry, I was delighted to find a five-domed church quite in the Byzantine manner, the domes surmounted by octagonal towers. In the cathedral at Roskilde I saw what were, I think, the grandest and most stylish of all series of royal tombs. The majesty of buried Denmark is in a number of noble Baroque heraldic sarcophagi made of marble and bronze, like that so powerfully evoked by M. R. James in the story of 'Count Magnus' which is set in Sweden. I wonder, by the way, why these Scandinavian sarcophagi lie slightly tilted, with the head-end raised a little above the floor, as though for burial at sea?)

I have been in a good many burial vaults in my time, nearly always on business. One such visit took place, as it happened, on the day after the Harrow and Wealdstone railway disaster in which a great many people were killed. Though the

---

* Jeremy Bentham lives! I learn with delight that the principal gaol in La Paz is called El Panoptico. (*Observer*, February 21, 1988.)

railway in question does not pass Kensal Green Cemetery, the Harrow Road does, and this association pressed powerfully on our minds as we walked through the vaults under the Greek Doric temple and its wings. Among the more recently deposited coffins was one of a Chinese gentleman, on which reposed his walking-stick and a large number of eggs.

My greatest disappointment in this line was in Lisbon. The 1908 Baedeker promised that in the monastery of Sao Vicente I should see the monarchs of the house of Braganza from 1656 onwards in coffins with glass lids 'shown by the light of a wax candle (fee)'. Alas, when we got there we were told that this innocent pleasure had been put an end to, no doubt as a by-product of the 'revolution'.

The frustration of Lisbon was amply requited in Palermo a year or two later. Under the Capuchin convent is a vast network of vaulted corridors, quite wide and quite well lit, in which lie, or sit, or stand, some eight thousand deceased Palermitans, who died between 1631 and about 1880, all fully dressed in their best clothes. Few of them have any faces to speak of: just brown leathery skin drawn tight, and no eyes. Those who are standing are wired back to the wall, and some give the impression of having been garrotted, recalling Goya.

I could not help wondering whether they had been partially embalmed before being put there, or what measures had been taken to dispose of noisome fluids at the beginning. There was a current of dry air constantly flowing through the vaults, and through the occasional lunettes eight or ten feet up I could hear the shrieks and see the bare legs of small boys playing some game in the adjoining field. No doubt these little lads were well acquainted with those below, though I did see one being shooed away by one of the friars' guardians.

Towards the end of the nineteenth century the fashion for being put in these vaults died out. Perhaps in post-Risorgimento Italy it was no longer felt to be seemly. How long, I wonder, will it be before the exhibition of these cadavers is thought to be beneath the dignity of our enlightened times, and the whole business is put an end to? Far be it hence.

Not the most spectacular, but among the more memorable of my descents to the underworld was an occasion when the Knight and I went into a vault in a neglected Limerick graveyard. In wellington boots, and flashing electric torches, we waded about in a kind of purée in which floated skulls, bones and bits of splintered wood. The Knight fished about in this and netted half a dozen brass coffin-plates which he bore off to the back of the station-wagon. His response to my mild expostulation was magisterial: 'I am the heir-general of that extinct family.'

The coffin-plates now adorn the walls of the demesne church at Glin, where they look very well.

It would be an interesting study to trace the originals of the different types of coffins in favour in various parts of Europe. In these islands we have for some time used the box which is widest at the point where the occupant might thrust out his elbows, if he had a mind to. This may perhaps descend from the hollowed-out stone boxes which I have seen at, for example, the Black Abbey in Kilkenny, which have a round space for the head and then get wider at the shoulders and remain that width as far as the feet. There are medieval grave-slabs which taper very gradually in width from the head to the feet, and I have seen this elegant shape in a vertical headstone as late as the 1790s. Our coffins normally have flat lids, or did until recently; but I have noticed a tendency for the lids to be built up with a succession of fruity mouldings, so that the area of the plateau on top is markedly smaller than that of the whole lid. Jewish coffins, at least to judge by the two Jewish funerals I have attended, are completely rectangular boxes with flat plain lids. In Holland they are slightly wedge-shaped and have flat lids.

Southern Europe favours the *cassone* type, parallel-sided but elaborately moulded as to the lid. This seems to have affinity with the pattern popular in America: doubtless under Sicilian influence, and in America they do not even call them coffins.

My first sight of the Mediterranean type was in rather dramatic circumstances. Two of the custodians of the Villa dei Misteri at Pompeii had been overcome by charcoal fumes during the night, and as we entered the forum the two coffins were borne slowly across the scene, from left to right, like a poem by Leconte de l'Isle.

Russian coffins are very shallow and the sides are widely splayed. The lid is virtually the same shape and as deep as the coffin itself, so that when it is closed the lid forms the top half. Whenever I have been in a Russian church there has been one or more such coffins lying open, with an old person inside.

The Russian type occurs, apparently, as far West as the Rhineland. It would be interesting to see a distribution-map such as human geographers produce for the distribution of traditional games or the shapes of scythes. The frontier between the Nordic and Mediterranean types would, I expect, be found in France, in this as in other matters.

XLIII

Like other people of my age and upbringing, I have a horror of getting into debt. I have only done it twice, when circumstances outside my control obliged me to. In vain do people tell me that for most of my lifetime it has been prudent to be in debt, that you borrow at a higher value than you repay at, that the business of banks is to sell money just as any other tradesman sells whatever is his trade to sell, that zero is merely one notch on a scale, like any other notch. To me what is above that notch is different in kind from what is below it.

When I have very little money there is a limit to the amount of money I have. But once I have sunk below the zero mark there is no limit to the amount of money I have not got. It is as though the floor had suddenly been removed and I could fall for ever and ever. It is not a comfortable feeling.

There is no logic in this, but the more one thinks about it the clearer it becomes that people, in their attitude towards money, are ruled not at all by logic but by their profoundest emotions.

Everybody must, at some time or other, have played the game of thinking about what they would do if they had unlimited money. It is not a very satisfactory game because there are no rules. If you can set the boundaries wherever you like it soon ceases to be interesting. Nevertheless I have played it, by arbitrarily setting up three stages: rich, very rich and what we used to call stinking rich but is now, I understand, called 'seriously rich'.

I very much like the smell of cigars, but I am not so fond of the taste of them. Therefore, if I were rich, I should not myself smoke the cigars but would hire a man to smoke them in my presence.

If I were very rich I would cause to be made accurate replicas of the tools used to decorate the Irish parliamentary bindings of the mid eighteenth century. This in itself would take a long time because minute comparisons and recuttings would be necessary until they were exactly right. I would then cause a dummy volume to be made, of the same size and shape and of the same materials, as one of the great mid-century series. I would then employ the best finisher available to make a replica of one of the bindings. I would not, to begin with, choose one of the two or three which I most admire, because I have learnt from experience in trying to make things for myself that you should develop your technique at first on objects of, at most, secondary importance, so that it will be at its best when you address yourself to the most important task of all. While all this was going on I would be kept as busy as anyone concerned, because my task would be the critical one, of making sure that everything was done exactly right, identifying what was not yet right, and sending it back to be amended. But the results would be marvellous.

J. Pierpont Morgan (I think) said that if you had to ask what it cost to run a steam yacht you were not rich enough to own one. Very well then: I shall be rich enough to have one built to my own specification. When I say a steam yacht I mean a steam yacht: not one with diesel engines. She must have a proper triple-expansion engine with polished cylinder-heads and fluted con-rods, served by a scotch or water-tube boiler – I don't mind which – oil-fired in the interests of cleanliness and to avoid drudgery. There would be no such unpleasant smells and sounds as accompany diesel operation.

As to the accommodations and appointments, I am not particular so long as they are gentlemanly.

I would do all the obvious things such as cruising among the Isles of Greece and in the Baltic, and revisiting by water all those cities which must be approached by sea: Leningrad, Stockholm, Amsterdam, Genoa, Venice, Constantinople. I would go either Westwards through the Panama Canal or Eastabout via Indonesia and Japan and would instruct my professional crew to take the ship, using the extremely precise satellite navigational aids with which she would be equipped, to the International Date Line, where I could stand on the bridge with one testicle in Wednesday and the other in Thursday. And from there I would send postcards to all my friends.

XLIV

One of the effects of inflation is to make our ideas of cost and value move in a jerky and spasmodic manner, so that the customary relativities become dislocated. The price of something goes up and we conclude that it has become too expensive for us. Some time later we notice that it is, by now and in comparison with other things, rather cheap: and so perhaps we buy it or use it. But we are not often allowed to enjoy this state of affairs for long. Up it goes again, and again we bid it goodbye, probably regretting that we did not notice in time that it had come within our means.

This happened to me with the London to Paris Night Ferry. I had been accustomed to doing it the hard way, humping my suitcase along an interminable catwalk at Dover in the small hours of the morning, and sitting, cold and hungry, in the train for Paris. My feelings towards those quietly sleeping in the first-class carriages all the way from Victoria to the Gare du Nord verged on the uncharitable. Then I suddenly realized that the first-class return fare was well within my means. It had not gone up for some time, whereas my income had. I think it cost about £17. . . . So for a time I enjoyed the luxury of going to bed between clean white sheets with a shaded lamp and a private wash-basin, being dimly aware during sleep of being carefully trundled on and off the steamer, coupled and uncoupled, waking refreshed and pulling up the blind to see the familiar names of Creil, Chantilly, Saint-Denis and so into Paris. But then the price went up and, rightly or wrongly, I thought I could not afford it. Never again, for, like most other gentlemanly modes of travel, the Night Ferry has ceased to exist.

In more everyday things inflation keeps us on the hop, desperately trying to do proportion-sums in our heads to determine whether something we have not bought for a while is now relatively cheap or relatively dear. For things do not stay in phase with one another: they leap-frog by fits and starts, and so, if we are honest enough to admit it, do our means. I have never been much good at mental arithmetic, and with the onset of old age and the objective acceleration of the rate of change it has not become any easier. Coupled with this is the autonomy of words and figures, so that we go on thinking that such-and-such a sum is the 'right' amount for such a commodity. Such concepts were once, and within my recollection, stable enough for a firm to call itself, for example, the 'Fifty Shilling Tailor' without having to repaint the sign more than once in a generation. Are books now dearer or cheaper in comparison with petrol, or drink, or hotel bills? And how do these items measure against one another at any given moment? Should not there be more important things to have to think about?

I do not understand economics, but I suspect that even if I did I would not know why it was judged necessary, during the First World War, to send about one million pounds' worth of gold, by dribs and drabs and through the post, from the Bank of England to the Bank of Ireland, and, later on in the same war, to detach a sizeable part of the British navy to ferry it back again across the Irish Sea. Even a qualified economist might be hard put to provide a rational explanation for this piece of farcical solemnity, remembering that, at the time, Great Britain and Ireland formed a single legal jurisdiction and fiscal unit.

But the mystique of gold defies reason. It is an uncommon metal, and usually hard to come by. It has properties which make it useful in electrical and medical contexts, and it is highly resistant to corrosion, which makes it very useful out of doors and in people's mouths. The visitor to Leningrad is struck by the amount of gold to be seen on the spires and domes of the city and in the teeth of the citizens. But to eat one's food off gold plates with gold spoons and forks cannot, surely, be as agreeable as to eat off and with silver. Yet the attempt to use silver instead of gold for the lettering and embellishment of bookbindings and for the heightening of decorative plasterwork seems to be an unqualified failure, and not only because silver so readily tarnishes. Both metals are, nowadays, most commonly replaced by ingenious modern substitutes.

It remains the fact that anywhere in the world people will give you money's-worth for gold. And why? Because they know that anywhere in the world . . . *da capo* ad infinitum.

XLV

When I joined the Inspectorate of Ancient Monuments in 1952 the old Oxford-and-Cambridge system by which men addressed one another by their surnames was still largely in force in the upper ranks of the civil service. We addressed those lower in rank than ourselves as 'Mr Smith', 'Mr Jones'; but between ourselves it was 'Smith' and 'Jones', and there was much to be said for this, especially as we had dealings with large numbers of people whom we hardly knew.

Oddly enough, the first of my fellow-inspectors whom it came naturally to me to call 'George' was thirty-odd years older than I. This was George Chettle, the predecessor of my immediate boss, who having retired was re-employed on a temporary basis and sat in the same room as we did. In part this familiarity was the result of his personality, but on reflexion I think that it may have been also because, being retired, he was outside the power-structure.

My Dublin book had just come out, and George bought it and read it with close attention and I believe also enjoyment. He had been in Dublin before the First World War, as an assistant to C. R. Ashbee who was one of the entrants to the Aberdeen competition for a new Dublin Town Plan. The winners' Dublin plan was a visionary and thoroughly impractical affair, heavily under French Beaux-Arts influence: but it made a splendid book.* George had been in charge of the restoration of the Queen's House, Greenwich.

George died about five years later, and I remember wondering to what purpose had been the care and attention with which he had read my book. But of course it was not the knowledge itself but the pleasure of assimilating it which had really mattered.

For many years afterwards I still called most of my colleagues by their surnames, and they me. I prefer this to the American system, gaining ground here, by which 'first names' are used from first acquaintance. I cannot get used to it, though I remember that had I lived in ancient Greece I would have had no choice. Demosthenes was Demosthenes, and that was that.

XLVI

My two visits to No. 10 Downing Street amused me at the time, and the relation of them may amuse others, particularly as nowadays nobody with my background and beliefs would be let in to that house.

In 1952 I was assistant to the Inspector for London whose business it was to look after all the buildings of historic value in the ownership or care of the Ministry of Works. Some trifling matter of doorknobs arose in connexion with No. 10, and my boss, a kindly man, gave it to me to do, solely, I am sure, because he knew it would amuse me, as indeed it did.

I went there on my bicycle with my briefcase strapped on to the back, chained my bicycle to the railings at a discreet

* *Dublin of the Future* (1922) by Patrick Abercrombie, Sydney Kelly and Arthur Kelly. Volume One of the publications of the Civics Institute of Ireland, a sumptuous and copiously illustrated large quarto. The work was mostly done before 1916, in which year it won the Aberdeen competition for the planning of Dublin.

distance, knocked on the door and went in. There was the usual small crowd gawping at the front door, but at this stage all they saw was my back. Inside, having disposed of the doorknobs, I saw two or three of the main rooms. I remember a sensation of awe at the thought that the Cabinet Room was the very room in which Gladstone had presided. No other ghosts had a look-in except Soane, whose two dining-rooms I saw and admired.

When I had finished I came out and paused on the doorstep. The curious crowd was still there and I gave them time to speculate who the tall dark man with the briefcase and the long overcoat might be. With an almost imperceptible movement of my head I seemed to acknowledge their interest. Their minds were working furiously. Then I took my bicycle-clips from my pocket and put them on. (There were, a little later, though not, I think, at this time, one or two cabinet ministers who habitually went round London on push-bikes: but I was neither of those.)

My second visit, a few years later, was as accompanist to Nikolaus Pevsner who was then doing the *London and West-minster* volume of his Buildings of England. We were taken round the whole house, from attic to cellar, by Sir Anthony Bevir, the Patronage Secretary (whose business it was, *inter alia*, to make bishops). I remember that one of the chimney-pieces in the private suite on the top floor was a Bossi, obviously imported from Dublin. The maids also, who were chatting as they went about their business, had obviously been imported from Ireland.

At the end we sat with Sir Anthony Bevir in the basement, still shored up with heavy baulks of timber, in which Churchill had spent a good deal of his time during the war. Of Sir Anthony's reminiscences I can now remember nothing; but Sir Anthony himself I remember most vividly. He did not smoke but he took snuff, and the whole of the front of his person, clothes and all, was dark brown as a result. 'Did you ever see such a *dirty* man?' asked Nikolaus as we walked away.

(Soon afterwards Sir Anthony retired and went to live in the West of Ireland, from which his wife came. The next and last time that I saw him was in a hotel in Galway about twenty years later. By this time he looked much cleaner and I was told that he spent much of his time drinking, as many people in the West of Ireland do.)

It was either on this occasion or on one very close to it that I accompanied Nikolaus to Schomberg House in Pall Mall.* There was the usual muddle about access: the building was standing empty and either the man with the keys failed to turn up, or the keys I had been given were the wrong keys. But from previous visits I remembered that there was a fire-escape which descended into the backyard of the Royal Automobile Club next door. So we explained ourselves to the automobilists and were let in, which would not happen now.

It soon became clear that the fire-escape was past its best. As we ascended, bits kept falling off it. I had gone up first in my capacity of, as it were, host, and pieces kept falling off the cast-iron structure including, I think, one whole step. For some time afterwards Nikolaus used to dine out on the story of how I had 'kicked the ladder away' or alternatively showered him about the pate with bits of metal. We left by the front door.

Schomberg House was hardly worth the trouble, as only the front wall (and not all of that) was seventeenth century. But Nikolaus quite rightly wanted to see for himself.

When I reviewed his last book I did so at some length and while not being by any means uncritical, and inserting a mild tease here and there, I was eloquent on the subject of the altogether special position which he held in our trade. I had a very warm-hearted letter from him; and not very long afterwards he died.

XLVII

I heard of the burning of Coleshill when I was at the bottom of a trench beside the moat at Eltham Palace, excavating the inverted underground buttresses at the behest of the

* Another Irish connexion, since Schomberg won the battle of the Boyne and his son Meinhardt was created Duke of Leinster.

Chief Inspector, Brian O'Neil. Someone had seen the news in the paper that morning but was not quite sure about the name of the house.

I was appalled at the news. Of all the houses in England, Coleshill was the one I had most been looking forward to seeing. It had always been in private hands, but its latest owner, rich old Mr Cook (of the travel agency), was going to give it to the National Trust. Work had been in progress on the roof, and a plumber's blowlamp, we heard, had started a hidden smouldering which had erupted into flame when nobody was there. An old story.

Though the walls were still standing to eaves height, rich old Mr Cook, it appeared, was determined to bulldoze everything into the ground till nothing remained of it. There was never a house to equal Coleshill, for nobility of scale, suavity of design, a majestic silhouette and breathtaking perfection of masonry. Nothing had been done to it since 1660, and it was perhaps the most influential single building of its century. Its progeny were legion. Yet very few people had ever seen it, and now it was too late.

It was, strictly, none of our business in the Ancient Monuments Branch, still less any of mine as a recently arrived Assistant Inspector. Yet I badgered O'Neil in the desperate hope that demolition might be at least arrested. George Chettle went down to look at it and returned with gloomy news. The walls, and especially those internal transverse walls which looked so substantial on the plan, were not as solid as they looked (they would have been, in Ireland, but this was England) and the ruins were unstable. The Ministry of Housing, whose business it was, were reluctant to move.

At this point Arnold Taylor, the Inspector for Wales, and his assistant Oswyn Craster, invited me to join them for a tour of inspection in Monmouthshire and Brecon. This was really quite irregular but my kindly boss John Charlton let me go. Among other places we went to Tintern Abbey in honour of Wordsworth and Llanthony in honour of Landor. It was all new to me, and unforgettable.

On the outward journey we went to Coleshill. It was a heartbreaking spectacle. The ashlar was as perfect as the day it was cut. Two or three of the great panelled stacks were still standing. The balustraded platform and cupola had of course gone, but some of the great modillion cornice was still in place. More of it had either been burnt or had fallen to the ground, and some of the carved modillions were lying about in the grass. Arnold and Oswyn decided to take one home in the boot of the car. They were bigger, of course, than they had looked from the ground, and this one was strangely heavy: even heavier than expected. They had nearly reached the car with it when a man came in sight: perhaps an estate worker. They hastily dropped it in the ditch.

Only then did we realize that it was a cast-iron replacement, evidently put up during some nineteenth-century repairs. But by this time it was too late to go back for one of the oak ones. I had been more modest. I had taken only a curled leaf-end from one of the broken consoles, and another smaller fragment.

Soon afterwards I made a model of the house, which I bequeathed to my successor in office seventeen years later. I had intended to carve the smaller piece of oak so as to make the cupola, but it was so hard that it blunted several knives and I never got round to finishing it.

The curled leaf-end I have still.

At the time, I remember, I used to say to anyone who would listen that the English people had lost a work of art comparable to 'Lycidas'. Nobody took much notice. Perhaps they had not read 'Lycidas' very recently.

It fell to my lot one day to take a party of MPs on a conducted tour round Chiswick House. We – that is to say the Ancient Monuments Branch – had removed the Wyatt wings and probably also the rooms in which C. J. Fox and Canning had both died, and thus reduced the size by two-thirds, spending a good deal of money in the process. This needed some explaining; so I explained it. I mentioned also that there existed an excellent perspective drawing done fifty years or so earlier in which the viewpoint had been so cunningly chosen that the

Wyatt additions were virtually invisible. This, I told them, was by an architect called Bossom who, now I came to think of it, had later gone into Parliament and even become a lord.

My audience were delighted. They converged on a small bird-like man who had been standing near me, listening attentively. Why, bless their souls, Alfred, they said, they did not know he had it in him! why had he been hiding his light under a bushel etc. etc. and the little man bridled and looked very pleased.

This was, of course, the Alfred Bossom of whom Churchill said that his name was not quite one thing or the other.

On another occasion, I was one of many who converged on a large country house in East Anglia on which we were spending a good deal of money. There were our architects, our administrators, men from the contractors, and of course the noble lord himself, and his architect. His architect was the great Sir Giles Gilbert Scott. More than once back in the office, I had heard mutterings to the effect that Sir Giles did not give overmuch attention to the work, but contented himself with playing golf with the client. He had arrived in a large Rolls-Bentley, and I happened to be standing beside him when he opened the boot which contained only a large bag of golf-clubs. 'You see,' he said to me, 'I always carry the tools of my trade round with me.' Fair enough, and full marks to the knighted architect for self-knowledge and candour. My own distaste for golf is all too well founded, and resembles the puritan disapproval of bear-baiting which, it will be remembered, rested less on the suffering caused to the bear than on the enjoyment had by the spectators. It is not so much the inherent futility of the game of golf – though I had protracted, repeated and tedious experience of this during many years of my youth – as the character of those who play it and who congregate in the clubhouse afterwards, and for what purposes.

Logically, I can see, I should object less to golf than to other games which I was also forced to play when young. Golf, at least, is not used to develop Team Spirit. Like all right-minded boys, I detested Team Spirit and all its then visible manifestations. In later life I have come to value team spirit very highly indeed, when it is invoked and cultivated for the attainment of some worthwhile communal goal or joint enterprise. What I could not stomach then, and cannot understand now, is how sane persons could devote their attention to getting a ball between two posts or down a hole, or to preventing someone else from doing so. As the Shah of Persia is reputed to have said to Edward VII, 'Of course one horse can run faster than another, but why should I care which horse it is?'

XLVIII

Not many people have put me into their books. In fact I know of only two instances, both misleading. Among the illustrations to Victoria Glendinning's life of Elizabeth Bowen is a photograph taken at Bowen's Court showing her with Iris Murdoch, Edward Sackville-West, Hubert Butler and myself, which makes it appear as though I were one of her circle of friends and a frequent visitor. The truth of the matter is that this was my only visit to Bowen's Court and the only time I ever met her. Hubert Butler and I had motored over in the Delage from Bennettsbridge in 1956 or 1957 and on page 149 of my *Classic Irish Houses* the tail of the Delage is just visible on the right of the picture.

The other book is *A Peacock on the Lawn* by Anne Hadfield, one of those books which so many English ladies write about how she and her husband found a lovely old house and with great effort brought it back from the dead and now live in it and how fond they are of it. It tells how they made an application to the Historic Buildings Council and how in due course two languid gentlemen from the Ministry arrived in a large green Bentley and flopped into deck-chairs on the lawn and drank gin and stayed to lunch and made civilized conversation and finally gave the house a rather perfunctory inspection and went off down the drive weaving from side to side, and how there was no grant forthcoming for their house. I need hardly say that we went painstakingly through every nook and cranny of that (rather ordinary) house on that very hot day, before gratefully accepting the offer of a drink. It was at her suggestion, not mine, that I hid the dark-blue Delage in a shed and covered it with sacking to save it from being pecked to death by her peacock. And they did (after whispered consultation) ask us to stay to lunch, and it was all very pleasant. In her position I would have done exactly as she did, transposed the order of events and heightened everything for effect, so I do not bear her any malice. But it was unkind of her to call my car a Bentley. This should have been one more of the appearances of Delage in literature, which I collect and hoard.

As a general rule, when I have picked out a house on the ordnance map and want to look at it, I memorize the name of a house a mile or so away and then drive boldly up the avenue, circle round in front of it memorizing its features, and drive smartly out again, stopping only when I am safely outside the gates to write down the particulars and perhaps make a small conventionalized sketch. If the owner or anyone else stops me I am ready with the name of the house next door which I pretend to be looking for. The risk of being ordered off the premises is rather less than that of being invited in, shown over it at perhaps wearisome length, and fed a large quantity of history irrelevant to my purposes. By these tactics I may miss an internal feature of interest, but otherwise the amount of country I could quarter in a day would be very much reduced.

I once drove up to the gravel sweep in front of a house on the Wicklow-Carlow border and as I swirled round I had time to see what appeared to be a fox, curled up either asleep or dead on a pedestal such as supports a sundial. There was a small dog trotting about, and as he barked neither at me nor at the fox I could only conclude that he was used to it, whatever it was, or was more than usually phlegmatic.

While trespassing in the same way in the same part of the country I had the misfortune to get bogged down, and the lady of the house was so much a lady that she called her tractor-man to haul me out and waved me on my way without so much as asking my name, for which I award her full marks.

XLIX

It pays to insult people's grandmothers, at least when they are safely dead. Such has been my experience. Many years ago I wrote a life of the first Earl of Charlemont in which I commented disapprovingly of the conduct of the last Countess of Charlemont in getting compensation for the burning of the Charlemont Fort and selling the materials to a contractor so that it was levelled to the ground. I got a solicitor's letter from a firm in Lincoln's Inn writing on behalf of the French family who were descended from her. I replied that I stood by what I had written and that in any case they had no cause of action. I do not like insulting people, or to be more accurate, I do rather enjoy the idea of insulting them, but if I give in to the temptation I sometimes feel rather ashamed of it.

About twenty years later I happened to have to visit, in the course of my work, an old house in East Anglia which had, at the time of my visit, been let to Lord French. When he heard my name he recognized me as the author of the book, and I have an idea that he was somewhat apologetic at having got his solicitors to write to me, which I think he had done to placate some of his relatives. I, of course, was equally apologetic, and the upshot was that there and then he made me a present of a charming quasi-silhouette portrait of the old Earl, done in 1790, which I have treasured ever since.

I have been in a number of buildings which few other people have had the opportunity of penetrating. Mereworth, Kent, for example, which I had the good fortune of visiting in the company of my minister, an engaging rascal called Nigel Birch, when it belonged to Mr Michael Tree and before it was bought by an oriental gentleman who, I understand, keeps it to himself. I saw Welbeck, including all the underground parts, before it became a kind of military public school. I have also been up in the roof-structure of the Albert Hall which is of great elegance, an intricate web of cast and wrought iron giving the impression of being inside an old-fashioned airship. The actual weathertight covering, few people know, is of glass, with another membrane of glass lower down to make the internal dome. Both were painted to obscure them during the war.

I have also been across the high-level span of the Tower Bridge, though I had to twist someone's arm to wangle it. I gather that the works of the Tower Bridge are now open to the public, but the steam-engines which worked the works have gone. These I saw in action. They turned very slowly, only a fraction of a revolution at a time, and their job was to pump a little water into a hydraulic reservoir, against the weight of a huge plug which pressed down on the water and provided the hydraulic pressure to work the slave-engine which looked at first sight not unlike the steam prime mover.

I have also been inside the Henry VIII wine-cellar in Whitehall. This modest structure has an extraordinary history. It was found to be in the way when they were going to build the enormous block by Vincent Harris which houses the Ministry of Defence. Because it was minutely described in the Royal Commission volume and was the only remaining part of the medieval palace of Whitehall, the civil engineers braced it full of struts and encased it in a corset of steel and moved it on steel rollers so many feet to the South, and then lowered it by hydraulic lift so many feet downwards, finally moving it back again Northwards until it was almost directly below its original site, and far below the ground-floor level of the new buildings, where I saw it. All this, it can be understood, cost a vast deal of money; but I imagine that it was done chiefly for the exercise.

At all events, that is the only benefit anyone has ever got out of it. Being right under the Ministry of Defence, it was, even then, hardly ever seen by anyone. Indeed it is a wonder that even I ever got into it. Yet: in a country where people delight in anything which is underground, where the associations of wine are potent, and where the exploits, real or fancied, of that folk-hero/villain Henry VIII are sure-fire box-office, what a pity that the public cannot flock into it to gape.

On the way back from somewhere in the West of England with two of my colleagues, I noticed that a certain house lay very near our way, and with some difficulty persuaded them to agree to a small diversion so that we could look at it. One at least of them felt that a deviation of a hair's breadth from the shortest route while on official business was an improper use of official time and petrol. Nothing could persuade him to drive through the gates (which were open), so we left the car outside and went on foot, he following, nervously protesting. From just inside the gates we got a good view of the house, perhaps three or four hundred yards away. I studied it through binoculars. It was of brick, from the seventeenth century, with a row of circular niches containing busts between ground and first floors, much as at Ham House.

A portly figure in a tailcoat detached itself from the house and came towards us down the drive. My nervous colleague, with that exaggerated respect for private property so common in England, counselled flight. We could still escape by car. I insisted that we stand our ground. The butler approached us. Who were we? I replied that I was an Inspector of Ancient Monuments in the Ministry of Works but that I was merely sightseeing in a private capacity, having read about the house in books. 'The last man we had here claiming to be from the Ministry of Works is doing time in the County Jail,' he told us. Would we accompany him? With the greatest of pleasure, we would.

By the time we reached the house a large car had drawn up in front of it. Down the steps came the baronet, red of face, in full hunting pink with shiny black boots and a black silk hat, and was driven away. The baronet's lady turned to us. We would like to see the house? Of course; and she showed us everything, from the great eighteenth-century octagon room with its florid plasterwork to the niche on an angle of the stairway which, she explained to us, was there to accommodate the end of a coffin on that awkward turn, should the occasion arise. I reflected that, to judge by the baronet's complexion, the occasion might arise at no very distant date, depending on whether he should come by his end in the hunting field or in bed.

Before we parted, on the most cordial terms, the lady pressed us to a glass of sherry. As he served it, the butler, I thought, did not seem too well pleased.

All that was nearer thirty than twenty years ago, and I fear that were it to happen today our reception would almost certainly not be so courteous or so trusting. The butler's view of things has probably, by now, prevailed.

L

Some people attribute significance to coincidences. In particular Arthur Koestler devoted a book to them. I remain unconvinced, but, like other people, have experienced my share, and some are worth recounting.

When I was living in London Thomas Pakenham was also living there. I was in the habit of going to the London Library during my lunch-hour. One day I met Thomas in the entrance lobby. We agreed to go to a nearby pub for a sandwich. As we walked along King Street I asked him how he was getting on with his book about the Ninety-Eight Rising. He had finished or nearly finished it, he said, and went on to tell me that the impression the whole business had left with him was that of the absurd frivolity of the leaders. There they were, he said, all set to overthrow the British empire or, more probably, be caught and hanged. And what did I suppose, he went on, warming to his subject, what did I suppose Lord Edward was doing in that house in Thomas Street just before Major Sirr came rushing up the stairs to arrest him? Checking over stores of arms and disposition of forces? Not a bit of it. He was reclining on a *chaise longue*, reading some rubbishy novel called – oh, let me see – yes, called *Gil Blas*, by somebody called – what was it? – Lesage. I ask you . . . !

'But, my dear Thomas,' I said, 'every cultivated gentleman carries a copy of *Gil Blas* in his pocket to read at odd moments,' and I pulled it out of mine, having just borrowed it to reread, my own copy being in storage at home in Dublin. The effect was all I could have hoped for. He nearly fell flat on his back, and dined out on it for long afterwards. As did I.

Anyone can appreciate the satisfaction which I got from this particular incident. Others seem worth recounting for slightly different reasons. My wife Jeanne gave me an Old English sheepdog puppy as a birthday present. I had never owned a dog of my own before, let alone such an enchanting animal as this. As happens to the owner of, for example, a rare kind of car, there is a strong impulse to compare notes with other owners. Only a week or two later I drove North out of London on a tour of duty, and approaching Biggleswade saw in the distance a lady with an Old English sheepdog. I stopped, got out of the car, waited till she came up to me and accosted her on the subject.

To cut a long story short, this dog, Sally, the first of the breed that I had seen since becoming an owner, turned out to be the mother of my puppy. Mrs King, the wife of a police-sergeant, had been living in Portsmouth when the puppies were born. At the appropriate time she had sold them to Miss Tilley, the breeder at Shepton Mallet in Somerset, from whom my wife had bought mine. Mrs King's husband had in the meantime been transferred from Portsmouth to Biggleswade.

Not very far from Biggleswade, at Barley, lived Miss Inno-cent, the owner of my puppy's father, an enormous dog called Horace. In due course we went there and made his acquaintance, and in failing light I managed to take a photograph of father, mother and daughter all in one frame.

A coincidence is not the same thing as a fortunate accident with which it is sometimes confused. The element which is com-mon to both sides of the coincidence must be something which is virtually unique: one dog out of many thousands, one book out of millions, and no other dog or book. The odds against the coincidence must be very long.

There are something like seventeen radial roads out of Dublin, depending on how you count them. There would be more if Dublin were not on the East coast, so that not much more than 180 degrees is available. Even if we agree to count only five or six of these radial routes as really important, the following story is still remarkable. I had left home early one morning and was driving along the main road to Roscommon and Sligo. Somewhere between Kinnegad and Mullingar I passed a car on my left: stationary, empty and with its lights on. As I passed it I automatically read off its number. Then it occurred to me that there was something familiar about the number.

There was indeed. It was Agnes's car. It had been parked outside the house the night before. I went back to it, turned the lights off, locked it with the key I had on my ring, and drove on into Mullingar where I reported it to the Guards who kindly said that they would bring it in and report its whereabouts to the number I gave them.

When Agnes came in to work at the boutique which she was then jointly running she was astonished to get a telephone message saying that her car had been found and was in safe custody forty-five miles away. She had not noticed that it had been stolen and had gone in to town by bus.

I would never have taken any notice of the car but for my habit of reading numbers and anything written or printed which comes into my field of sight.

The appeal of these incidents is aesthetic. It is the delight in seeing the arrow landing, against all odds, dead in the middle of the target.

LI

The aesthetic element, I believe, lies at the root of all my responses and decisions, including the moral ones. It is perhaps worth exploring some instances of the diversity of this response.

Three instances of the ambiguity of the response occurred to me, all on the same day, each exemplifying a different aspect of the problem.

In the morning I heard on the BBC the waltz by Diabelli which stands at the head of the 'Diabelli Variations'. I heard it with the thrill which accompanies the opening bars of the opus 110 sonata or the *Missa Solemnis* or indeed *Otello*. But in itself the waltz is a banal little piece. It stimulated me exactly as the sound of a tin being opened stimulates my cat: by pure association. They did not play the Variations till later in the day.

Later in the day I saw from a distance a bridge with a grey lattice-work balustrade which I took to be, from its dimensions and its colour, made of concrete, and noted it, half-consciously, with distaste. When, a little later, I found it to be made of timber which had weathered to a grey colour, I thought quite differently about it. Knowledge had superimposed itself on the sense-data, as though my cat had, to his disappointment, discovered that I was opening nothing more exciting than a tin of peaches.

Then, as I was being shown round a garden, there floated into my head the words 'chill drosera' from a poem by Landor. I would not recognize a drosera if I saw one, nor, so far as I know, was there one in the garden. But 'chill drosera' always excites me, not because it brings an image before my mind but because I know from the form of the word that it derives from the Greek word 'droses' meaning dew (and in fact the drosera is otherwise known as the sundew). 'Chill drosera' makes its effect partly by association between 'dew' and 'chill' and partly by the vocalic and consonantal harmony which is the essence of poetry. It was as though the cat could read the label on the tin but had never tasted its contents.

Other people's minds are much like other people's houses. They may look quite similar to our own from outside, but once you get a glimpse of the interior . . .

I know many people who are better citizens than I: more industrious, more compassionate, more conscientious, better husbands and fathers, and, in many cases, a good deal cleverer. But I know also that the moment I enter the house of one of them, I shall immediately see that they have no discrimination whatever in a field which I cannot help thinking of as important. They buy, and fill their houses with, objects which I can only think of as rubbish.

For example, when I was young the artist Birket Foster was a joke. I see that his paintings are now sold at auction for very large sums. For another example, seventy years ago cultivated people such as Yeats and Sir Hugh Lane went in no fear of contradiction when they asserted that the Metal or Halfpenny

Bridge in Dublin was an 'ugly' structure and would not be missed. They had, it is true, a strong motive for saying so: they wanted to put Lutyens's crack-brained gallery in its place. Fortunately they failed.

But what can they have meant by calling it 'ugly'? Because I have no doubt that they really thought so. But the next bridge upstream from it, Grattan Bridge, has, demonstrably, every aesthetic fault a bridge could have. What would they have said about it, if asked? Would it not have been clear to them that, by comparison, the Halfpenny Bridge is a miracle of grace? Can people's way of seeing things really change so much?

Certainly I can remember thinking beautiful some things which I do not now think beautiful. There is a distinction here between remembering thinking something and remembering *that I thought* it. One is much more immediate than the other. In these cases I really do remember the thought itself. To put it another way, I was, at that time, and to that extent, a different person.

It seems that there are virtually no human likes and dislikes that are not culturally determined. Prescott tells somewhere of a young man whose turn it was to be immolated as a sacrifice on top of one of those stepped pyramids in Mexico. The arrival of the conquistadores put a stop to that and he was bitterly indignant at being done out of his passport to felicity. This young man must himself already have witnessed, several times, the bloody fate of his predecessors. Natural revulsion, supposing there to be such a thing, was quite obliterated by a much stronger motive.

We now know that culture, besides dictating eighty per cent or more of our desires and actions, is almost infinitely plastic, indefinitely protean. There is almost nothing which it does not, at some time or another, prohibit or enjoin. Even the desire to know the truth is, as George Steiner has reminded us, only a part of culture, and not a very large part nor, much more disturbingly, even a permanent one.*

* G. Steiner, *Has Truth a Future?* (1978).

Let us return to those good citizens who fill their houses with junk. Had they lived 250 years ago, or even 200 years ago, their houses would have been less full but would have contained nothing ugly. At that time, and, perhaps, at all previous times, the culture of high art and the culture of peasant craft formed a continuum. There was no perceptible break between them, no chasm in which people wallowed about, not knowing what was what. This much is known and as provable as any scientific fact.

To put it another way, the predecessors of our good citizens enjoyed much less freedom in these matters than do their descendants. They did not chafe at their want of freedom, not knowing any different.

A few spirits, however, did chafe; and it was they who made the Romantic movement which, in retrospect, looks so similar to Eve's business with the apple and has had such similar results. I suppose that what John Summerson has called the 'rebellion against good taste' was bound to take place sooner or later, but only when alternative possibilities had presented themselves, explorations in time or space, the examples of ancient Egypt, the world of Islam, China, the four Gothic centuries.

When to this was added the expanding possibilities of what could be done and made with machines and industrial processes generally, the floodgates were opened and could not again be shut.

When something was made a long time ago, and particularly if it was made by hand, it goes against the grain to call it 'ugly'. Yet most Jacobean architecture is, to my eyes, as ugly as sin, and I think I know why. It was the product of an age when a sudden increase in wealth was matched by the appearance of a number of new ideas: ideas which were less than perfectly understood by those who set out to express them. Something very similar has been taking place, in the last decade and a half, in modern Ireland. Hesitant and faltering steps into a new realm can, sometimes, have the charm of a child's first efforts to walk or to talk. But much more often not.

A child's head is too big for its body, or rather it would be if it were not a child. Knowing it to be a child, we find it beautiful, just as a gap in the teeth of a child of a certain age is charming, but in an adult would not be charming in the least. Or take the case of the donkey:

> With monstrous head and sickening cry
> And ears like errant wings,
> The devil's walking parody
> Of all four-footed things.

When Chesterton wrote this he presumably meant it. He was a pious man, and presumably he did not ascribe one of God's creatures to the arch-fiend without some reason. True, he was working up to a dramatic climax in the poem and therefore not playing quite fair, but nonetheless he expected his readers to find this opening stanza credible. In other words, he expected to get away with calling the donkey 'ugly'.

Why?

Clearly, I think, because he and his hearers had been brainwashed by the propaganda of the hippodules. If you look at a donkey expecting it to be a horse, you find it misshapen. The horse is so closely identified with human prestige, potency and political clout, that nobody has noticed that if you look at a horse expecting to see a donkey, it, also, is the wrong shape. The horse, like many of those who ride him, has an enormous backside and a small head. The donkey, by contrast, has slim hindquarters and a large head stuffed full of sagacity. Even the horse-cultists know, in their innermost hearts, that the donkey is much cleverer than the horse. As for its cry, what is wrong with that? If you love the donkey you come to love its voice. Besides, I never heard of anyone crying up the melodiousness of the horse's whinny except Swift, and he was not playing fair either. He, too, had an axe to grind. How many mammals (as distinct from birds) make a sound which is positively pleasing to our ears? The trilling and purring of cats, and the roaring of their larger cousins, are pleasing, and the lowing of kine and the bleating of sheep appeal because of their pastoral associations.

And the ears? All the better to hear you with, my dear.

The Bible seems to have got the sheep and the goats the wrong way round. Who would not sooner be a goat than a sheep? If something unusual is happening, a goat walks circumspectly towards it to investigate, while a sheep takes fright and trots away. It is extraordinary that two animals so similar as to be virtually indistinguishable anatomically (as I am told by those who know) should be so different.

As for their skins: ask any bookbinder. Morocco (which means goatskin) is the aristocrat of binding leathers, while sheep is dyed and teased about and disguised under a variety of names such as roan and skiver in the vain effort to pass it off as morocco, and not at all esteemed.

The Germans (an ill-natured wit has said) are a race of carnivorous sheep. Let us hope that is no longer true; and let us hope, also, that their mantle has not descended on the shoulders of someone else.

Being a town-bred child I have had little direct experience of sheep or goats. But two moments remain in my memory. The first was nearly forty years ago, in a lonely place somewhere above the Gulf of Policastro, when a flock of goats, each with a little bell, came ambling past, in charge of a goatherd: a scene from biblical times. The second was when Agnes and I spent a week in January, about fifteen years ago, at Ballymaloe in Cork. Every morning, while we were still in bed, the sheep with their lambs would come drifting by, bleating gently, on some routine movement of their own.

Can it be that some trigger implanted when our ancestors were a pastoral people has endowed these moments with the quality which invites recall?

I had an early lesson in how useless a word 'beautiful' is when, on returning from Paris, I remarked that I thought Paris must be the most beautiful city in the world. My father was puzzled at this, so I asked him which city he would propose. His answer, Rio de Janeiro, left me equally baffled, until I realized that it was not the city itself but its setting which he had had in mind. Like ninety-nine per cent of the world's population, he did not see or look at architecture. I look at little else.

With wider experience I would now propose Leningrad and Rome to set beside Paris. Constantinople and Cairo are not exactly beautiful but they are inexhaustibly interesting. Florence has a certain beauty, but as an entity is hardly up to the aggregate of its component parts. In its setting, and when seen from a distance, it has the same kind of beauty as Bath, which contains finer set-pieces than any in Florence.

But, in the end, perhaps Paris has the edge on all of these by virtue of the dimensions of time, experience, emotional associations and intellectual distinction.

The word 'beautiful', I have noticed, is nowadays more often on the lips of engineers and mathematicians than of artists or indeed art critics. A good example of this response is, of all unlikely things, the Victorian brick sewer. Medieval drains were very large, arched-over and with flat floors, because hydrostatics was among the very many things which medieval man did not understand. He supposed, like many since, that more of anything was necessarily better, so he made his sewers as capacious as he could, thus giving rise, incidentally, to the ubiquitous tales of secret passages. The Victorian sewer, by contrast, employs the principle that the smaller the cross-section the brisker the flow and the less risk of precipitation and silting-up. Such drains are egg-shaped in section, with the pointed end of the oval at the bottom, so that when the flow is small the channel is narrow and the velocity high. When the rate of input rises, the sectional area rises with it and so accommodates a larger volume per second. When the flow drops, the level drops, but the cross-section diminishes at a greater rate, thus keeping up the velocity.

I cannot believe that anyone to whom this is explained and who fully understands it can fail to find it beautiful as one finds Kepler's law of planetary motion beautiful, and beautiful, furthermore, with a beauty that does not fade. This is a very simple example, but note that, like other simple things, it arrived only at a late stage of civilization.

Civilization is a word which seems to me to have three distinct meanings which have very little to do with one another.

The one which occurs first to most ordinary people (and also to archaeologists) has to do with drains and aqueducts and metallurgy and communications. The second, which is the one which first occurs to me, is about having good libraries and opera-houses and also riches of a less tangible kind such as a healthy literary and artistic tradition and an esteem for those who practise and transmit it. The third, which may be the most important, involves the toleration of diversity and in particular the technique and habit of coexisting with your political (and religious) opponents, not torturing or killing them.

Clearly it is possible to have any one of these without either of the others, or any two without the third. Examples of each of the possible combinations are not hard to find, though perhaps invidious to mention.

It is sometimes asserted, and widely believed, that art cannot flourish except in conditions of political liberty. For good or ill, this is simply not true, and there is even a certain amount of evidence in the contrary sense. Some kinds of architecture, for example, flourish best under a despotism. The age of Augustus was favourable to literary culture, and both Beethoven and Verdi flourished under reactionary regimes. The necessity of circumventing censorship elicits tactics and stratagems which have positive artistic value, as any reader of Gibbon knows well.

A favourite piece of current cant is the assertion that the artist must, *ipso facto*, be subversive: that art which is not subversive does not deserve the name of art. I am well aware of being quite adequately subversive on a number of issues, mostly political. There have been, there still are, and I hope there will continue to be, artists who are subversive both in their intentions and in their effect. But there are, it seems to me, other kinds of artist as well.

What I care most about, and what gives me most trouble, is trying to make something properly. What I am trying to make may or may not be art: that is, perhaps, a question of opinion: certainly a question of definition. Definitions of what is art are a notoriously thorny territory: look at the mess old

146

Tolstoy made of it. And our civil servants, in trying to implement the Haughey Act, have apparently decided that if it is fiction or in verse it is art, but not otherwise. By these standards Gibbon, Johnson, Swift, Carlyle, Norman Douglas would hardly scrape in.

The role of the commentator is universally despised. He is asserted to be a parasite, a passenger, a superfluous organism. As one who cannot claim to be other than a commentator, I naturally feel sensitive about this, though well short of resentful. The Alexandrian age was an age of commentators and grammarians, sharply to be distinguished from the great creators of the fifth century. But the Alexandrians cannot be blamed for being born when they were, and but for them, how much of the fifth century would we know? Yet the stigma of being mere commentators remains.

The authors of programme-notes or descriptions of musical works such as the series of booklets published by the BBC are exposed to this imputation. If the listener (so the argument runs) is musically well informed he will not need to be told where the modulations come or what happens in the coda or in the third variation, and so on. If the listener is not musically well informed, so we are told, he will not understand what he is reading.

The fundamental fallacy here is that all mankind can be divided into the fully informed and the totally ignorant. Having spent most of my life trying to enlarge and enhance the experience of those partially informed but well disposed in a certain field, I naturally believe no such nonsense. The truth is that though each of us may be an expert in something, there is always a much larger field in which we are grateful for guidance from someone else. Providing that guidance is analogous with the making of maps. Some maps are better than others, and good maps, of the same territory, differ according to their purposes. But nobody suggests that the study of the map is a substitute for a visit to the territory.

I have met people who positively disapproved of maps and refused to use them, on the grounds, apparently, that this interferes with their perception of the place when they actually reach it. I confess that I find this incomprehensible, but must plead guilty to being affected by the contrary heresy. I am given to poring over maps of places which I am never likely to visit. But, more oddly, I do, in a sense which is rather more than metaphorical, get the illusion, when I am looking at a really good map on one of the larger scales, that if I looked even more closely I could see what is actually on the ground. In other words, I endow the map with a kind of reality. It is true that we are spoiled, in Ireland, in this respect. The older one-inch maps, of which I am the fortunate possessor of a nearly complete set, do give the illusion of reality, while the original six-inch maps, the earliest large-scale survey of any country in the world, are a unique source of joy.

LII

It is for love of beauty that people fill their houses with hideous things, and spoil the outsides of them, and even succeed in making their gardens ugly.

If beauty is that which gives pleasure to the eye, then I know nothing more beautiful than a good specimen of the raised-quarter-deck steam coasters which were built in their thousands between about 1890 and 1950. Such a vessel is neither quite a natural growth nor yet quite a work of art as most people understand the term. The type is one which was evolved to meet practical needs within the limits of available technology, and the formula is quite standardized. Reading from left to right the events are: straight stem, raised fo'c'sle, well-deck with one hatch, bridge amidships, raised quarter-deck with one hatch, boiler-and-engine casing with one tall funnel, counter stern. There would be a little variation in the number and position of the masts and the boats: otherwise they varied only in size and that only within narrow limits. But since during the period the pride of craftsmanship and a feeling for proportion and for detail were widespread among both builders and owners, some are more beautiful than others. Seen from any angle, the best of

148

them give great aesthetic pleasure. They gave still more pleasure when one saw them in action, as I well remember, and I have tried to re-enact that pleasure by making a working model of one of them.

Such things are not taken seriously by art historians, and it is worth while to examine why. One obvious reason is that they are made of perishable materials. Even an iron ship could not easily, even in favourable conditions, often last more than a century, while mild steel, which superseded iron about a hundred years ago, has a very much shorter life. Timber, of course, has a still shorter expectation; but in the case of preserved ships such as the *Victory*, it was thought admissible to renew nearly the whole fabric piecemeal, as is done with holy structures in China and Japan, without prejudice to their metaphysical survival.

Such vessels are entirely without ornament, for the era of scrollwork at bow and stern came to an end at just about the time when they began to be built. But suitable mouldings were sparingly applied: builders and owners set great store by them 'looking right', and individual yards had their own recognizable style. In profile, the informal balancing of masses was such as to delight the eye of a modern architect. Theorists like Le Corbusier, and professors of design such as David Pye, did indeed give evidence of understanding that the static architecture of earthfast structures could take lessons from seagoing exemplars.*

Conventional opinion concedes, indeed proclaims, that sailing-ships are beautiful, and you will sometimes see it implied that steam yachts and those few cruise-liners which anachronistically retained the clipper-bow and the bowsprit are, to that extent and for that reason, 'beautiful' and 'graceful'. I do not share this view. Any fool can see the resemblance of a square-rigger to a sea-bird, and the plenitude of swelling sails is only too obviously picturesque. I suspect, too, that in this view there is an element of moral preference for the 'natural' over the 'mechanical'. But for me sailing-ships have never held as much interest as steamships.

* David Pye, *The Nature and Art of Workmanship* (1968); *The Nature of Design* (1964, 1967).

In neither case was the social content of the artefact acceptable to a well-informed observer. Looking at a typical coaster one cannot help remembering that the crew's quarters in the raised fo'c'sle were ill lit, ill heated, ill ventilated, overcrowded and dangerous into the bargain. But the social content of the *Aquitania* was no more acceptable. On critical examination she gives an all too truthful account of the priorities of the society which created her: what was thought due to stokers, deck-hands and stewards, what to the steerage passengers, and what to those who travelled first class. Yet no more splendid vessel ever sailed the seas, and she embodied the aspirations of the time, both the noble and the less noble, more faithfully than contemporary structures on land.

Over the past twenty-five years I have taken, or made, opportunities to travel by paddle-steamer, a class of vessel then rapidly disappearing and now almost extinct, and to see surviving examples, and have built a working model of the PS *Cynthia* which had a long Irish career. I travelled on eight such ships, including the most out-of-the-way of all, which I found by accident. Jeanne and I were touring in central Jutland, and came to Silkeborg to see the Tollund Man in the museum there. And very remarkable he is, with his thoughtful, lifelike face and about a day's – not more – growth of beard. Moored to the little wooden quay was a small and very ancient paddle-steamer with a clipper-bow, the *Hjeilen*. It was a Friday, and we were told that she ran on Saturdays, so we stayed the night. The *Hjeilen* was and is, I believe, the oldest operational steamship afloat, built by Burmeister and Baumgarten before they became Burmeister and Wain, and with a single-digit yardnumber. I think the date was 1864. She had a two-cylinder oscillating engine with the bore given in 'thumbs' (inches): *tommer*. The boiler and crankshaft have been renewed but for the rest she is original. The journey was of perhaps ten miles there and then ten miles back, to a lake on which is the Himmelberget, the highest peak in Denmark, about 600 feet. I was allowed down into the engine-room while we were under way.

The launching of a ship is such a remarkable spectacle that I am surprised more is not made of it. The number of those who have seen it, apart from those occupationally concerned, must, I suppose, be rather small. You stand under a smooth steel structure as high as most buildings and a good deal longer than most, which is not quite on the level because the whole thing must necessarily slope towards the water. Nor is it, especially near ground level, at all straight because it has that smooth fish-like underwater shape common to all ships, even the ugliest (and nowadays there are plenty of those).

The launch I remember was in April 1930, when I was eleven. The ship was the *Warwick Castle*, an intermediate vessel of the Union-Castle line. She was torpedoed in 1942 and her name afterwards transferred to another ship. Union-Castle ships were painted a rather remarkable lavender-grey (in fact a good many ships are painted grey at the time of launching, which makes them look even bigger).

When the trigger was pulled the whole mass began to move, slowly at first but with gathering momentum and in complete silence until she began to take up the chains which were coiled on the ground to act as a brake, finally losing way and floating free, ready to be taken by tugs round to the fitting-out berth.

I had a camera with me and managed to take three or four frames during the launch, of which the only one worth anything is the last, where in the middle foreground, back to the camera and watching the ship, is a man in a cloth cap who probably (since this was 1931) was watching his employment ebb away.

LIII

I read in an English newspaper – one of the posh ones, too – that the Russian sailors who come ashore landing fish at some East coast port are 'surprisingly well educated'. What did they expect? Did they think that they would be as ignorant as English fishermen? Do they not know that the Russian government has, for good or ill, a policy of trying to protect its citizens from the contagion of commercialized mass culture, and that this policy is, at least partly, successful?

I like the story of the Russian sailor who landed at Tilbury and asked a dock-worker to direct him to the nearest Shakespeare theatre. It may not be true, but it is far from impossible and though I find it funny, I also find it sad. My own experience of Russia is extremely limited: a total of less than ten days in and around Leningrad. But I could not help being struck by the number of ordinary people who were reading serious literature out of proper books. The world I live in is increasingly governed, whether visibly or invisibly, by right-wing populists. Being myself a left-wing élitist I am naturally tempted by the doctrine that the people should be given not what they want, but what they ought to want.

I would like to believe in some aesthetic analogue to the scientific law of the uniformity of nature. In fact I do already believe in some such law. I believe, or want to believe, that people will not forever put up with a diet of rubbish. The trouble is that the metaphor breaks down. In dietetics an organism fed on rubbish either stops eating it and finds something nourishing, or perishes. There is no guarantee that we will take the first course rather than the second. To judge by the media, we are mostly being fed on frivolity and nihilism, not only in entertainment but also in real life.

To claim to be an élitist does not mean claiming or aspiring to belong to a circle from which other people are excluded. It need mean no more than the recognition of having tastes (or, for that matter, abilities) which are not widely shared. All that the élitist demands is that there should be some room in the scheme of things for him to indulge his taste and exercise his talent, in company with others similarly situated. As a general rule, the élitist wishes that more people would join his company, though he recognizes that in the society in which we find ourselves this is unlikely to happen on a large scale. He does not wish to interfere with the majority's enjoyments unless the majority interferes with his.

But he does, in his heart of hearts, believe that he is on to something better than that which contents the majority. He takes no pleasure in the rupture of continuity between the few and the many, a rupture which happened a century or a century and a half ago and which he would like to heal and to bridge. If any political system seems to offer the prospect of such a reversal, he is inevitably tempted by it.

LIV

When my first books came out there was a certain amount of muttering about my not being 'a trained historian'. They are more polite now, and if they think it they do not say it. On the contrary, I find myself described as a historian when I would not claim to be one. The writers think I am a historian and the historians think I am a writer. They are both right.

Thirty-odd years ago the academic historians paid no heed to the kind of matters I sought to explore in my books. They were very narrowly documentary, political or economic. They have learnt a little since; but not very much, to judge from the amount of space allotted to all aspects of the history of art in the *New History of Ireland*: an admirable enterprise in most other respects.

Standards in architectural history have risen dramatically during my lifetime, and I have found it difficult to keep up with them. Hardly any of the architectural history written more than forty years ago is of any value today: it is nearly all tainted with dilettantism and slovenly optimism. It has been very pleasant to find myself, by the accident of age, carried forward on this wave, where Ireland is concerned. I have done my best to demystify the subject: to persuade the reader not that it is too elevated or too arcane for him to understand, but, on the contrary, that most of it is common sense and comes with practice, and that above all he must use his eyes.

Of all spheres of learning, academic literary criticism is that in which the tyranny of the technical expert has taken the most deadly hold. The hungry sheep look up, and are not fed.

LV

'Irish country houses in arrogant disrepair make everything else look vulgar.' This quotation from Cyril Connolly (*The Evening Colonnade*, 1967, p. 503) gives me great satisfaction, not least because Connolly, in spite of his name, neither was nor claimed to be in any real sense Irish: he was an Englishman and an Etonian. I know exactly what he meant. But is there any future in it? 'Arrogant' is the kind of word Yeats liked to use: it recalls the mood in which he elected to go down with all flags flying and all guns blazing in the divorce debate in the Senate in 1925. There was no future in that. Connolly's sentence lives, in my mind, beside one from Yeats which has haunted me for far longer. It comes from *Dramatis Personae* (p. 49): 'To transmute the anti-English passion into a passion of hatred against the vulgarity and materialism whereon England has founded her worst life and the whole life that she sends us, has always been a dream of mine.'

Because I was sent to school with the sons of successful businessmen from the midlands of England, I have always thought of the English as vulgar. Cambridge went a long way to undoing this impression, but could not quite efface it. I could never really think of Cambridge as being in England. The discovery, in later life, that I could drive there from London in an hour and a half by land seemed to be in defiance of nature. It still does.

But as for vulgarity and materialism, in the senses in which Yeats uses the words, they are surely even more prevalent in late-twentieth-century Ireland than in England. The 'mid-Atlantic' amalgam that is swamping us all has found Ireland even more vulnerable than Britain. Yet there is a precious grain of cynicism in the Irish character, a vein of scepticism, which is perhaps immune to corrosion. If only we may be spared the discovery of offshore oil or any other of the curses which come in the disguise of benefits.

There is, or was, a shred of evidence tending to show that the English are, or were, aware of their own vulgarity. Until not long ago, in the matter of getting jobs and being accepted by the BBC, the possession of an English provincial accent was a severe disadvantage, even a bar, whereas an Irish or Scotch (I am not sure about Welsh) accent was acceptable. To be sure, we are speaking not of a thick demotic brogue, rather of an intonation. Apparently an Irish or Scotch accent is thought romantic in England, much as an English accent is apparently thought romantic in the United States, and gets people jobs which they might not otherwise get. But the distinction – rooted in snobbery as it is, and I concede all that – does seem to reflect some faint perception that when the majority of Englishmen open their mouths the result is not pleasant to listen to. Speaking personally, I should make an exception for the accent of Bristol, which is pleasant to my ear. I well remember the pleasant surprise I got when I first stepped out of a train at Temple Meads station and heard the voices around me; and when I first heard Sir Bernard Lovell on the wireless I thought he might be Irish, until I looked him up in *Who's Who*.

Is it all a matter merely of what we are used to? I don't think so. We use language, as Talleyrand (I think) said, to conceal our thoughts. But we use it for many other purposes besides: among others, to convey our own estimation of where we belong in the scheme of things. A story which I relish concerns a gentleman (whom I know well) who is prominent, and creditably so, in Irish public life and further afield. 'X — Y —, is it?' said a contemporary, 'I know him well. Wasn't I in the digs with him the night he changed his accent?' With this I couple in my mind another story about an even more public man. Henry Kissinger, as all the world knows, has a rather perceptible German accent. He has also, what is not quite so well known, a brother who speaks in ordinary American. Someone asked his brother how it came about that Kissinger sounded so palpably German, and he not. 'Quite simple,' was the reply, 'Henry never listens to anything that is said to him.'

LVI

A tiny practical example of the inextricable intermingling of good and evil in the world as it actually is. Agnes gave me a beautiful expandable attaché case for Christmas. The handle is joined to the body by a pair of steel pins which are each housed between a pair of little pillars. A careless assembler in Taiwan had made one of the pins fractionally too short so that it came out and one end of the handle came adrift. This was very vexatious, and emotionally disturbing because it was such a valued present and so splendid in every other way. After some thought and rummaging about in my box of bits and pieces I contrived an assembly consisting of a tube in which slid two rods, held apart by a spring which I found by dismantling an old lamp-switch. With a click the whole device slipped into place and can never again spring out, and it works perfectly.

As a result I get even more pleasure from this present than I could have got if nothing had gone wrong. Besides my self-satisfaction I can boast about it to such of my friends as are capable of understanding it.

This is an, admittedly minute and trivial, illustration of the *felix culpa* principle celebrated by the medieval poet in 'Adam lay ybounden', where the argument is that but for the transgression in the Garden of Eden the greater good of the Redemption could not have taken place. It is also the basis of there being more joy in heaven over one repentant sinner than over the ninety and nine just sheep that went not astray.

This raises an aesthetic question of more than passing importance. I am in doubt whether to call it aesthetic or moral, which may seem surprising. It turns on the pleasure to be had not from looking at something, but from the knowledge of its internal economy: or rather, from thinking about its internal economy while looking at it. Thus much of the pleasure in contemplating, let us say, a Bugatti engine, comes from having seen a cross-sectional drawing of it. And conversely, my pleasure in looking at certain three-funnelled ships is lessened by the knowledge that the first and third funnels are dummy. When

Lethaby began his book on Haghia Sophia with the resounding statement that it 'is the most interesting building on the world's surface' he was choosing his words with care. He did not say the 'most beautiful' or even the 'best architecture'. 'Interesting' is a word beloved of art historians and critics, who, as already noted, prefer to leave such words as 'beautiful' to mechanics and others. This is typical of our introspective, Alexandrian culture.

I see nothing wrong with this. It seems to me right that my pleasure in actually visiting Haghia Sophia should have been so immeasurably enhanced by prior knowledge not only of its history but of its construction and of the static principles involved, and by the study of sectional drawings of what cannot actually be seen on site. Much the same applies to the great Gothic cathedrals and to the Florence dome and to St Paul's, London, and to the Forth Bridge. It is the basis also of the appreciation of a good architectural plan, which does not, as such, make a direct appeal to the senses.

The critique of this attitude is expressed by Goodhart-Rendel thus: 'To call a building beautiful while you believe it to be of stone and to declare the same building ugly directly anyone tells you it is really faced with cement shows an odd conception of the meaning of the word beauty.' Hence, no doubt, our avoidance of that word. I do not, personally, get aesthetic satisfaction from knowing about the internal workings of the human body, though some do.

It raises, tangentially, another philosophical problem which has much exercised my mind, namely the question whether there is any difference in kind between mere malfunction and out-and-out evil. We now know that a tiny physical malformation, a missing chromosome or maladjusted piece of brain-circuitry, can cause aberrant behaviour which we would otherwise be tempted to call wicked. Leaving undone those things which we ought to have done is usually the result not of *mens rea* or malice prepense, but of carelessness or inattention. I do not find either of these listed among the seven deadly sins, though, if they come under the general heading of laziness I suppose that can be equated with Sloth.

I am inclined to categorize laziness as a virtue rather than a vice. More damage is on the whole done by busybodies than by those who leave well alone.

Laziness is to be defended on the principle of economy. Chinese helmsmen used to be highly prized because they never made an unnecessary movement and thus saved Alfred Holt and Company appreciable amounts of money. Cats are to be admired for similar reasons. Though they walk about, and run, and even leap and jump when they feel like doing so, and can move very quickly indeed when it is really necessary, their principal occupation is lazing, which they do, as they do everything else, with exemplary elegance and grace. People like me willingly give them bed and board simply for the pleasure of watching them and, if possible, of learning from them. This is not so easy, as we have so many tedious preoccupations from which the cat seems to be free.

What I most admire in cats is their individuality, their independence, and what it is difficult not to call their aesthetic sense, their sense of style. However hard I try, I cannot quite rid myself of the anthropomorphic notion that their poses are contrived with an eye to sculptural effect. Here, if anywhere, I am in danger of confusing the beauty of nature with the beauty of art.

A thousand authors have written of the cat in similar terms, but more eloquently than I. Yet for each of us there are, I fear, rather more who dislike and distrust the cat and think of him as deceitful, aloof, cold-hearted and cruel.

The root of the matter, I believe, is that cats do not flatter the human will to power as dogs are so apt to do. As usual, people give themselves away by linguistic usage. Nine people out of ten will insist on calling a cat 'she' and a dog 'he', even in English which has no grammatical gender to furnish an excuse, as German has. I am reminded of an unintentionally comic passage in a Victorian architectural writer, Robert Kerr: 'vastly as I admire all French art, I can never divest my mind of the feeling that I am admiring something whose charms are feminine'. And a few lines later he speaks of 'England, the very home of rough-and-ready muscularity', which is the very language now used by Americans who see themselves as 'rugged' and 'red-blooded' and all the rest of it.

The idea of the English thinking the French essentially feminine is, if I may be pardoned the expression, enough to make a cat laugh. The French, whose cars are so much more rugged and durable than those of the English, whose rugby play is so much more aggressive and 'dirtier' . . . as I learn from complaints about it in the public prints.

LVII

What an expressive word the verb to 'scamper' is! It perfectly suits the gait of the 1927 Austin Seven Chummy tourer we once had, as it also suits that of the 2CV Citroën derivative which I drive at present. It does not at all suit that of the Mini in which I drove many thousands of miles, even though the Mini is a good deal smaller than either. In a Mini one scurries or scuttles: one does not scamper. Travel by Delage is as smooth as the sound of its name suggests. And how wise it was of the Rolls-Royce company to keep the name of the Hon. C.S. Rolls in their title, though he died almost before the company started making motor-cars. How many extra sales resulted from the retention of that magic syllable we shall never know.

There is a striking contrast in the gait of our two cats. One gallops along, caracoling and curvetting almost like a porpoise. The smaller cat, his mother, scuttles along *ventre à terre* like a tube train. These two modes of progress seem to express very exactly their contrasting characters.

But of course to say this is, strictly speaking, a tautology, since what I know or presume of their characters is founded on observation of just such external traits as these, so no wonder their behaviour agrees with the roles I have assigned to them. If it did not, I would adjust my beliefs accordingly. Yet it is justifiable to draw some conclusions from the behaviour of animals, if it is carefully noted. Konrad Lorenz, I think, observes that bears are particularly dangerous animals because they have, accidentally, a benevolent appearance and therefore seem to be giving us a message which we are in danger of misinterpreting. This is not quite the same thing as saying that they are treacherous.

Abraham Lincoln was once asked why he had not included a certain man of known ability and influence in his cabinet. 'Because I don't like his face,' said Lincoln. The other was shocked and protested that a man cannot be held responsible for his face. 'Oh yes he can,' replied Lincoln: 'Every man over forty is responsible for his face.'

It remains true that if, divesting them of their characteristic apparel, you present twelve mug-shots of bishops and twelve mug-shots of burglars, nobody can tell which is which at least until they move or speak. I leave aside the question whether burglary is not a more honest trade than bishopping. Readers of Trollope (who by the way is my warrant for using the verb to 'bishop') will not find it easy to answer.

LVIII

The idea of waste is a moral idea and cannot be anything else. In nature everything is wasted, or nothing is wasted, whichever way you choose to look at it. 'Tutto trapassa – e nulla può morir.' This is one of the most obvious ways in which nature differs from art. Most good art proceeds on the principle of economy: the greatest possible effect by the simplest possible means. Yet some good art does use the 'shotgun' or 'spraying' effect, throwing up great gouts of volcanic activity, splurges of colour or cascades of sound all over the place, creating an effect of richness, almost of confusion. Shakespeare versus Racine. Rastrelli's Winter Palace versus Zakharov's Admiralty.

As David Pye has made clear, choice in design is mainly a matter of deciding between priorities where waste is concerned. This is very clear where machines and the like are involved: the designer may fix his eye on low labour cost, or economy of raw materials, or durability of the finished product, or cheapness of operation of the same, or on some combination of some of these. Compromise is always necessary.

The considerations which apply in making works of 'fine' art are not so different as may at first appear. For example, to say what you have to say in the fewest possible words may be self-defeating. It may be so compressed that the reader or hearer has not space or time to take it in: there may not be enough sugar on the pill. Durability in works of art is an elusive concept. It may be simple physical durability, as when colours are chosen so as not to fade, and structures or finishes chosen for low maintenance cost or long life. There is a kind of writing calculated to make an immediate impact, and another kind calculated to sink in and work more slowly, given the chance to work at all. The writer should try to be well and promptly paid for the first kind, and to ensure that the second kind ends up between hard covers.

I distinguish three motives in writing:

(1) Getting it off the chest or out of the system. A kind of excretion or at least secretion.
(2) Conveying information (in the broadest sense of that word); briefly, the desire to communicate to a supposed audience.
(3) Making something.

All these, I presume, are present to some extent on all such occasions, though in widely differing quantities. In (1) the interests of the writer are paramount; in (2) the interests of the audience; in (3) the interests of the work itself.

This will sound absurd to many people. How can a thing have 'interests'? Yet there seems to be no other way in which to express the truth of the matter: when the interests of the reader and the writer have been accounted for, there is a residue, sometimes a very large residue, which is due to the work itself. Of course it is true that the ultimate reference is human and that without people there would be no work. We are not talking about ß Aurigae but about things made by man. And of course I am aware of the internal compulsion which makes me adjust and hone something to my own satisfaction. All I am saying is that this satisfaction seems to me different in kind from self-expression or communication, and it is 'as if' the thing itself had claims on me. For practical purposes, that is how it works.

It is notorious that we are most blind to the faults which other people see in us, and self-congratulation is a risky business. But I do believe that I am not much given to managing other people's lives for them, or to bullying or domination of others. This, I suppose, is what makes me such a bad chairman. I am faced with panic at the thought of having to regulate even a small group of even the least contentious of my fellows, and I nearly always succeed in avoiding conscription to the chair.

But I am made uncomfortable when other people do not share my tastes, to the point at which I feel an urge to compel them. I hate, for example, to see someone putting sugar on his porridge, for no better reason than that I cannot see it done without imagining how nasty it must taste. Needless to say I long ago gave up trying to dissuade them. Similarly, it pains me to remember that two people who are close to me so dislike the sound of the violin that they are prevented from enjoying that rather large sector of musical experience in which the violin plays a predominant part. I am sorely tempted to compel them to come into the fold. I would like to become a bully.

The motive, as usual with me, is at bottom an aesthetic one. There is perhaps a small moral element in the desire to share experience, but I would not put it any higher than that. The desire to share my pleasures with others shades off into the desire to dominate, and is not easily to be distinguished from evangelical zeal. It led me once, all unconsciously, into making the only genuine 'Irish Bull' that I have ever made. It was many years ago, at Cambridge. I very much wanted to persuade a friend to go and see a film I had greatly enjoyed. But I felt almost certain that he would not take my advice. 'If you'd only go and see it,' I said, 'you'd be really sorry to have missed it.' This has the authentic structure of the bull: elliptical, forceful and completely comprehensible though logically absurd.

What are our motives when we set out to do justice to some writer, architect or artist of the past who has been undeservedly forgotten or ignored? In part it is a device for giving employment to art historians, academics and the like. In part it is a genuine desire to increase the available range of enjoyments for readers and others, and therefore a laudable wish to increase the sum of human happiness. Critics are apt to pour cold water on the process, and to say that if an opera has not been performed for 200 years there is probably good reason for its neglect; but this is not invariably true.

I think that the desire to see justice done is a large part of the motive. Odd, when you come to think of it, because neither the subject himself, being dead, nor, as a rule, his relatives, get any benefit from it. Justice is an end in itself.

It can operate on a very trivial plane, and be no more than the desire to see that the subject gets, as they say, his guinea's worth of law, his day in court, before having his case dismissed. Thus, for example, when junk mail, or communications which I have no intention of doing anything but ignoring, arrive through the post, they do not go straight into the wastepaper basket, but are put on one side for a little while before being looked at once more and finally disposed of in the inevitable way. This is foolish because it gives me unnecessary work. But it is almost a compulsion.

In the same way, if I have to go out of the room while someone is talking on the wireless or playing a piece of music or singing, I do not quench him or her brutally by the switch. Let him say his say. Let her finish her song. Even if I am not there to hear it. There is no logic in this: only a certain delicacy.

In this spirit I have invented the Kerryman's video-machine, which records the programmes you do not want to see and plays them when you are out.

LIX

Proselytism is a dirty word in Ireland. The reason is that the conversion of someone from his original religion to another religion, at a time when he was, to say the least of it, at a disadvantage, is seen as the *taking away* of something, and not as the *giving* of something.

There is no doubt whatever that those who, during the nineteenth century, strove by fair means or foul to turn people away from the errors of popery, believed sincerely that they sought to give something of much greater value than what they sought to take away. To this day, the theoretical position of Irish Protestantism, especially in the North-East, is that if our fellow-countrymen could be converted to Protestantism all would be well, or at any rate much improved. It was to this end that the elaborate structure of the Church of Ireland, with, as an ideal, a parish church in every parish, and a complete organization, right up to the top where there were twice as many archbishops as in England, was set up and maintained. Even in the North-East, whenever and wherever individuals, whatever their origins, have embraced Protestantism, they are unaffectedly received and welcomed. The Protestants can continue to wish sincerely for the wholesale conversion of the Catholics only because they know that it is not going to happen. They would sincerely like to give each one of their benighted countrymen the greatest gift in their possession, provided they could be sure that they would not all accept at once.

If that were to happen they would no longer be a separate and identifiable power-group, and their occupation would be gone. For 250 years or so the *de jure* position in Ireland as a whole was that unless you were a Protestant you could not expect to get a significant share of the money and the power. In the Six Counties this is still, *de facto*, the case, which is why the Protestants are so reluctant to yield any ground whatever to the Catholics as a group, whatever about individuals.

Resurgent Islam is faced with a somewhat similar problem. Much of its message must consist in denunciation of the practices of the modern world, yet many of these practices must presumably be built into the structure of modern industrial society, to defeat which Islam must in part at least come to resemble. In theory, at least, Islam intends to take over the whole world, like all other universal religions. In practice, at present, it seems to be torn between denunciation of the gravy train and trying to climb on to it.

OUT OF IRELAND

I

IF REQUIRED to make an entry under the heading 'Recreations' I might be tempted to put 'Travel', as many other people have done. And yet . . . the fact is that in nearly forty years I have never spent more than five or six weeks away from wherever I was living, even that only once, and it has generally been three or less. I had no *Wanderjahre* such as many young people embark upon nowadays, and as I have grown older I have become more and more sessile and less inclined to stray from my base. For most of this I cannot blame anybody but myself, though I can plead that the more gentlemanly modes of travel have become less and less available till now they have virtually ceased to exist. I have never spent more than five days on board ship without landing, and it is now no longer possible to have dinner on what used to be the Rome Express.

A merciful dispensation of nature sees to it that time spent on holiday seems longer than time spent at work, not in the sense that it hangs heavily on our hands, but that when we have been away for two days it is hard to believe that we have not been away for at least a week. As a rule we pack a great deal more memorable experience into a fortnight away from home than into the same space of time lived routinely at our usual occupations.

A great deal of mischief has been done by that foolish sentence in the Declaration of Independence which speaks of 'life, liberty and the pursuit of happiness'. Life and liberty are all very well, but no sensible person ever set out to pursue happiness. You may set out to pursue money, or girls, or success, or power, or the 'inviolable shade', or truth, or God, or perfection of form or expression, or the fox, or a great white whale, or even, at a pinch, pleasure. But surely not happiness, which, if it comes at all, comes as a concomitant of success, or even of failure, in one or more of these quests.

Going on holiday, for many of us, means going to places where the technology is markedly less advanced than it is at home, and much of our time is spent in watching other people at work. Donkey-carts, lace-making, men spinning ropes on a beach, fishing-boats bringing in the catch, irrigation-pumps worked by oxen, water-mills (if we can find them), reciprocating steamships (if we can find them), even trams . . .*

This has been so for a long time. When Lord Charlemont went travelling in the Levant in the 1740s there was not much to choose between the local technology and that available to him at home, so that when he sat on the beach on a Greek island and they grilled a kid to eat in the Homeric manner there may have been a shade less formality than at home, but there was no thermos flask and no primus stove. A century later, however, when Kinglake was taking the journey which ultimately became *Eōthen*, he was very much aware of roughing it, and his hosts were correspondingly aware, if only at a distance, of Western technology. 'The armies of the English', said the Pasha of Belgrade, keen to show off his knowledge, 'ride upon the vapours of burning caldrons, and their horses are flaming coals! – whirr! whirr! all by wheels! – whizz! whizz! all by steam!'

Now that travel has been virtually abolished and tourism has taken its place, the moral problems which troubled King-lake are as intractable as ever, and vastly increased in scale. 'Whizz, whizz, all by wings – whoosh! whoosh! all by jets!' applies to everybody regardless of their country of origin. The dictum of the physicists: that you cannot observe a system without changing it in the process, is even more obviously true in human affairs, whether the motive is scientific enquiry, idle curiosity, or the mere desire to play at one of the many versions of pastoral.

Like Marie Antoinette.

I remember vividly my first entry into Italy. After a night on a couchette in the Rome Express I emerged from the Fréjus tunnel to see the sun gilding the jagged tops of the Alps. The only other occupant of the compartment was a young man who

* To some extent the Americans are doing the same thing when they visit us.

turned out later to be a policeman, from Naples. As in Ireland, the police are stationed in places where they have no relatives. When he said 'Bussoleno!' I thought, in my ignorance of Italian, that he was drawing my attention to the sun, not giving me the name of the place. Thousands upon thousands of tiny slender trees in regular rows intersected by narrow canals covered the plains of Piedmont. Like Thomas Hardy I had my first view of the Mediterranean through a gap between houses as the train moved slowly through Genoa:

> . . . housebacks pink, green, ochreous, where a slit
> Shoreward 'twixt row and row revealed the classic blue
> > through it

and like him I saw it through festoons of colourful Italian washing:

> Chrome kerchiefs, scarlet hose, darned underfrocks;

describing them in his poem, which I did not come across till later, as 'squalid undress'. I did not see it that way at all. I thought that the Romans had probably hung out their washing in much the same way, in Virgil's time.

A few days later I had my first sight of Rome. I had come by train from Florence, and after traversing the shores of a large lake – whether Trasimene or Bolsena I do not know – and passing under the walls of Orvieto, which I have never since had the opportunity to revisit, we entered the Campagna, at that time still relatively free of recent buildings, and passed through a succession of compositions taken straight from Claude. Into one of these, suddenly and almost unbelievably, came the dome of St Peter's and with the meandering of the railway's course it seemed to move slowly backwards and forwards, as the outer planets seemed to do in the days of the Ptolemaic cosmogony.

Arrived in Rome, I did in rapid order the things which were highest on my list of priorities: San Pietro in Montorio, the Palazzo Farnese, the Pantheon, the Basilica of Maxentius. And presumably also the Piazza San Pietro. I cannot now remember whether I went to St Mary Major's on that occasion:

certainly I would now rate it among the first five sights of Rome. But I have never spent as long in Rome as I could wish. One week, afterwards, in 1969. *Sonst nichts* . . .

Venice I have never done justice to, and perhaps now never will. We had been working our way Northwards up the coast through Rimini and Ravenna, past the place where Garibaldi embarked after the death of Anita in 1849, and had seen the marvellous tower of Pomposa in the delta of the Po. We came to Chioggia. A small steamer was at the quay, labelled for Venice. We locked the little car, left it on the quay and jumped on board. The steamer, as it turned out, did not go all the way to Venice. She sailed Northwards along the lagoon, and decanted us onto one of the islands, the length of which we were taken by bus to a quay opposite Venice itself where, still on the same ticket, we re-embarked on another and so approached the Serenissima as she ought to be approached, landing at the quay below the Doge's Palace. I was not allowed into St Mark's because I was wearing shorts, which was a pity, but I got a quick glimpse of the aureate interior. Four hours later we re-embarked for Chioggia.

My first sight of certain other cities has also been very memorable, partly through circumstance but partly, I must admit or proclaim, through my own contriving.

Constantinople, sailing up the Sea of Marmora in the *Karadeniz*, with the domes and minarets of Stamboul (or Eminonu as they call it now) slowly taking shape in the haze, and the delight in sorting out Haghia Sophia from Sultan Achmed and from Sultan Suleiman, till Seraglio Point and the Asiatic shore of the Bosphorus emerged more and more clearly, and we finally tied up at about lunch-time close to the mouth of the Golden Horn.

Athens, earlier on the same journey, approaching Peiraeus and seeing the Parthenon still floating high above the distant city, much as it must have appeared to returning Athenian sailors in the fifth century. Fortunately for us, this was before it became necessary to prohibit visitors from walking about inside the Parthenon. I have been there once since, and it was intolerably crowded, though in April. Even that is over ten years ago: so what it must be like now . . .

Leningrad: a couple of years earlier, sailing up the Gulf of Finland in the *Baltika* in the early morning, through the middle of Kronstadt where there was a four-masted barque, a distant view of Oranienbaum to the South, then the long slow approach up the Morskoi Canal and the gradual emergence of two golden needle-spires and one golden dome: the Peter-Paul Cathedral, the Admiralty and St Isaac's. My feelings much coloured by recollection of the then fairly recent siege, the most terrible in recorded history.

The grandest building in North-Western Europe, for my money, is Durham Cathedral. I could wish the East end other than it is: the original Romanesque apse would have been more to my taste, and the spidery wheel-window goes a long way towards spoiling the view down the nave to the choir. But in every other way, and particularly in the splendour of its situation high on its rock almost completely surrounded by the river Wear, it is incomparable.

I have most often seen it from the railway to the West, which ought to be one of the most famous views in Europe. But my first arrival in Durham was by bicycle, on a holiday tour designed to include also Seaton Delaval, which it did, while thanks to the advice of a lorry-driver met in a transport café, we also made a detour to see the Saxon church at Escomb.

South of the Cathedral at Durham, within the loop of the river, is the Bailey, a winding street of old houses, all or most of which belong to the university which is the oldest in England after Oxford and Cambridge. Wheeling a bicycle with a basket on the handlebars such as one sees in university towns was a young girl of twelve or thirteen, and perched on the edge of the basket was a small owl, of which the girl had made a pet. The perfect foil to the majesty of the ancient building we had come to see. I recently found a photograph which I had taken of this owl.

Long afterwards, on the other side of England, I had a privileged experience also connected with Durham. I had occasion to go on business to Stonyhurst College. When my business was finished, I recalled that St Cuthbert's Gospel was at Stonyhurst, and asked if I might be shown it. It was kept in an ordinary cardboard box, and turned out to be no bigger than a Penguin paperback. But it was in a red morocco binding so fresh that it might have been made last year, and of the rarest possible kind, with a raised knot-like centrepiece the nearest relatives of which are early Coptic bindings from North Africa. The book itself, though plain, is beautifully written and there are apparently good grounds for believing it to have been written by St Cuthbert himself. The binding is certainly contemporary, therefore of the sixth century, and the book was found, along with the other treasures which I have seen in Durham Cathedral Library, in St Cuthbert's coffin. I was in such awe of this treasure that I did not dare to handle it. The Jesuit who showed it to me had no such compunction, and I am relieved to know that it is now in the British Museum. I hope it arrived before my friend Howard Nixon, who helped me so much and was always so generous with his praise, retired from there.

My first meeting with Howard Nixon was memorable. In about 1951 I went to the British Museum and asked one of the doormen where I could find whoever dealt with bookbindings. 'That will be Mr Nixon,' I was told, and the man rang through to his department. Evidently he had just left. 'Never mind,' said the doorman, 'we might just be in time to catch him,' and led the way to the right and then left into the King's Library. Half-way down that enormous room, coming towards us, was an unobtrusive figure, looking, as John Hayward used to say, most deceptively like a motor-car salesman. At first he did not seem overjoyed at being waylaid, but as soon as I told him that I had two spring-back volumes of about 150 rubbings with me, he brightened up. We went back to his room.

Two hours later, having compared rubbings with other rubbings and with photographs and having arranged for books to be brought for me to inspect and rub at the desk of Salvador de Madariaga in the North Library, he turned to me and said, 'By the way, what is your name?' I have had similar experiences the other way round. As soon as I know that an enquirer really knows what he or she is asking about, the way lies smooth. But Nixon was an exceptional example of such virtue. This was before the bulk of his important work had been published, but he was already a man of prodigious learning, very lightly carried.

II

Sensitive people shudder nowadays at the very mention of the Canary Islands, and I am not surprised. But things were very different when we went there first over twenty years ago. The only guide was Mrs Stone's two bulky Victorian volumes, a model of their kind. There were, I believe, no aeroplanes directly from England: only from Brussels. We used to go by cargo ship, either from the West India Docks or from the wharf just below London Bridge, and it took five days or so.

It is true that the first time we went was from Southampton on the maiden voyage of the *Transvaal Castle* (absurd name!) returning on what was almost the last voyage of the old *Carnarvon Castle*, a ship with an interesting history, but the journeys I remember with intense pleasure were those in the small cargo ships of the Olsen line. All the accommodation for the twelve passengers was concentrated amidships immediately below the bridge: a dining-saloon on the port side, a sitting-saloon on the starboard side, above that the passenger cabins, above them a large 'verandah' with wicker chairs and pot plants (this was the boat-deck) and above that the bridge. These were the *Bruno* and *Bencomo*, and like all Olsen ships they had bronze sculptured figure-heads. For their size and type they were unusually fast: 17 knots.

We never knew (nor did the captain until the last moment) whether we would call first at Santa Cruz or at Las Palmas. We always hoped the former, as it would give us a day to enjoy ourselves in Tenerife, and so it usually fell out. The company was under contract only to take us to the first Canary port, but they always let us stay on board and brought us overnight to our destination.

Leaving London in the dead of winter, half-way through January, often in the snow, it was beautiful to look at a piece of icy deck and think that in five days' time it would be in sub-tropical sunshine, and so would we.

Communication between the seven islands was by a fleet of six steamers, three of them small and three of them very small: the *La Palma*, the *Viera Y Clavijo*, the *Leon Y Castillo*, the *Lanzarote*, the *Fuerteventura* and the *Gomera* (originally *Gomera Y Hierro*), all built in 1912 in such places as Aberdeen, Middlesborough and South Shields, and all still going strong in 1962 and later years, with their original triple-expansion machinery and even, in some cases, their original boilers, at the age of fifty-plus. They were totally silent and vibration-free, and very steady little sea-boats. In one or other of these we visited all the islands: the arid African islands of Lanzarote and Fuerteventura, and the lusher Western group, Hierro, Gomera and La Palma. Among the things I remember best are leaning on the rail with Pádraig MacMiadhacháin as we sailed along the South-East coast of Fuerteventura in the grey dawn, much as though we were sailing past Kilkeel and Annalong, and the occasion when we landed on Hierro and were taken by bus up a zigzag road to the tiny island capital, where we were plied with wine and sardines by the Cabildo Insular, taken off to see the island sights, and finally whirled vertiginously down the mountainside to the ship in the small hours of the morning. On Gomera the fiesta was in progress and the inhabitants dressed in strange transsexual costumes and communicating with one another in their famous whistling language. On La Palma we had, unfortunately, only a few hours as we had to return on the same ship. We never saw the great caldera where the observatory is now.

Fuerteventura is still, I believe, undeveloped, because it has no water. All they have done is to rechristen its capital, Puerto de Cabras, as Puerto Rosario, which I do not find an improvement. (*Cabras* means goats.)

I do not expect ever again to enjoy anything as we enjoyed those idle days between Hierro, Gomera and La Palma, eating our picnic lunches on the foredeck and watching the flying fishes. Enjoyable as it is to cruise on the Shannon or the Erne in a motor-cruiser, the objectionable thumping of the diesel, even when well throttled down, obtrudes and cannot be ignored. Now if it were only possible to do it in a steam cruiser . . .

On board the *Bruno* and *Bencomo* there was a small bathroom opening inwards from the corridor. This little steel compartment hung, in fact, inwards over the engine-room where the long nine-cylinder diesel thrummed steadily all day and all night. It was delightful to lie in a hot salt bath, the water swaying gently as we crossed the Bay of Biscay or the seas farther South, beyond Cape St Vincent and Casablanca. By day we might glimpse in the distance, wreathed in mist, the lighthouse of Corcubion, which we visited some years later by car, and soon there would be shoals of dolphins curvetting beside us, and the air would be warm with the warmth of Africa.

Such pleasures are denied to those who go by air.

III

Our first day in Constantinople was a marvellously varied sequence of experiences. The *Karadeniz* docked on the Pera-Galata side of the Golden Horn, not far from the Dolmabagche Palace, at about lunch-time. Immigration formalities were chaotic and long-drawn-out. We had picked, from a list, a hotel as near as possible to Haghia Sofia. It was a fly-blown little dump opposite the Mosque of Sultan Bajazet ('O Bajazeth, O Turk, O Emperour') near the Great Bazaar. We discovered afterwards that nobody stays in old Stamboul, but I am very glad that we did. Dumping our luggage we went straight to Haghia Sofia, where we took our time, exploring the building as thoroughly as possible before reluctantly going in search of the address we had been given in London, which was an office-block somewhere between the Sublime Porte and Sirkeci station. By this time it was late afternoon and all the offices were shut, so we left a note which, on the morrow, was to bear splendid fruit.

We walked down the hills and over the Galata Bridge from which the ferry-boats were rattling in and out at an incredible speed, jostling one another like taxi-cabs and belching clouds of black smoke from the soft Turkish coal which they burned in their boilers. More by luck than good management we jumped on one which took us to Salacak which turned out to be an enchanting little landing-stage just beside Leander's Tower. We settled down to drink a bottle of raki (which is what the Greeks have under the name of ouzo) and ate platefuls of those variegated small delicacies which are the legacy of Byzantine cookery. One or two steam ferries came and went, while the sun slowly sank over the Gran Serai and the domes and minarets of Haghia Sofia, Sultan Achmet and the Sulemaniye. When it was dark we walked up the hill and down the other side into Scutari (Iskudar) and by our side walked a man with a full-grown sheep on a leather lead, feeding it raisins out of a paper bag.

On the ferry back across the Bosphorus a man insisted on polishing my shoes and would not take any money, and I do not remember that we ever bought a ticket. By this time it was pitch-dark, and we set out to walk, by dead reckoning, back to our hotel. To this day I cannot be sure whether we went to the East or the West of the Gran Serai (Topkapi Museum): probably we went through Gulhane Park. It was a kind of garden, completely unlit, but after rather a long time we did emerge into the light, somewhere near the Yere Batan Serai and were able to find our way back to the little hotel.

The next morning a delegation of three very courteous Turkish gentlemen waited on us in our hotel. For three days a car and a driver were placed at our disposal, and we were accompanied by Hadji Tamer, the head of the Topkapi Museum laboratory, and, whenever possible, by his wife Cahide, the architect responsible for the restoration of the Yedi Kule Gate and the castle at Rumeli Hissar. We were taken to see anything we had a mind to, escaping all the time-wasting frustrations which beset travellers in a strange city who know nothing of the language. In consequence, we saw three or four times as much as we could possibly have managed on our own. Sometimes our objectives were very hard to find – the Gul Djami or Rose Mosque (St Theodosia) for example – but we found them. Much of the old city was then (1966) an unplanned congeries of old houses and narrow winding streets, but I had the 1893 Murray's *Handbook to Constantinople* with its two 'ancient' and 'modern' maps and by this means we navigated.

There were moments of respite: sitting, for example, on the terrace outside Hadji Tamer's office, high over the Marmora, pulling mulberries off a tree and eating them in the sunshine; and meals down by the Bosphorus or in the Tamers' home. I am glad to say that later they came to London and we did our best to return their kindness to us. Admiring the cats sunning themselves among the tombs in the courtyard of the mosque at Eyub, at the headwaters of the Golden Horn. A man with a bear on a lead walking across the Ataturk Bridge. A quick glimpse of the Euxine, *Thalatta! Thalatta!*

IV

The Neapolitan church of Santa Chiara has a special place in my imagination. In part this is owing to the poem by Arthur Symons, which I knew long before I ever went to Naples:

> Because it is the day of palms
> Carry a palm for me.
> Carry a palm in Santa Chiara
> And I will watch the sea.
>
> There are no palms in Santa Chiara
> Today or any day for me.
>
> I sit and watch the little sail
> Lean sideways on the sea,
> The sea is blue from here to Sorrento
> And the sea-wind comes to me
> And I see the white clouds lift from Sorrento
> And the dark sail lean upon the sea.

177

I have grown tired of all these things
And what is left for me?
I have no place in Santa Chiara.
There is no peace upon the sea;
But carry a palm in Santa Chiara
Carry a palm for me.

It is perhaps not a very good poem, with its facile *fin-de-siècle*
sentiment. But the hypnotic repetition appealed to my adolescent sensibility.

When I did visit Santa Chiara at last it was at a time of
great emotional turmoil. The church was a burnt-out shell full
of rubbish, for it was not long after the war. The walls were
calcined; remains only could be seen of the Baroque decoration
which had hidden the medieval structure; and the tombs of the
Angevin kings were invisible or in ruin. In the narrow street
beside the church was a beautifully false-perspectived archway
of another building destroyed by bombs or fire.

The next time I was in Naples I went again to Santa
Chiara but, as so often in Italy, it was shut. It had evidently
been restored, to its fourteenth-century aspect, of course, but
the archway had gone.

Presumably I never will see Santa Chiara, and it will keep
its special place. No doubt most of this is due to the music of
its name. As for Sorrento . . . I once spent a night there, by
mistake, and my nose bled: the only time it has done so since I
was a child.

V

There are, I know, people to whom Italy is just another
foreign country out of many. I cannot see it this way. Italy is in
a class of one.

Our grandest Italian journey was the Apulian expedition.
Apulia (or Puglia) in the 'heel' is perhaps the least visited part
of the peninsula. In 1968 hardly anybody went there and there
were few hotels and even fewer restaurants. The drive down the

East coast was penitential: a nightmare of oncoming lorries on a narrow road. We made perfunctory reverences to Rossini and Leopardi as we ground through Pesaro and passed by Recanati. Our principal quarry was the great emperor, Frederick of Hohenstaufen, Stupor Mundi, the Boy from Apulia. Beyond Vasto we could begin to relax, and at Termoli, where Apulia begins, there was clear water to swim in.

The layers overlie one another in Puglia in a readily recognizable way. There are Byzantine traces (of which more later) but the main architectural theme is Romanesque. Every few miles along the coast there is a cathedral city, and several more inland, nearly all the cathedrals dating from the Norman lordship of the Hautevilles. After the Hohenstaufen come the Angevins, who worked over most of Frederick's buildings, especially the castles. And everywhere, of course, there is what Wittkower calls 'the charming, volatile and often abstruse Apulian Baroque' (which is nearly the sum of what he says about it).

Not much remains of the remarkable keep of Frederick's castle at Lucera, where he kept his harem of Saracen beauties, but the spectacular Angevin walls are still there, and tiny lizards scurry over their vertiginous tops.

Two of the Apulian cathedrals are right down by the water: Trani, with its tall tower standing on an open arch and its Byzantine-style bronze doors, and Molfetta, with three domes covered with contrasting pyramidal roofs, where a hot wind was whipping the water of the little harbour into short steep waves. I seek out domed churches wherever I can find them: in France at Souillac, Cahors, Angoulème and as far North as Fontevrault. Molfetta belongs to the same family and so does Canosa, which is inland, and has also the mausoleum of that maverick giant of the Hauteville family, Bohemond Prince of Antioch, with its own dome like that of a Turkish *turbeh*, and its own pair of bronze doors, and the single word BOHEMOND graven on the flat slab. There are more such doors at Monte Sant'Angelo and at Troia and even at Amalfi and Ravello on the West coast. Some were made at Constantinople itself and some by local craftsmen in the Byzantine tradition.

Most of these cathedrals were bedizened internally in the seventeenth and eighteenth centuries, much like Santa Chiara in Naples, with plenty of plaster and paint, and nearly always the spirit of modern archaeological rectitude has dictated their removal, with mixed results, exposing mutilated capitals and other details. At Altamura we found one where the Baroque decoration had survived, and I hope it has still been spared.

In all these towns, needless to say, there are numerous other churches besides the cathedrals, most of which we did not see and which I know about only from reading the literature after coming home. But that is inevitably the way with holidays, unless you prepare meticulously beforehand as though studying for an examination; and in that case we would have covered much less ground and never got round to seeing many of the things we did.

We could see Castel Del Monte, the greatest of Frederick's surviving buildings, on its dome-shaped hill, long before we reached it. Of all Frederick's buildings it is the most memorable, unlike any other building of the Middle Ages: neither castle, nor villa, nor palace, but a geometrical fantasy partaking of all three. Like the other buildings of Apulia, it glows with a rich golden colour, but it is difficult not to remember the long miserable years of captivity suffered by the last of the emperor's posterity in this place, after the fall of that great house.

Beyond Bari it became more difficult to find places in which to stay and even to eat. We slept in Polignano which was clearly geared for a kind of tourism other than ours, so we were quickly out of it. The famous *trulli* of Alberobello lived up to expectations, and more so, since a good many of them were clearly of recent and continuing construction. Sated with these, I refreshed myself with the Egyptian portals of the local *campo santo*.

Through Locorotondo and Francavilla to Oria where there is a Hohenstaufen castle in a dominating position but in private occupation. Hereabouts, I noticed, there are plenty of corbelled structures, much less vertical than those in Alberobello, and much more like our Irish examples. Most of them were clearly built for agricultural purposes, and many were already falling into decay and disuse. We avoided Brindisi on purpose.

Lecce was, to me, something of a disappointment. It is, to be sure, a very attractive town, built, like so many places in Italy, of a beautiful golden stone. But the much-vaunted Baroque of Lecce proved to be not Baroque at all, but quite straightforward rectilinear architecture with rococo decoration made possible largely by the fact that the local stone is soft when first quarried and can be tortured into intricate shapes before it hardens.

The Castle of Otranto is not at all as some might expect it to be. To begin with, the accent is not on the middle syllable but on the first. It is a squat building with cylindrical towers, occupied by the military and facing over the sea towards Albania which is almost within sight. The town is small and pleasing, not without hotels, and with two treasures, for neither of which I was prepared.

The great mosaic pavement of the cathedral, made between 1163 and 1166, covers the entire floor of the nave. It takes the form of a great tree, its trunk borne by elephants and its fruit a vast sort of strip-cartoon into which the artist had put everybody of note that he had ever heard of. Right up at the front of the procession, near the chancel steps, is 'REX ARTURUS' on horseback holding unsteadily aloft a sceptre and with his other hand waving, for all the world as if to say 'Hi, folks!' A long way from home. How this splendid pavement survived the sack of Otranto by the Turks in 1480 is a mystery. Probably it was so drenched in blood that nobody noticed it.

The other great treasure in Otranto is a tiny and very complete Byzantine church in a backyard in the middle of the town: cruciform in a square, with a little dome roofed with a flat cone of tiles, and a frescoed interior; a reminder that this part of Italy remained longer in the Eastern empire than any other. There is a Byzantine flavour, too, right at the other end of Apulia, about the two square churches of Siponto, standing lonely in the flat ground near Manfredonia.

We turned West towards the instep of Italy.

Gallipoli – 'the beautiful city' – has a waterfront of agree-ably shabby coloured houses all round its peninsula jutting out into the Ionian Sea. Somewhere between there and the Quattro Colonne, which is a large keep with all its four walls quarried away leaving only the corner turrets, we found a secluded place to swim in the blue-green water. A signpost to the right pointed us to Copertino, but in spite of the temptation to pay our respects to Norman Douglas's flying monk, we pressed on to Gioia del Colle up in the mountains, another of the emperor's places of pleasure. How much to believe of his hall of state with its canopied throne and wall-benches is very uncertain. It is dismissed by modern authorities as a concoction incorporating genuine details, and it is certain that the various owners of the castle have rearranged it nearer to their own ideals. We nick-named it Fred's Diner, and went to look for something to eat, finding nothing but pizza, which I detest.

From now on we were driving through the mountains, sometimes on very bad roads, especially beyond Gravina. Here we left Puglia and crossed over into Basilicata. We made a detour over an even worse road to Acerenza to see the Hohen-staufen bust in the wall of the cathedral, and a small boy made us a present of a lapful of hazel-nuts. At Pietragalla a vast horse-fair was in progress, and soon after that we turned North towards Lagopesole, the most remote and least visited of all the Frederician castles, tenanted only by a few *carabinieri* and some hens. Thunder-clouds were gathering round the head of Monte Vulture, and soon after we had left the castle on our way to Melfi the rain came down. But by Melfi it had cleared. Remembering the Duchess – for this is the Malfi of Webster's play – we paused only to look at the outside of the scaffolded castle before circling round the North side of Monte Vulture and heading across the mountains to Eboli where, as everyone remembers, Christ stopped.

We did not. We hurried on down to Paestum where we had time to drive round the walls in the sunset before dinner and bed in a comfortable pensione by the beach.

The rest of the journey was inevitably less adventurous. After an early-morning swim we took our time over the Paestum temples, which I had seen before and Jeanne had not, and which, for my money, excel anything else of the kind. Because I was determined to see the early round church at Nocera we found and persisted in a road not marked on our map which did indeed bring us to Nocera where, after some trouble, we found the church. Seeking out early circular churches has been something of a cult with me. Santa Costanza in Rome is very easy, but I am constantly reading accounts by people who have failed to get into Santo Stefano Rotondo, as we succeeded in doing in the year following, and hardly anybody seems to know about Nocera, though it has been in Fergusson's *Architecture** for well over a century. It was well worth the trouble.

We joined the *autostrada* and skirting Naples drove steadily on to Caserta. Here, again, the thunder was on our heels. We had just finished looking at the great grottoes and cascades when the rain came down. The only part of the inside of the palace which we saw was the great staircase. When we got home we reread Sacheverell Sitwell.

Next stop the gardens and fountains of the Villa d'Este at Tivoli, where we did not even try to disentangle our own emotions from those of Liszt. We also looked at the travertine quarries before finding a hotel overlooking the Villa Adriana. 'Villa' is a misleading name for this astonishing collection of structures covering an area equal to that of a sizeable town.

So swift is travel on the *autostrada* that without hurrying over Hadrian's Villa we were able to eat our picnic in the villa of the Orsini at Bomarzo, among the stone freaks and monsters. By this time I had run out of film for my Minox so had to make do with a little concertina-shaped brochure bought on the site. On this part of the journey Jeanne was suffering intermittently from the pain of the cancer from which, eighteen months later, she died; but she would not let that interfere with our

---

* James Fergusson (1808-86). His *History of Architecture* was published, ultimately in four volumes, between 1855 and 1876, and remained for many years the only treatment of the whole subject in English on so large a scale.

pleasure, and, so far as I could, I followed her example. There was nothing else I could do. We passed Florence in another rainstorm and so over the Appennines to Bologna where we stayed the night, and, driving on the old Via Emilia and pausing only in Modena to look at the churches and in Parma to have a drink in honour of Giuseppe Verdi, we regained Milan.

THE INWARD ASPECT

I

OVER THE fireplace in one of the rooms in Annaghmakerrig is a portrait of Verdi by Boldini: a lithograph, I think, from an original in crayon. I have no idea how highly Boldini is thought of, but this is a splendidly forceful portrait. It shows him aged about sixty, in a black silk top hat and with a white scarf tied round his neck, the ends sticking diagonally outwards across his chest. The greyish-blue eyes are determined and the face is strong and humorous. It reminds me that I have only to think of the personality, life and works of Verdi to feel a lift of the spirit. There are not many people about whom I have this feeling. Claud Cockburn is another. I saw his tombstone in the graveyard in Youghal recently. My first feeling was to think what a beautiful thing it was: a beautiful piece of stone beautifully lettered. On this followed feelings of regret that he was dead, but since he did not die prematurely these feelings were swept up in what I can only call gratitude that such a man should have lived and that I should be a member of the same species and should have known him.

But pleasure is the primary ingredient in these feelings. Those who can evoke them are a very curiously assorted lot. Groucho Marx for example. I have only to think of Groucho and it is as though the sun had suddenly come out from behind a cloud. It is, of course, the cinematic persona of Groucho of which I speak. His vulpine lope is a joy for ever.

I find it profoundly reassuring to know that Verdi, surely one of the sanest artists who ever lived, was a prey to neurotic illnesses and to psychosomatic disorders of a quite gross kind, which paralysed his creative faculties for months on end. It is a great consolation to us to know that our little talents and our trifling afflictions are paralleled on the grandest possible scale.

II

The muscular imagination is something people seldom argue about, though it is very mysterious. All children, I suppose, are under the impression that when they open their mouth they are raising their upper jaw as well as dropping their lower one, until, at some point, they discover to their surprise that it is not so. Even as adults, though we have known for years that only our lower jaw moves, we feel as though we were moving the upper one. The crocodile does the same, though some have thought otherwise.

Geoffrey Scott, in *The Architecture of Humanism*,* identified this factor as a critical element in our apprehension of that art. We identify ourselves, in some sense, with the building we are looking at, and on an unconscious involuntary level, share its experiences and carry its burdens. This is generally accepted, though of course only as a partial account of the matter.

The psychophysiology of listening to music works in a similar way. It seems to be universally accepted that notes which have many vibrations per second should be felt to be 'high', while those which vibrate more slowly are felt as 'low'. There is, indeed, an inescapable connexion in nature between largeness and low frequency, as in pendulums or the motions of the wings of birds. We do not expect an albatross to flap its wings as quickly as a wren. But when a child accepts 'instinctively' a 'high' note as high and a 'low' note as low it is not from any knowledge of physics, but rather from an unconscious acceptance of metaphor. As we listen to music we rise and fall, as it were, inside ourselves. This is why we feel uncomfortable during some parts of the Ninth Symphony or the Mass in D where Beethoven is asking the singers to do things which are almost impossible to do.

When one hears, as I did recently, a composition originally written for the flute being played on a tin whistle, it sounds 'thin' or 'narrow' by comparison. The diameter of a tin whistle is, in fact, about half that of a flute, but our feeling is independent of this knowledge. Nevertheless we would be surprised to hear a deep sound and then be shown something very small

* Geoffrey Scott, poet, biographer (*The Portrait of Zélide*, 1925) and editor, published *The Architecture of Humanism* in 1914 (second edition 1924, reprinted 1929 and since).

as the source of it, just as we are surprised when, as occasionally happens, a large deep-chested man turns out to have a squeaky voice. I know, because I have seen and heard it done, that very high-pitched harmonics can be coaxed out of a violoncello, but it is always a little surprising.

Our psychophysiological identifications, though accepted, at least within a single culture, can be quite fallacious. Thus, I imagine that most people have shared the feeling that certain melodies 'flow' and are like 'long curves'. But in fact, if properly played or sung, they are not curves at all but a series of steps, and to swoop from one note to another glissando is either a vice or a special effect, specified by the composer.

(Some people identify a barometric depression with depression of spirits which so often seems to accompany it. But, so far from the sky pressing down on us at such times, the air pressure is in fact lower.)

It accords with our common-sense experience when we are told that the tonal difference between, say, an oboe and a flute, when both are sounding the same note, is the result of that note being accompanied by differing combinations of harmonic partials.

When a similar mathematical description is applied to colours, the talk about wavelengths and frequencies is not disbelieved. It is felt to be, though doubtless true, completely irrelevant to our sense-experience. I do not know what the numerical relationship between the wavelengths of red light and blue light may be; but I do know that they contain no intimation whatever of the redness of red and the blueness of blue. But if you tell me that the wavelength of the C above middle C is half that of middle C, that is just what I expect to be told.

III

The Romantic movement has a lot to answer for. In particular it has done a great deal of damage to architecture, and even more obviously to architects. We may feel that in the pre-Romantic era architects hovered uncomfortably in a limbo between being artists and being tradesmen; but so did composers such as Haydn and Mozart. The academies which were founded towards the end of the eighteenth century and the beginning of the nineteenth provided for architects among their members. When an architect appears in a late nineteenth- or early twentieth-century novel, he is expected to produce a great masterpiece or to die young, or perhaps, like Harvey Lonsdale Elmes,* both. But most architects do neither of these things, but merely get by in a humdrum sort of way. Yet they seem to have lost the knack of designing buildings which merely get by in a humdrum sort of way, just as they seem, for the most part, to have lost the knack of setting their buildings in relation to the contours and to each other, in the felicitous way which seems to have come so naturally to the 'untrained' designers of the past.

Architecture is the most accessible of the arts; yet paradoxically it is the least noticed by people at large and is commonly thought by them to be an arcane mystery. This seems to be to the advantage of the architects, at least in the short term. But in the long term it has led to complete mutual incomprehension between architects and public.

The resemblances between architecture and music extend somewhat further than the fact that neither need be about anything except itself. Both rely on the regular recurrence or alternation of mathematically related quantities, on repetition and recapitulation, on themes ornamented and unornamented, on balance, symmetry and conventional terminations. There are other analogies less easily demonstrable, as when a modulation in key suggests a sudden enlargement in space or a flood of light following upon a passage of relative darkness.

The form in which the correspondence between architecture and music is most commonly presented is in such a situation as, for example, listening to Bach in a medieval cathedral, when the intricate polyphonic patterns seem to be echoed by the complexities of lierne vaulting and window-tracery. Many years ago I heard John Summerson giving a wireless talk in which, as I recall, he spoke of hearing such music and simultaneously looking at the stained glass of York Minster or Chartres.

* 1814-47: principal architect of St George's Hall, Liverpool.

In fact, of course, there is little or no connexion between the architecture and the music, which were produced three or four centuries apart and by virtually distinct cultures. The parallelism is essentially sentimental and associational: people are accustomed to hearing polyphonic music in medieval cathedrals, and indeed, if almost by accident, they do go very well together.

The form in which it suggested itself to me was the idea of hearing one of Handel's coronation anthems – 'Zadok the Priest' perhaps – in the Painted Hall at Greenwich: a setting contemporary with the music, and embodying much the same ideas of the apotheosis of a Protestant dynasty, with dissolving cloudscapes and opening perspectives such as it is easy to hear suggested by Handel.

Mendelssohn's Hebrides Overture ('Fingal's Cave') is surely among the most effective pieces of 'tone-painting' ever realized. Yet, if nobody had told us that it was inspired by Mendelssohn's visit to Scotland, would we ever, unaided, have fitted the imagery to the sound? More recently we have heard Khatchaturian's *Spartacus* music very convincingly pressed into service to depict 'oceanic' feelings.

The truth is that music can indeed express emotion, but only in the most generalized way: intense or expressive emotion, feelings of exaltation or dejection, of languor or of breeziness. It can be ponderous or frivolous. It cannot, of its own nature, be convincingly 'sacred' or 'secular'. And the same is broadly true of architecture.

I refuse to be made to feel guilty for treating music as wallpaper. I treat architecture as wallpaper, too, and so does everybody else. That is to say that for every one time I look at a building with attention, I pass it a hundred times without looking at (as distinct from seeing) it. But if anything had been done to it I would notice it immediately. In the same way, I hear a great deal of music, and only sometimes do I listen to it. But if a significant alteration is made to something I am hearing without listening to it, I become alert.

I see nothing wrong in this. But to some people it is almost critical. *Il faut qu'une porte soit ouverte ou fermée* is their motto. For myself, the half-open door.

Wide as is the field of music open to me, much of it still awaiting exploration, my musical tastes are in fact rather narrow. Jazz, for instance, I quite enjoy, but I do not know my way round it at all. I am amazed at the wealth of learning which some of my contemporaries have acquired in this sphere: comparable to what I have picked up about motor-cars or bookbindings, subjects on which in the past I have been thoroughly hooked so that information has attached itself to me like burrs.

When my musical taste was first formed in about 1936, neither Mahler nor Bruckner were much noticed, at least in this part of the world. They have since risen in the firmament, though I cannot very easily see why. Bruckner still seems to me mostly long-winded and banal, while Mahler seems, except for some of the songs, the most self-indulgent of composers and a very fountain-head of schmaltz. When I was young we hardly ever heard mention of Vivaldi except in historical terms: now his stock has risen and he is heard in all quarters. Pleasant enough stuff: but for me not so very different from most of the music of before 1750, which I tend to dismiss as a kind of undifferentiated tapestry. (This is not offered as musical criticism: merely as a record of personal experience and limitations.)

Two composers who have come up in the world have come up also in my appreciation: Haydn and Liszt. Their cases are very different. Haydn has always been reckoned among the greatest composers. But fifty years ago very little of his work was actually heard: his magnificent masses, for example, not at all. Concentration on his quartets left no time or attention to spare for his trios, and his operas are even now only beginning to be explored. Mechanical recording has of course made all the difference in this field, in expanding the individual's share of opportunity and choice. The older I grow, the more enjoyment I get from Haydn: not only the quartets and the masses, but also the symphonies, which I once foolishly undervalued.

Liszt, also, has risen in esteem since those days. He used to be thought a rather meretricious composer, and perhaps some vestige of this feeling still lingers. He is, perhaps, more uneven than any other composer of comparable stature; but this is, among other things, a reflexion of the great range of his adventurous daring. His *Orpheus* seems to me about as perfect as such a thing can be, and I remember that the tone-poem is only one of several things he invented. He is more to my taste than Chopin: he strikes me as having had a much more interesting mind. Only now are we beginning to appreciate the breadth of his generosity to both the living and the dead. With such a combination of sensitivity and gusto, and with such technical facility, is it any wonder that he occasionally struck a false note? And who cares if he did?

There are two composers I treasure specially, whose output was pitiably small. One is Arriaga who died in 1825 at the age of nineteen, leaving three lovely quartets which, without sounding ethnically 'Spanish', yet could not possibly be mistaken for Haydn or Schubert. The other is Duparc, who wrote a handful of wonderful songs before being overtaken by a clouded silence which lasted till he died at the age of eighty-five in 1933.

Longevity, as lovers of Verdi know well, can produce its surprises. Richard Strauss is a case in point. Who could have foreseen that at the very end of his life the rather shop-soiled old master should have shed all the dross and soared up to write *Metamorphosen* and the 'Four Last Songs'? For this, all must be forgiven him.

The greatness of Verdi was never, it seems to me, more fully indicated than by the fact that he spent years brooding over the project of making *King Lear* into an opera, and in the end decided not to. *Otello* is if anything even better than Shakespeare's play, and as for *Falstaff*, it is nothing less than miraculous to have turned such a prosaic and mechanical piece as the *Merry Wives* into what he made of it. The secret is, of course, that with Boito's help he infused the great Falstaff of the Henry IV plays into the new conception of his opera, with magical results.

Whenever I hear a piece of nineteenth-century music which is clearly very good but clearly not by one of the greatest masters, it nearly always turns out to be by Saint-Saëns.

I have never felt tempted to join in the fashion for trying to push Beethoven off his plinth, though I can understand that some such reaction is bound to occur from time to time, if only because such colossal pretensions invite it. But I would sooner not find myself in the company of Ezra Pound. After all, if I should find myself tiring of the symphonies and concertos I can always turn to the sonatas and the quartets.

I do make a clear distinction in my own mind between music which appears to be developing an argument and, as we say, 'getting somewhere', and music which seems to be getting nowhere. Most of Beethoven comes in the first category, and some of Sibelius, such as the sixth and seventh symphonies, and Fauré's string quartet. Schubert is a special case: he seems to me to be less directional and, to vary the metaphor, to be conducting the listener through a landscape in which the main objects are seen from varying angles and under varying atmospheric conditions. Examples of music which seems to me to be getting nowhere are the symphonies of Elgar, and almost anything by Delius.

I am not musical enough to know what are the technical means by which these effects are created: they are well known to musicians and can readily be identified. Yet there is obviously much more to it than that. I am quite ready to believe that in Elgar's symphonies all the prescribed evolutions are correctly performed; but, so far as I am concerned, to no purpose.

There is a good deal of music, especially from before about 1770, which seems to me merely busy and bustling. Into this category falls, I fear, much of the output of Johann Sebastian Bach. The fault here must lie with me and not with him.

The tastes, at one time, of Rudy Kousbroek* and myself, in music and architecture, were curiously contrasted. He disliked the parade of emotion which is found in so much nineteenth-century music, whereas I can put up with a good deal of that, with certain limitations which I have already touched upon. I can

* Dutch writer and journalist, born 1930 in Indonesia, long resident in Paris: one of the author's oldest and closest friends.

even enjoy, in small doses, the great swooning washes of orchestral sound in some of the overripe Late Romantics. He did, on the other hand, like the output of the earlier court and church composers, whose range of expression seemed, and seems, unsatisfying to me. In architecture on the other hand, Rudy did not at that time see the point of the Classical style, which seemed to him dull and frigid. He preferred the more extravagant fantasies of the Gothic and other revivals: the further they were removed from common sense the better he was pleased, and he enjoyed some buildings which I could not, and cannot, take seriously. Most of my favourite buildings date from before 1770, and most of my favourite music from after that time.

To some extent, of course, we have since then converted one another to a wider spectrum of tolerance and of pleasure.

I can remember the actual moment at which music suddenly hit me. It was, of course, an affair of hormonal change. I must have been fourteen at the time. Till then my acquaintance of and involvement in music had been rather small. I was familiar with a handful of pieces of which my parents had gramophone records: cumbrous 78s of course. They were: Mozart's 'Eine Kleine Nachtmusik', Tchaikovsky's *Casse-Noisette*, César Franck's Violin and Piano Sonata, Brahms's First Symphony and Double Concerto, Rachmaninov's Second Piano Concerto, and a disc which had on one side Delius's 'Cuckoo' and on the other 'Shepherd Fennel's Dance' by Balfour Gardiner. (It was to be many years before I found out who Shepherd Fennel was.) I thought of all these pieces as being on much the same level. I had also heard and enjoyed Beethoven's First Symphony.

Then, one evening, at the school Music Club which met to listen to gramophone records, I heard the Seventh Symphony and was completely bowled over, especially by the Allegretto. A whole new world seemed to open up for me. Not long afterwards I heard a real live quartet play the Haydn opus 76 no. 5 in D, and the Largo of this made an immediate emotional impact, with the same kind of emotional resonance. From there I went on to the Beethoven Violin Concerto and before long to the Second Symphony of Sibelius.

It was, nevertheless, to be a long time before I came to the enjoyment of quartets as a class. Like most adolescents I was first seduced by the headier intoxications of the full orchestra. But the world which then opened before me has remained open ever since: an alternative universe which I constantly revisit.

IV

Soon after my book on ¹rish bookbindings came out I became interested in motor-cars, and this interest lasted for about ten years. The kind of ca⸱s I was interested in, those of the Vintage period (i.e. from 1919 to 1930), resembled rather closely the kind of books in which I had been and still was interested. In both cases the books or cars were produced in largish numbers – hundreds for the most part rather than thousands – and in bare form: in 'boards' ready to be bound by Derôme, Monnier, Roger Payne or Mackenzie: as a chassis ready to be clad in coachwork by Henri Chapron, Zagato, Saoutchik, Labourdette, Mulliner or Park Ward. During the run of a production car small modifications would be introduced which were closely analogous to the variant points which determine the 'issues' and 'states' of an edition. Like the books, the cars were produced in series but not in mass: there was an appreciable handwork element in their manufacture, and if you owned a specimen you had the interest of knowing that your example would have a strong family relationship to others but would have its own individual features also.

It was still possible at that time to own and run a high-quality car, twenty-five or thirty years old, both for practical purposes and for fun, but only if the subject interested you. The more you did for yourself the better. I had, for my D8 4-litre Delage with Figoni coachwork, not only the driver's manual but also the spare-parts catalogue, which had some thirty or more fold-out pages of meticulously produced sectional drawings, so that I knew the whole of the car and its parts, both accessible and inaccessible, by heart. It is easy, when remembering what such things cost, to make the mistake of forgetting the difference in money-values. Nevertheless, when I recall that the initial cost of buying one car, plus another for spares, plus an engine-rebuild, plus coachwork, a new hood, new carpet, gearbox rebuilt, wheels re-splined, repainting and the rest – in short the combined sum of all capital costs spread over a period of thirteen years, was only about £660, for which at the time one could barely have bought an ordinary small mass-produced car all made of pressed steel, it seems that we did indeed have our luxury at a very moderate price. Even petrol, road tax, insurance and the rent of a garage were within our means. I regret that we never took the Delage to France, but we did take her on several occasions to Ireland, always by Rosslare-Fishguard, motoring in the old style in Cork and Donegal and most places in between.

But the time came when, having acquired an ordinary motor-car for everyday use, I was driving the Delage only half a dozen times a year, never for less than fifty miles each way, but at a cost of about twenty pounds a time. The car had become like a country cottage or a yacht: not to resort to it whenever possible made me feel guilty. Already the return to Ireland was in sight, and in Irish conditions and at Irish costs the ownership of such a car would not be practicable. So, with the utmost regret, a good home had to be found for her.

For some years I also owned the grandest of all Delage passenger-cars, the 6-litre overhead camshaft GL with mahogany boat-shaped body by Henri Labourdette. I am glad to have been one of those who played a part in restoring this beautiful machine to the land of the living. She had had a chequered life, and at one stage the rear half of the body had been sawn off and this noble vehicle turned into a breakdown truck. I drove her only for a few hundred yards, because the torque-tube and universal housing had been damaged. Apart from a lot of stripping, preparing and painting the rear half of the chassis and the 36-gallon petrol tank, I made a measured survey of the car and did the lines for the restoration of the bodywork and had the transmission put in order, before handing her over to others in whose hands she has since resumed her rightful place and can now be seen on page 83 of Rousseau's *Les Automobiles Delage* (1978).

The GL is a truly glorious machine. The engine, designed by Maurice Sainturat, rising out of an upswept aluminium platform made of the extended flanges of the crankcase, is like a cathedral. It is curious, in parenthesis, to observe how, during this period, English automobile-engines had the character of French railway-locomotives, and vice versa. Like the French locomotives, the English motor-engines were festooned with a tangle of pipe-work and untidy auxiliaries – 'brushwood' we used to call it – whereas the French with their 'suitcase-engines' managed to hide all that away and present an appearance as neat as a Great Western 'Castle' or a Great Northern Gresley Pacific. Owners of Bugattis, Hispanos and Delages used to describe the Rolls-Royce as 'the triumph of workmanship over design'. But that is by the way.

This Delage was the most expensively made motor-car I have ever got to know well. The cam-followers and tappets are rollers; the forged ends of the front axle are drilled out and the kingpins have ball-bearings. The instrument-panel, dashboard and toeboards are magnificent aluminium castings, and so is the massively deep X-braced cross-member of the chassis. Both the autovac tank and the petrol tank have fabricated hollow ways to allow the passage of the fuel control rod and the exhaust-pipe respectively. The ball-and-socket joints of the throttle-control bell-cranks are retained by screw-in plugs instead of spring-clips. The ends of the springs work in elaborately made trunnions. And so on and so on. Warum einfach wenn es auch kompliziert geht?*

Ownership of this car, at a time when we had also in the family an Austin Seven of similar date, was, among other things, an expression of passion for the very extravagant and the very minimal as well. I have never owned an ordinary-sized family saloon, and my present car is the cheapest and lowest-powered (and also the most intelligently designed) on the market. The same passion underlies my love for enormous steamships such

* 'Why do it the simple way when there is a complicated way?'

198

as the *Normandie*, *France* or *Aquitania*, and for the minuscule Canary packets.

A friend of mine once bought an old Humber which was equipped with a device called a Startix. When you pressed a button it would operate the starter, and, if the engine did not start, it would do it again, and again, and again, till further orders. After the first few moments of amusement, this performance became very painful to witness. I am made uncomfortable by seeing or hearing machinery suffer.

My daughter, on the other hand, has a device attached to her telephone which, when a number is engaged, will go on dialling it, silently and untiringly, until it gets through and only then will it advise her of the fact by ringing. Now that, for once, is a technical device which makes the world a pleasanter and quieter place to live in.

I am reminded of the Startix by the behaviour of our very ancient dog. She is seven-eighths blind, very deaf, unpredictably incontinent, but still ruled by desires which she seeks and sometimes succeeds in gratifying. When she tries to open a locked door she behaves exactly like the Startix. Left to herself she would go on till the battery was flat.

It reminds me, too, to what a great extent we are all machines, as La Mettrie suggested so long ago.* She follows me round the house for all the world like a magnetic toy, never more than a few inches from my heels. But I behave in much the same way. When I go to put my hand in a pocket, and for some reason – perhaps the presence of a flap – it does not go in first time, my hand goes backwards and forwards independently and in vain, until I notice what is happening and apply my mind to it.

The body seems sometimes capable of autonomous action, by which I do not mean the well-known involuntary reflexes. Like other people, I often find myself in bed or in a chair saying to myself that it is time I got up. The odd thing is that sometimes, while I am still debating the point and forming resolutions, my body gets up apparently of its own accord, as

* In *L'homme machine* (1748).

though to say, 'I have been listening to you and I have had enough of this indecision: I will show you how it is to be done.'

I am not in favour of exercise and never take any if I can help it. At school I was an exceptionally unathletic boy who avoided games of any kind whenever I could. Yet I remember that up to the age of about fifteen or perhaps even older I habitually ran from one place to another, rather than walking. It surprises me very much that this should have been so, and I recall that it surprised me even then. It must be another instance of my body having opinions at variance with mine.

It is a commonplace to observe that the motor-car is an agent of alienation. People in motor-cars are hated by those without, and the hatred is returned. People in motor-cars hate other people in motor-cars. This is especially noticeable when, after a week's cruising on a large river, you get into your car to drive home. A world which was populated by friendly people in other cruisers becomes a world populated by your car-borne enemies. Everything happens so much more quickly and there is so much less room.

It has been less remarked that the motor-car can become a very effective means of non-verbal communication, not necessarily of a hostile nature. For many years I used to drive across central London during the height of the rush-hour, twice a day. All those who did so did it regularly and frequently and had become very good at it. The traffic moved very quickly but not once, I believe, did I see an accident or even a sign of overt anger. People did not even sound their horns. In ways not easily definable we were able to tell others what we intended to do and what we expected them to do, simply by being where we were, pointing at such an angle, and going at such a speed.

By contrast, whenever I drove over the same routes at 'slack' times, mutual understanding was noticeably lacking. The reason was, of course, that many of those who shared the road with me were not very accustomed to doing so and did not know the (non-verbal) language. Hostility and anger were the result.

Does this contain a moral applicable to the avoidance of war?

V

I recently heard a modern prize-winning architect say that large-scale buildings seem designed to make people feel small. I cannot see that this is so. It seems to me to depend largely on the relationship between the building and the person concerned. Blenheim was not designed to make the Duke of Marlborough feel small: quite the contrary. Nor need we suppose that any such large country house was intended to make the owner's neighbours or guests feel small, however large or small their own habitations might be. Cathedrals, of course, are designed to make the whole human race seem small by contrast with the majesty of heaven, which is fair enough.

But the speaker more probably had in mind public secular buildings. Here again I cannot quite agree with him. The Opéra in Paris is a good deal grander and larger than Covent Garden, but, leaving aside the quality of the productions and performances on offer, I was certainly not made to feel small by the splendour of the halls and lobbies and staircases, with a *huissier* standing to attention in full uniform in front of each pilaster. A little of that sort of thing does not come amiss once in a while, and makes you feel you are getting full value for the price of your ticket.

What is wrong with most modern public buildings is surely the contrary fault, that they are apt to be short on 'wasted' space and hence on the sense of occasion. Lofty ceilings give you the sense that you are getting your money's worth, like Louis XIV. But if you are made to live in a building which looks like an anthill, you feel like an ant.

Modern architects sometimes remind me of those primitive tribes whose arithmetical attainments extend only to 'one', 'two' and 'many'. Few modern buildings are divided, as many classical buildings are, into three or five units: a centre, two ends and perhaps two units linking the ends to the centre. Once the number of 'bays' or windows rises above about seven, the eye stops counting them, and they read as merely 'a large number', and since many modern buildings are required to be very large, the building ends up with no focus of attention. Moreover, when a modulus of, say, five metres is adopted, so that the structural stanchions occur at that interval, the modern architects almost invariably divide this into four: never into three or five. There is no good reason for this, and since the experience of centuries has established that small odd numbers are more engaging to the eye than small even numbers, it seems to me to be merely perverse.

Another drawback under which modern architects labour is not, perhaps, to be blamed on the architects. This is the frequent absence of a focus in the form of a front door or main entrance. There are three conspicuous buildings in Dublin with front doors which are never used. In one case – the Old Parliament House – this is because internal alterations have made it impossible. At the Custom House the changes made in the reconstruction after the fire have, without actually making the door unusable, had very much the same effect. Finally there is the Moyne Institute in Trinity, which has a grand central entrance with a portico and a great flight of steps. Nobody ever uses it because it faces the cricket field, and everybody goes in and out through the back entrance.

The recent obligation to provide for people in wheelchairs has made it more difficult than ever to endow new buildings with dignity, for it is not easy for a building to assert itself unless it stands on some kind of plinth or podium. Similar constraints inhibit any display of grandeur in the interior. I was recently in a building which, however well it fulfilled its programme and however efficiently it may have 'worked' for those who knew it well, remained incomprehensible even after several visits. Its anatomy did not proclaim itself in any helpful way. It was, for example, difficult to remember how to get to the staircase. As everyone knows, the staircase is or has been habitually a critical element in the articulation of most classical plans, a fixed reference point for the visitor.

That this was not so in the building in question was, I came to the conclusion, mainly because of the demands of safety against fire. The interior was cut up into small compartments with self-closing fire-proof doors between them, and the staircase was lurking behind one of these. It was rather like being on board ship, and done for similar reasons.

John Summerson in one of his essays has accounted for if not justified this kind of change by saying that whereas in the past the town hall (for example) was intended to glorify the mayor and corporation, it has nowadays no such purpose and if we go there at all it is probably to complain about something. Therefore, so runs the argument, monumentality in such architecture is out of place.

Perhaps; though I doubt it. Some day the wind will change.

VI

Plastics are a moral problem. There may be some who would dispute this, but Ruskin, Morris and Lethaby would nod in vigorous agreement. No true materialist doubts it. It is not merely their diabolical behaviour: their tendency to fail without warning and to tear in unpredictable directions, their resistance to being cut or filed, the behaviour of some of them when exposed to sunlight, low temperature or even the mere lapse of time, their disinclination towards being repaired, their reluctance to accept most adhesives, their horrible slitheriness, their tendency to get grubby – and so on and so on. These are faults or vices which irritate us in just the way that we are irritated by the faults of our fellow-men or indeed ourselves, and they are compounded by the fact that there are now such large numbers of different plastics with different characteristics that nobody but a specialist can keep track of them.

The moral question arises at the very beginning, from the fact that plastics are derived for the most part from finite non-renewable sources such as coal and oil, and require much energy for their manufacture. It arises again at the end, from the fact that most plastics are not recyclable and have to be regarded as expendable, and are not even biodegradable (to use three nasty, ugly but almost indispensable twentieth-century words).

Their unpredictability works both ways. I bought an appliance which had a case with a pair of handles which came together when the hinged lids were shut, and were connected to them by incredibly thin hinges of the same plastic material. A friend of mine, a professional engineer, gratuitously volunteered the information that, flimsy as they might look, they would never fail. That particular plastic, he said, had been tested with several million flexures and counterflexures. I ought to have been warned by this. After being opened and shut a few hundred times the hinges failed. On the other hand I bought, many years ago, a yellow cycling-cape which looked like oilskin but was in fact plastic. It was very cheap, and over many years' hard service it never became hard or brittle, or cracked, or tore, and even the zip went on working perfectly. It showed no sign of wearing out, and in the end I believe I must have lost it.

It took some time for an aesthetic appropriate to plastic to evolve. Unlike other materials, a plastic can have its colour right through it and normally does. But this can limit the choice, since certain colouring agents sometimes affect the mechanical properties of the material coloured. During the primitive plastic or 'bakelite' period, it seemed that you could have any colour you liked so long as it was brown.

More recently an acceptable aesthetic based on silver and black has been evolved: the silver being sometimes aluminium and sometimes stainless steel and sometimes the plastic itself. It is surely undeniable that there are some purposes for which plastic is better than anything else. Nobody would think of making the knob of a gear-lever, or the case of a portable wireless, out of anything else. This black-and-silver aesthetic is very similar to that of my Royal Portable typewriter which was made in 1939. But the black, there, is japanned steel (or, for the case, timber covered with black cloth which I have freshened up with a coat of matt black) and the silver is chromium plating.

Cameras, tape-recorders, portable calculators and the like now mostly have this style, and very satisfactory it is. But fashion cannot leave well alone, so before long, no doubt some new and diabolical discord will become all the rage and sweep through the shops like wildfire.

VII

After reading *A History of the Crusades, The Eastern Schism, The Sicilian Vespers* and *The Fall of Constantinople*, all by Steven Runciman, I found myself feeling a great deal of sympathy with the Orthodox Church. They were so clearly in the right and had been so badly treated by their opponents. Besides, I had a natural Protestant tendency to play off the two ends against the middle. Their architecture, too, was and is much more to my taste than that of the Latins, at least after 1200 or so.

My enthusiasm did not survive a reading of *The Orthodox Church* (1963) by Timothy Ware. This author became a convert to Orthodoxy at the age of twenty-four, and must be presumed to be putting the best face he can on the faith to which, by choice, he adheres. His book is very informative and often entertaining, but it left me with the impression that the Greek Church yields little if anything in reactionary obscurantism to its Latin counterpart.

Not long ago St Mary's Church in Dublin, long since surplus to Church of Ireland needs, was made over to the Orthodox, which seemed a convenient solution to the problem which it presented. The latest news, alas, is that the Orthodox in Dublin have split into two factions, whether from some ancestral memory or from the contagion of the Irish air, and have dumped the building back into the reluctant lap of the Representative Body. Now it is to be a paint-shop, and its prospects are not at all promising.

This reminds me once again of how many of the buildings I most admire were built for purposes of which I cannot approve. If we are to subtract from the canon of the world's architecture all the buildings devoted to religion or war, there will be little left except the palaces of tyrants, which hardly command my unqualified approval. And what about the gaols which embody some of the finest architecture of all? Am I to be left with a handful of court-houses, bridges, granaries, limekilns and railway-stations? Or is the whole question of a building's purpose best regarded as irrelevant? One of the 'post-modern' architects said recently that the mausoleum is the only class of building in which the architect is free to produce pure architecture, which is much like saying that the only entirely satisfactory songs are songs without words.

Not all experiences involving architecture are strictly architectural, or purely architectural, not even if we include among architecture's main functions that of interacting and collaborating with the climate and the weather. There is a famous remark of Goodhart-Rendel about preferring a view of the Free Trade Hall in Athenian sunlight to one of the Parthenon in a Manchester dusk.* He did not live to see the present pollution of the Athenian atmosphere.

Pollution was no doubt, in part, responsible for one of the most magical sights I can remember. From somewhere near the Westminster end of Lambeth Bridge I saw the Vickers Tower on Millbank through a thick haze or thin fog. Though I was looking Southwards at it, for some reason the sunlight, which must have been strong and coming from low down either to the East or West, caught the verticals of the tower in great golden streaks. It was much more like looking at a painting than looking at a building, so that the sharp distinction which is usually so clear in my mind, between the beauty of art and that of nature, had for once broken down.

Not that the Vickers Tower lacks architectural merit: far otherwise. It is not square on plan: the sides are alternately concave and convex, and even though this is done by two straight lines in each case instead of by curves, it generates varied interest from every angle. In its rigorous cleanness of outline it makes a splendid foil to the bristly Victoria Tower when both are seen in enfilade. Or at least it did, when I knew it. By now it is probably surrounded by a forest of roughly similar towers, and so devalued.

The trick with the adjacent convex and concave elevations is one that can be played only once, like a good many other tricks in modern architecture. Such, for example, as the patterning of

---

* *Vitruvian Nights* (1932), p. 176. This book, and other writings from the same hand, abound in sharp and felicitous observations.

an exterior by vertical bronze H-section girders, invented by Mies van der Rohe and used by Ronnie Tallon for the Bank of Ireland in Baggot Street, which has been played a good many times already and which was to have been played again, posthumously, by Mies himself, at the Palumbo tower beside the London Mansion House, if it ever had got built.

I watched the television programme on the controversy about this tower. Two of the principal figures in the dispute were known to me; one well, the other from long ago and in a quite different context. John Summerson, now in his eighties, had lost none of his incisiveness, and though he was saying much the same kind of things, so unhelpful to 'conservationists', as he had said years ago in Lower Fitzwilliam Street with such woeful results, I found myself agreeing with him. That was only half of what he said: with the other half I found myself agreeing much more whole-heartedly.

I had met Mr Palumbo rather more than twenty-five years ago when my raffish friend Hamish Moffat and I had been invited to his house in, I think, Hyde Park Crescent in pursuance of a scheme (which succeeded) for selling to Mr Palumbo a Bugatti motor-car. Mr Palumbo was then very young, and lived in a very pretentious neo-Georgian *palazzo*, built, no doubt, by his father who had more ability than taste. He was then, I should judge, in his early twenties, and his desire to buy a Bugatti was not, it is clear in retrospect, the usual modish fancy of a rich young man, but the nascent stirrings of a passion for quality which led him to his involvement with Mies. In 1989 he was appointed Chairman of Britain's Arts Council.

VIII

Fashion may be defined as that which cannot leave well alone. Nothing could be more perfectly adapted to its purpose, or more elegant, than the sports bicycle of about 1950, with its rhomboidal frame, the top member parallel to the ground, its narrow tyres and dropped handlebars: the culmination of a century of evolution.

But somebody had to go and invent a bicycle with small wheels and fat tyres. The ostensible reason was that it could be folded up and put into the boot of a car. So it could, but very few ever were. Its great merit was that it was new and that it was different. It faded away, more or less, and is not so much seen now. But another fashion spread, based I think on the film *Easy Rider*, a fashion for handlebars which curved upwards and outwards like the horns of some kind of deer, so that the rider had to reach upwards well above his head to control it. Serious cyclists, it need hardly be said, will have nothing to do with it.

The bicycle is unique among machines in having structural gender. While ladies did not go so far as to ride side-saddle, they had, and have, bikes adapted to their special circumstances, even if the more determined girl riders rode masculine machines. The only aesthetically pleasing improvement made in recent years has been the stiffening of the frame by replacing the awkward extra tube of the 'lady's' model by a pair of tubes running in a straight line from the steering head to the back axle, one on each side of the saddle-post and welded to it where they cross it. Besides looking better, this is a structural improvement.

Some other fashions seem, alas, destined to hold the stage for rather longer than the small-wheeled bicycle. One which I particularly dislike and would be glad to see the last of is the habit of allowing rough stonework and brickwork to be exposed in domestic interiors. This perverse taste runs clean counter to three thousand years of human experience. It seems to have begun with the Victorian craze for stripping the plaster off the insides of churches. Those who did so did it out of ignorance, not knowing that the insides of medieval buildings were always plastered if possible, and from a Romantic preference for rough surfaces over smooth ones. (It is understood, of course, that this does not apply to highly finished ashlar masonry and carved detail, which was always intended to be seen.) Ceiling laths were ripped off, and structural carpentry, of a rough but sound kind which was intended to do its job but not be seen, was enthusiastically revealed. From this it was but a short step to regarding the result as 'beautiful', and it was not long before the disease spread to private houses.

Medieval man made the inside of his dwelling as different as he could from the wild and dangerous environment which surrounded it. Classical man, who succeeded him, took the same view of inside versus outside. If he did, occasionally, construct an underground grotto or line a room with shells or lumps of quartz, it was for a very special effect and it was well understood to be for that occasion only and not to be made a habit of. But Romantic man has taught himself that everything wild, irregular, unfinished or shaggy is 'beautiful', and thousands of acres of good plaster have been hacked off to expose wriggly timbers, wormeaten sapwood with wany edges and full of shakes, the more wriggly the better. I hate to think of the number of times I have been expected to admire the result.

Bare bricks indoors, even bare concrete blocks, seem now to be regarded as acceptable. I am glad that I do not have to live or work in such an environment. But when the internal space is very large, as at Westminster Cathedral, the scale of the brickwork becomes simply a texture or 'grain', and is perfectly appropriate.

THE DRUCE-PORTLAND CASE
AND OTHER IMPOSTURES

I

BEING A poor liar myself, I have always been fascinated by imposture and its cousin, forgery. The technicalities of imposture are interesting, but even more interesting are the motives. It is easy to understand the desire to appear before the world in one's own real or assumed character, and comprehensible to wish not to appear at all. Forgery for financial gain is perhaps not very interesting. I did, when very young, buy a book simply for the sake of the title on its spine, which read, laconically,

DODD

ON

DEATH

to be rewarded later by the discovery that it was by the unfortunate Dr Dodd who, as readers of Boswell will recall, was a fashionable London preacher hanged for forging a cheque.

The literary forgers: Macpherson, Ireland, Chatterton, are not so interesting to me as those who forged from a more complex mixture of motives, such as Sir Edmund Backhouse and Thomas James Wise. In both these there seems to be some tincture of a desire to score off the great world, without – and this is the puzzling part – letting the great world know that it had been made a fool of. It is a most delicious irony that the man who so elegantly presented Sir Edmund Backhouse to the world should himself, and so soon afterwards, have been led by the nose into the morass of the 'Hitler Diaries'.

Seeing a televised version of Josephine Tey's clever novel *Brat Farrar* reminded me of the Tichborne case which was clearly its inspiration, and which used to be familiar to the public. The heir to the Tichborne baronetcy, Roger Charles Tichborne, it will be recalled, was lost at sea in 1854, but supposedly reappeared in 1865 in the person of Arthur Orton alias Castro, an Australian butcher born in London, who succeeded in getting the confidence of his supposed mother, the dowager Lady Tichborne, by whom he was recognized in a darkened room in Paris. The heir was slightly built and dark-haired, whereas the claimant was fair-haired and weighed twenty-four stone. Backed by Lady Tichborne, but not by the rest of the family, Orton instituted proceedings in the Court of Chancery in 1871, by which time she had died. Though apparently supported by some of Henry Charles's brother officers, his suit failed after a trial lasting 102 days. He was then prosecuted for perjury and defended by the able but eccentric Irish barrister Edward Vaughan Kenealy. After a 188-day trial he was sentenced in 1874 to fourteen years' penal servitude, but released in 1884; and after publishing in 1895 a recantation (later said to have been withdrawn by him), he died in 1898 aged fifty-four. Kenealy was disbarred and disgraced, and published a private newspaper in the plaintiff's cause, and an account of the trial in eight volumes. Dublin folklore says that one of the things by which Orton was caught out was in not knowing that the quickest way from Castle Street to Ship Street was by the 'Castle Steps' (open till recently but now closed to the public). The real heir had been stationed in Dublin.

I have always found it puzzling that the Druce-Portland Case, which seems to be intrinsically more interesting than the Tichborne, should be so little known. There is a rather scarce book by Theodore Besterman which consists mostly of a transcript of the proceedings in the courts, and an indifferent recent novel based on the case, but the most serviceable account is my own, based on Besterman and designed and delivered as a broadcast.

II

The fifth Duke of Portland was a very odd fellow indeed. And to my mind one of the oddest things about him is how little he seems to be remembered, considering how odd he was during his life and what a carry-on there was about him after his death. He had a passion for building, and people who build a lot are usually remembered: people like our own Earl-Bishop of Derry, for example, or William Beckford. Most people remember something about Vathek, and the Halls of Eblis, and the Lansdowne Tower of Bath, and the tower of Fonthill Abbey which so spectacularly fell down. It's true that the Duke of Portland spent a great deal of effort trying to ensure that nobody ever saw him: but people who do that, especially if they are very rich, generally succeed in drawing attention to themselves – like Howard Hughes, for example, and others I could mention.

This Duke started, as I suppose we all do more or less, in a fairly ordinary way. He was born in 1800, but he did not at first expect to become a duke because he had an elder brother. And by the time he succeeded to the dukedom and all the money he was fifty-four. So he lived the usual fairly humdrum life of a man in his position. He was in the army for a few years and he was a Member of Parliament for a few years. But as soon as he inherited Welbeck Abbey, which is one of those enormous houses in that part of Nottinghamshire called 'the Dukeries' (because it is so full of dukes and their huge houses), he began to build furiously and went on building for a quarter of a century, until he died at the age of seventy-nine.

Even that, you might think, is ordinary enough, except that all his building was downwards instead of upwards. He built a suite of libraries 236 feet long, a ballroom 160 feet by 64 (which was originally meant as a chapel), a huge picture-gallery – all underground; an underground railway from the kitchens to the dining-room, with points and a long branch line leading to a lonely lavatory; a long tunnel leading to a vast conservatory and a riding school which are more or less above ground. Most extraordinary of all, perhaps, he built an underground drive, wide enough for two carriages to pass, from the house to the station. It is a mile and a half long, and I hardly need say that when it comes to the lake it goes clean under it. Whenever the Duke wanted to go to his house in London – or rather to one of his houses in London – he got into his carriage and was driven with the blinds down through his tunnel to the station where his carriage was hoisted on to the London train with the Duke still inside it, and at the other end, still of course with drawn blinds, to Cavendish Square or Hyde Park Gardens.

Needless to say he did not do all this single-handed. He had an army of workmen busily tunnelling and boring and burrowing and building, and he was on good terms with all of them. Every workman who entered his employment was presented with two things: a donkey and an umbrella. The donkey was to carry the workman to and from his work on the estate, and the umbrella to keep him dry if it should rain. The workmen were not allowed to address him as 'Your Grace' or 'My Lord': if they did they were dismissed. As far as I can make out, he never met or talked to other dukes or members of the landed classes.

It so happens that I have been in all the Underground Duke's underground rooms, rather more than thirty years ago. If you stand in the windows of the house proper and look down, all you can see are rows and rows of glass skylights, not very obtrusively breaking the surface of the green lawns. Inside the rooms themselves, the effect is not very extraordinary, apart from their enormous size, because there is plenty of daylight coming in from on top. The underground railways and other tunnels are another matter, especially that branch line.

In one of his London houses he built a sort of observation post on the roof, which could be seen from the street, and even during his lifetime there was an odd rumour current that there was a dead body up there. I have known other houses in England which had rumours of dead bodies up in the roof, and I know one which actually has a dead body: and the dead body up in that roof is that of no less a person than Oliver Cromwell. But that is another story. Anyway, in view of the strange goings-on that were to take place after the Duke's death, it's odd, to say the least of it.

Was the fifth Duke of Portland mad? I really haven't the faintest idea, and I'm not sure that the question has any meaning. If you are unbelievably rich, there is a great temptation to spend money building – and why not downwards? They say he had a disfiguring disease: perhaps he had. That is the kind of story that crops up all over the place and it may be true.

He died in 1879 and was buried – underground, suitably enough. The famous Lady Ottoline Morrell was a sister of the next duke and though she was only six at the time, she left a highly circumstantial account of going to Welbeck just after he died. She says that nearly every one of the rooms above ground had a lavatory standing unconcealed in the corner; that he made all the housemaids skate on his skating-rink; that he had hundreds of waistcoats and suits apparently unopened since arriving from the tailors; that she had found two thousand gold sovereigns in a wallet just lying about on one of the tables; and that he had an uncountable number of wigs.

As I said before it was all very odd, though against the background of the usual form of the English aristocracy or indeed any aristocracy, perhaps not quite so very exceptional. But the things which began to happen nearly twenty years after his death were, to my way of thinking, odder still.

When the Duke died he was succeeded in his dukedom and his vast wealth by one of his cousins. By 1896, seventeen years later, we must suppose that most people had forgotten all about him. If so, they were not allowed to remain forgetful any longer. For in that year a lady called Mrs Anna Maria Druce, the widow of one Walter Thomas Druce, applied to the Home Secretary for permission to open the grave of her father-in-law, Thomas Charles Druce, in Highgate Cemetery. In support of this request she told a very strange tale indeed.

There was at the time (and indeed there still was until a very few years ago) a large furniture store in Baker Street, London, called Druce's. At this time it was called the Baker Street Bazaar, and Mr Druce – old Mr Druce – was the owner of it. He had died in 1864, well over thirty years before the moment at which this part of our story opens. At least everyone believed he had died. But no, said Mrs Druce: he had not died at all, nor had he been buried. Indeed he had not existed at all! Because the man whom the Baker Street people knew as Thomas Charles Druce was really the fifth Duke of Portland who had commuted backwards and forwards from Welbeck to London, popping up in Baker Street as Mr Druce the furniture merchant, and popping up again in Nottinghamshire as the Duke of Portland. Finally, said Mrs Druce, he had got tired of being Mr Druce and had killed himself off, arranged a mock funeral with an empty coffin and gone back to Welbeck to be a duke and nothing but a duke till he finally did die fifteen years later. But under the name of Druce he had married and had a son (Mrs Druce's husband, who was now also dead) and through him a grandson, Mrs Druce's son, who was in Australia. And therefore, of course, this young Mr Druce was really the Duke of Portland and rightful owner of the Portland millions.

Well, not surprisingly, the Home Secretary was not very impressed with this elaborate tale and his answer to Mrs Druce was: no, you may not dig up your father-in-law. Quite unabashed by this, Mrs Druce applied to the House of Lords to have the sitting Duke of Portland thrown out in favour of her son, with no better success. So Mrs Druce then applied herself to the Bishop of London who referred her to the Chancellor of his diocese, a Dr Tristram QC, and in March 1898 a Consistory Court began to sit in St Paul's Cathedral.

Mrs Druce said that the Duke, in the character of Druce, had burrowed and tunnelled under Baker Street just as he had done at Welbeck; that he had pretended to be mad, under the name of Dr Harmer, and had become a voluntary patient in an asylum run by a Dr Forbes Winslow; and that twenty years after Druce's supposed death, and five years after that of the Duke, she had seen him in Dr Forbes Winslow's asylum at Maidenhead. She added that she had seen him there, 'dancing like a bear' and practising homeopathic medicine. On the strength not so much of these bizarre details as of the fact that there was no doctor's name on Mr Druce's death certificate, the Chancellor granted a faculty to have the grave opened.

At this point the real Mrs Harmer put in an appearance, and so did Dr Forbes Winslow, who said that his patient Dr Harmer had indeed a remarkable resemblance to the Duke of Portland. From now on, things began to happen with bewildering rapidity.

A Mr Herbert Druce, who was a son of old Mr Druce but born before Mr Druce's marriage (though to the same mother), came on the scene and said that he was not going to have his father dug up. Since he was one of his father's executors and was supported by the other executor, Mrs Druce was foiled again. So she took the case to the Court of Queen's Bench who upheld the decision to allow the grave to be opened: but still the Home Secretary refused to act. So off went Mrs Druce to the Probate Court to try to get the will revoked and made enough impression on the Probate Judge for him to order that the grave should be opened.

The position now was that Mrs Druce, who believed the grave to be empty, wanted it to be opened to prove that this was so, whereas Mr Herbert Druce, the illegitimate son, who believed his father to be in it, refused to allow this fact to be proved. The effect of this was to create an impression that Mr Herbert Druce had something to hide, whereas, as we now in fact know, the real reason was simply his distaste for the idea of having his father dug up. If he had given in, the case would have collapsed immediately. As it was, it was to drag on for another nine years.

The ducal family of Portland maintained throughout a posture of aloof and majestic unconcern. Their attitude was that whether a Baker Street tradesman was or was not to be dug up was not of the slightest interest to them.

After the Probate Judge's decision, Herbert Druce went to the Court of Appeal to get it reversed and he succeeded. Mrs Druce returned to the attack, and she in turn succeeded. The ball was now again in the Home Secretary's court, so to speak; but he once again refused to grant a licence for the exhumation. The London Cemetery Company, to whom Highgate Cemetery belonged, went to the Queen's Bench to have the whole thing quashed.

By now Mrs Druce had taken to going almost every day to the cemetery accompanied by a mining engineer. She tried to stop some grave-diggers from digging a grave a hundred yards away. She brought an action against the London Cemetery Company. She took the case to the Court of the Lord Mayor of London. She took it back again to the Probate Judge and, in 1893, she went public by issuing 'Druce-Portland Bonds'.

By this time the press was abuzz with articles on 'The Double Duke' and every kind of speculation was rife. In 1899, however, the *Weekly Dispatch* published an article which cast an entirely new light on the whole affair. According to this, old Mr Druce had been married as far back as 1816, and had had a son, and this was why Herbert Druce's parents had not got married until long after his birth, because the first wife was still alive. Ridiculous, said Mrs Druce, and marched off again to the Probate Court.

Mrs Druce was by now pretty obviously mad; in fact it is surprising that she continued to be able to get into courts and get a hearing in them. If she had still been trembling on the edge of sanity, she would surely have been pushed over the edge by what happened next.

There suddenly appeared on the scene a Mr George Hollamby Druce all the way from Australia, old Mr Druce's grandson (or so he said) deriving from the first marriage in 1816. This was too much for poor Mrs Druce. She made one more appearance in court (this time it was again in the Court of Appeal), came out with a long story about how George Hollamby Druce was descended from a completely different Mr Druce and a completely different lady, failed in her case for the last time, was taken away in a van to a lunatic asylum and disappeared for good.

But was this the end of the Druce-Portland case? Not a bit of it. It still had five more years to run. Mrs Druce might have passed beyond the padded doors, but she had started up two ideas which still had plenty of mileage left in them. One was the basic idea of the Double Duke, and the other was the idea of issuing shares and forming a company to carry on the case. Between 1905 and 1907, George Hollamby Druce floated three companies in a row: G. H. Druce, Ltd, the Druce-Portland Company, and the New Druce-Portland Company – all with the same object. He had collected £30,000 from the public and it was calculated that the Portland estates were by this time worth sixteen million pounds. All the elements of a fine sporting contest, in fact, always supposing the case could be brought again to court. But how was this to be done? It was impossible to provoke the reigning Duke of Portland who simply sat tight at Welbeck and did nothing.

Finally George Hollamby Druce hit on a splendid idea, or a very dirty trick, according to how you look at it. He started an action for perjury against Herbert Druce, on the grounds that he had been lying under oath when he said that he had seen old Mr Druce lying dead in Holcombe House, Mill Hill, and there put into his coffin. (Incidentally, I have been, quite by chance, in Holcombe House and in the room where old Mr Druce actually died, which gives me a personal interest in the whole fantastic business.)

Well, the hearing went on for two months – but what is two months on top of eleven years? The details were by turns bizarre, macabre, preposterous. Mr George Hollamby Druce, who was most certainly a rascal of the first water, produced a string of very dubious witnesses, mostly from far away, such as a Mr Robert Caldwell from New York, described as a chartered accountant, and a Miss Robinson, also from the United States, whose occupation was less well defined. One by one they were caught out in fabrication. Herbert Druce was finally persuaded to withdraw his objection to having the grave opened, and the Home Secretary issued a licence.

An enormous enclosure was erected around the grave and an enormous crowd collected around the enclosure. An impressive array of black-coated officials, with spades and picks, lanterns and mysterious black bags, converged on the tomb. It was the dead of night. It was also the dead of winter, the midnight of the year. It was December 29, 1907. When the coffin was finally opened, a frail, aged and quavering employee of the Druce Furniture Company looked upon his old master's face and recognized him, so little had he changed in over forty years. The Druce-Portland case was over at last.

Three of the witnesses were prosecuted for perjury and sent to jail. But not Mr George Hollamby Druce: not he. He slipped quietly away and was never heard of again.

III

I have known fantasists who have given, with every appearance of conviction, circumstantial accounts of themselves which they must have known were open to disproof, yet in which they themselves apparently believed, at least for the time being. Sometimes there was an obvious reason for such deception: more often not.

Then there are those who fabricate false evidence simply for the fun of it, out of sheer mischief. Such a one was James Reynolds, an American author who flourished in the 1930s and '40s. He wrote books of popular architectural history in which he invented not only buildings but their owning families, which he supplied with journals and correspondence from which he freely quotes. These houses, families and documents are artfully mixed in among real houses, real families and authentic documents, so that many have been deceived. Of the authentic buildings he supplies photographs and also drawings of his own, and drawings of his own also of imaginary buildings with romantic histories and still more romantic situations, and romantic place-names and carefully imprecise locations. His masterwork, entitled simply *Andrea Palladio*, is a treasure-house of mythical Irish mansions.

Colin Johnston Robb, who lived as a recluse in Co. Armagh, used to release from time to time titbits of information, based of course on 'original documents' in his own possession, about his ancestor James Robb, 'Master of the King's Works in Ireland', of whom no trace has otherwise been found, but whom he managed to insinuate, however tentatively, into standard reference books. He did this over a period of thirty years or more. So much industry, and to what purpose? A lie, it has been well said, will be half across the world before the truth has got its boots on. So James Robb and his works will doubtless go marching on for many years to come.

Skelton and Painter, the two English exponents of the famous 'Vinland Map', came to the Society of Antiquaries of London to speak on it. The audience consisted of eminent authorities in this and related fields who listened respectfully to the story of how the two parts of the document had been reunited in modern times and how it had been deduced that crucial geographical information about the topography of North-East America had been brought by a Nordic bishop to Basel or Florence in the mid fifteenth century and embodied in the map, made then or soon afterwards, and either there or not far away.

I was astonished that in the discussion which followed there was no whisper of a suggestion that the document was perhaps not all that it was claimed to be. It seemed to me that, on the face of it, there was a way in which original material could have been doctored by a skilled hand to give it star quality, especially in American eyes, and I did not at all like the veils of mystery which shrouded the provenance of the two component parts. I was much too frightened of my elders and betters to get up and say so; but I did tell some of my colleagues in the Inspectorate of my suspicions.

Sure enough, in a year or two the Vinland Map was under fire and the controversy raged in public. It has not, even now, been conclusively settled. Explanations, plausible enough, have been offered for the murky circumstances of the provenance, when owners have good reason not to admit to owning such things, or to having sold them. Even in my own very limited experience the art historian's task has been complicated by the desire of owners to protect themselves from the attentions of burglars, terrorists and, of course, their own governments.

NOTES ON LANGUAGE

I

WHEN PEOPLE of my age take to writing about language, it is usually to lament or to denounce changes of usage which we are powerless to prevent. Our fury is proportional to our impotence. Most of what follows is about words or usages but I have tried to refrain from doing what King Canute so wisely refrained from attempting, in spite of the sycophancy of his courtiers. 'If I'd of known', said Cnut, 'how far up the tide was gonna come, I'd a never of put my deckchair where I did.'

I am profoundly grateful to the printer who described another printer's work as 'shopslid'. It is in that playful spirit that I hope most of what I have written on the subject will be read.

Logan Pearsall Smith, who wrote well and wisely about the English language, posits something which he calls 'the genius of the language', an impersonal entity which watches over it, guiding its development, and in particular rejecting or accepting new formations and usages, judging them by their survival-value. Against its edicts there is no appeal.

All writers on language, whichever side they are on, are obliged to invoke some such force, though everyone knows it is only a figure of speech, a retrospective personification of the collective wisdom of its users. How people who are as individuals both foolish and ignorant can collectively be wise, is never explained. This mystery lies at the root also of democracy and of the jury system.

Just as in order to arrive at a true verdict there must be not only a jury but also capable advocates on both sides, so there is a function for promoters and resisters of change. I belong to the resisting party, where language is concerned. It is so much easier to see, and to lament, when a fine distinction is being blurred and lost, than to notice gains which are being made in some other part of the territory.

There is perhaps an analogy here with the situation when a judge sends a journalist to gaol – not for crimes against the language, though God knows there would often be cause enough – but for protecting his sources. The journalist has an absolute duty to protect his sources. By sending him to gaol for refusing to reveal them, the judge is, paradoxically, giving that particular journalist the credibility of which, until it was so tested, nobody else could be absolutely sure. Useless to ask me whose side I am on: I am on both.

The fashionable name for this is 'creative tension'.

II

Singing-teachers, choirmasters and, I believe, also some composers, abominate the letter 's'. To their ears its hissing sound obtrudes just where it is not wanted, and they prefer setting or singing languages in which sibilants keep, so to speak, a low profile. I have heard it asserted, as though it were an established fact, that the sibilant sound is intrinsically ugly. It does not seem so to me. On the contrary, the word Austerlitz is one of the most beautiful I know, and I repeat it to myself with pleasure. Spanish, with its proliferation of plurals and the adjectives all agreeing with their nouns: 'las sanas y contentas vacas holandesas' and so forth, has perhaps too much of a good thing. I do not like to hear English-speakers sticking an 's' on to the end to make plurals of such names as Finzi-Contini and Hohenstaufen which are already plural in form. I wish that modern German did not habitually make plurals for imported words by adding 's', so that the German plural for Hotel is Hotels. Many French-speakers, on the other hand, carry distaste for the letter to great lengths. I have known French people who after many years of residence in an English-speaking country still refuse to sound terminal 's' in any context, saying (for example) 'we have three dog', as though dog, like sheep or fish, could form a plural free of sibilants. I remember a guide at Avignon referring persistently to the 'Pope-Palace', from a refusal to sound the possessive termination.

Is there some kind of physiological identification of the sibilant with hostility, derived from the experience of snakes, geese, and indeed cats? And if that is so, why is it that, as a clerical headmaster once pointed out to his pupils, the vocative of 'cat' is not 'O cat', but 'Puss'? If hissing denotes hostility, why does puss (sometimes) come running when thus invoked?

III

With a shock, I read where someone refers to Latin as 'a foreign language'. How could anyone think such a thing? Foreign languages are spoken in countries where the cigarettes smell differently from ours, the trains, buses and trams look subtly different, and it is hard to find the post offices until you know the knack. Foreign languages are languages which, if you are at all conscientious, you make an effort to speak with at least the correct accent if not the correct grammar. Latin and Greek, by contrast, are our own to do as we like with, to pronounce any way that comes conveniently, and to combine and recombine regardless. They belong to us and if you took them away from us we would be without a limb, from the most learned professor to the garage mechanic. Some of us are more sensitive about how to make plurals in them than others, but none of us could manage without them.

In one way, I had the worst of both worlds. I did not begin to learn Greek till I was about twelve, which is too late. At my first school we were taught both Latin and Greek by the 'new' pronunciation: that is to say the one established by the researches of phoneticians as an approximation to what the Greeks and Romans actually said at one period of their history: Wayney Weedy Weeky for example, and Maynin Ah-aydeh Thayah. But at my next school they pronounced Latin in the 'new' way but Greek according to the 'old' pronunciation: Meenin Ayeedey Theeay. Being English they wanted to ride two horses at once or have their cake and eat it or run with the hare and hunt with the hounds or whichever available metaphor seems to suit best.

This was all very unsettling, especially with regard to Greek. With Latin I am sufficiently at home to switch at will from the old unregenerate Nisi Prius to the Romish Italianate playnee soont chaylee to the one I was first taught, or from Fake It to Fee Sit (fecit). (I have never come to terms with the pronunciation used by the French cardinal at the First Vatican Council who said defiantly 'Gallus süm et gallicé loquor', pronouncing it as though it were French.) But with Greek I am never very sure-footed, and matters are not helped by the knowledge that in modern Greek, which looks so deceptively like ancient Greek, nearly all the vowels and diphthongs, eta, epsilon, iota, epsilon-iota, alpha-iota, omikron-iota, are pronounced eee.

Even at school I was much troubled, as I still am, by the claims of my masters and teachers to know whether something was good poetry while having either no idea or a very erroneous one of what it sounded like. Compare this:

> . . . she [Akhmatova] said that she wished to recite two cantos (*sic*) from Byron's *Don Juan* to me, for they were relevant to what would follow. Even if I had known the poem well, I could not have told which cantos she had chosen, for although she read English, her pronunciation of it made it impossible to understand more than a word or two. She closed her eyes and spoke the lines from memory, with intense emotion; I rose and looked out of the window to conceal my embarrassment. Perhaps, I thought afterwards, that is how we now read classical Greek and Latin; yet we, too, are moved by the words, which, as we pronounce them, might be wholly unintelligible to their authors and audiences.
>
> (Isaiah Berlin, *Personal Impressions*, p. 193)

To this day I have difficulty in French in distinguishing great poetry from rhetorical guff, while all German poetry sounds good simply because it is an intrinsically beautiful language which, for the most part, I understand, provided it is kept simple. My teachers could demonstrate to me the pithiness of the thought in Horace, as in Tacitus, and the beauty of the imagery in Horace or Virgil; but these are only the parts which can be translated, whereas everybody knows that the poetry is the part which defies translation. As for poetry in Russian or Arabic, all I get is the sound of those two languages respectively, and I like the sound of one much more than that of the other. It is not until you know what a word means that it can begin to work in poetic terms, and the full knowledge of the meaning of a word, even in one's own language, is not given to many people. 'The value of a word depends in part upon the obscure influences of popular expression and in part upon the fiat of poets and masters of prose,' wrote Lytton Strachey. Both these factors are much dependent on time and place, so that it is all the more astonishing that some poetry should continue to work its magic after such drastic changes of context and of background.

IV

'Is there anything more charming', Norman Douglas asks in *Alone*, 'than a thoroughly defective verb?' I agree, but there are people on whom this charm does not operate. The Americans, for example, seem to have dispensed with the verb 'must', which has no past and no future. So, instead of 'You must be joking' they say 'You have to be joking'. Would they also say 'He had to have been joking'? To my mind, 'must' and 'has to' do not mean quite the same thing. One expresses internal compulsion, the other compulsion from outside. 'I must go down to the sea again' as opposed to 'I have to go shopping this morning.'

What the Americans have done with 'must' is to turn it into a noun, meaning something which cannot be done without. I first heard this usage in England in 1952.

'Can', another defective verb, has fared rather better. It has no future (except when it means putting something into a tin) but it has a past form 'could' which doubles for the subjunctive or optative 'if only I could', or 'I could perhaps if I tried hard enough.'

Prepositions sometimes behave in curious and unforeseen ways. Thus we speak of a cow being in calf or a ship being in ballast, when we mean that the calf is in the cow and the ballast is in the ship. But this is a simple case compared to the tangle we get in when we start to apply prepositions with a spatial meaning to relationships in time. Myles na Gopaleen played on this when he maintained that what we call 'Old Irish' ought properly to be called 'Young Irish', and that the present form of the language, which had demonstrably been in existence for a long time (though changing, like the rest of us) should be called 'Old'. 'Middle Irish', of course, would stay as it was.

If the date for a fixture is postponed it is said to be 'put back', yet we continue to look *forward* to it, though it will take place *after* the original date. If by any chance the date has been brought forward without our being told, it may already be behind us. The future, like the enemy, is seen as advancing towards us. Or perhaps we see ourselves as advancing into, for example, the next century, which means movement in the opposite direction. The past can sometimes 'catch up' with us, coming forward from behind.

Lest it be urged that, however contradictory in theory all this may be, it never gives rise to serious ambiguity, let me record that when I had to give an architectural description of a court-room I had to explain that what I meant by the back of the court-room was behind where the judge sat, not behind the spectator. In the language of the theatre, the whole of the space in which the audience sits is called the 'front of house'.

Other prepositions have surprises for the unwary. If a project 'comes off' it is a success, but not if it is a play. A play which comes off is usually a failure. When someone said to me recently that the bureaucracy holds everything up I replied that that is indeed what they would claim to do, meaning that they sustain the body politic. A metaphor which seems to derive from aviation is at present enjoying a vogue: people talk of something getting 'off the ground' when more often than not they mean being what I would call firmly grounded.

The primacy of word-order means that you can do in English what you cannot do in German: use the same two words to mean on one occasion set up, and on another upset.

There is even a subtle though essential difference, in the vocabulary of printing, between offset and set-off. It would not be difficult to make a good case for the tiny verb 'set' being, in its various combinations, the most versatile operator in the whole language.

I had a competition with myself to see how many prepositions could be made to occur in a row in a natural-sounding sentence. So far the best I can do is 'receipts are down by up to ten per cent,' which is four, but I have hopes of five.

In Barbara Tuchman's *The March of Folly* (p. 295) I find: 'Out of sympathy with the doctrine of massive retaliation he [General Taylor] retired in 1959,' which could mean that he retired either because of his sympathy with the doctrine or because of his lack of sympathy. (The same author, incidentally, in the same book, speaks of a river being 'floated with corpses' which is certainly straining the syntax, though one sees what she means. Can she have had at the back of her mind the notion that the corpses were *bloated*, as they probably were?)

What we call 'the present' is in theory virtually inexistent, being an infinitely thin film separating the past from the future. In practice we use the word to denote an amalgam of a partly apprehended future with a constantly available past: I am approaching a traffic-light, I am expecting to meet X for lunch tomorrow, I will be seventy-one next year if I survive, *combined with* I cut myself shaving this morning, I have two grandchildren, I speak a language teutonic in structure and largely romance in vocabulary, and so on. There is always much more of the past than of the future in it, except perhaps at times of great stress. A favourite analogy is that of a man sitting in a rowing-boat. The banks of the river are constantly coming into view, but only as and after one comes level with each point, and the course already traversed remains indefinitely visible.

It is true that the imaginary reader for whom a writer sometimes writes is an inhabitant of the future and therefore inexistent. But, inexistent or not, he is a structural necessity. I came recently on another case of an inexistent person or persons about whom we could not help thinking. There had been a railway accident, with some deaths, and a railway-carriage was lying on its side. There were, naturally, fears for people who might be trapped, dead or alive, underneath it. It was duly lifted, and there was nobody underneath. We rejoiced that nobody had been killed. Or rather, that the 'nobody' (who was not there) had not been killed. Over whose not-death were we rejoicing?

These imaginary people are rather like the mathematician's imaginary numbers. They do not exist but they are a structural necessity. Whenever I think I have discovered a paradox of this kind I find that the Greeks have been there long before me.

V

When people say, as they often do, that this or that service or function 'has become expensive' what they really mean is that there is now a substitute which is much cheaper. A handmade pair of boots takes the same amount of leather and the same amount of a skilled craftsman's time as it ever did; but you can now buy a pair made by machine, perhaps with plastic uppers, which will serve you nearly as well though almost certainly not for nearly so long. I still have, and sometimes wear, a pair of boots made for me more than half a century ago. They take a long time to lace up (there is a high labour-content in this process: my labour) but they are watertight. So they are well worth the trouble when there is snow on the ground.

By the same token, there are now ships with unmanned engine-rooms. All the controls and indicator-dials are on the bridge. Down below there are computerized devices for keeping an eye on pressures and temperatures and levels and even for taking remedial action. But the ship has to carry an engine-room staff 'just in case'. What are they supposed to do with all their time? Drink? read comics? play cards? or study for higher qualifications?

In the infancy of the steam-engine, according to legend, it was the duty of a small boy to observe the motion and position of the piston, and to turn on and off the inlet, balance and exhaust-valves at the appropriate times. A more than usually intelligent and lazy boy (the terms are almost interchangeable) tied the valves to each other with string in such a way that they opened and shut of their own accord. All valve-gear, in all engines since, has been operated on a refined version of this principle. The plea of high labour costs is advanced whenever the staffing ratio is reduced. In museums and art-galleries, for instance, where there used always to be a custodian in each room 'working' by merely being present, a tedious enough occupation, it is now proposed that one person, by means of a closed-circuit television, can watch over three rooms at once. But it has apparently been found by experiment that the limit of concentrated attention when watching a television screen is about twenty minutes, at the end of which period the watcher must be relieved by another: a neat example of the principle that machines are only as good as those who operate them.

So technical advance, mechanization and automation come up against a law of diminishing returns. Before the children of the Southern hemisphere have begun to be released from drudgery and famine those of the Northern are looking round for new games to play to keep themselves occupied.

VI

I can just remember when 'Back to the Land!' was a popular clarion-call. It had to do with the resettlement of returned soldiers on small plots in the country, and it was closely related to Mr de Valera's famous pastoral vision of sturdy youths and happy maidens, and to Baden-Powell's moralistic pictures of weedy round-shouldered corner-boys loafing at street-corners with cigarettes hanging out of their mouths, which he contrasted with the wholesome open-air activities of his boy scouts.

These reactions were a response to the inexorable decline of agriculture as a demographic factor in the West, including even backward Ireland. Earlier intimations of unease can be found in the novels of Hardy half a century earlier, and of course as far back as Goldsmith, probably also in Lucretius and

Virgil; certainly in Juvenal. In Ireland's special circumstances we could observe the working of the law so elegantly stated by Ernst Gellner: 'The nationalist process is inversely related to its own verbiage, talking of peasants and making townsmen.' In other words while retrograde rural values are being trumpeted abroad, peasants who have had the wit to back the revolution are hurrying up to the capital to get jobs under the new government, the countryside is depopulated and the suburbs of Dublin spread even wider.

'Back to the Land!' was a recipe for what the working classes ought to do, or to be induced to do. To be fair to the middle classes, they had also a version of the gospel applicable to themselves. This was called, in those days, The Simple Life, otherwise Love in a Cottage. It was practised in various forms. My friends George and Mercy MacCann lived in a cottage buried in the heart of Co. Armagh, from which, in the dark on cold winter mornings, they diverged by bus and train to teach art in places like Dungannon and Belfast. The rewards came at weekends, for them and their friends. Others tried to live off the produce of their own cultivation and by themselves making as many as possible of the things they needed. This has been much caricatured but is not ignoble.

The simple life is, needless to say, far from simple. To be lived, it requires much preparation from far back, and many compromises, at one or more removes, with industrial civilization, if only in such matters as paraffin, binder-twine and candles. Self-sufficiency continues to be a dream that beckons. It is pursued nowadays for a blend of moral and medical reasons. It forms a continuum with a set of doctrines about organic farming and uncontaminated food which, in turn, shade all the way from plain common sense to the sheerest lunacy.

'Taking no thought for the morrow' is admirable counsel. Yet what a great deal of thought, and of action, must be taken before we can put ourselves in the position of being able to follow such advice.

VII

The game of using words to mean the opposite of what they really mean is a very old one. In its political context it was memorably anatomized by Orwell in his essay on the political use of language. Fresh examples have appeared in our own time: 'security' as in 'security forces', for example, or the exquisitely ludicrous calling an offshore island 'the mainland' when it has a perfectly good and accurate name of its own. This seems to have originated in the media in about 1972. It is easy to see how this absurdity came about. The British are nearly all too ignorant or too lazy to remember that the 'United Kingdom' as at present constituted consists of Britain *and* the six counties of 'Northern Ireland': so they use the term 'Britain' when they mean the UK. In consequence they are left without a word to use when they actually mean Britain. Even more absurdly, there are signs that the terms 'Britain' and the 'UK' have sometimes changed places. I have seen instances of mention of relations or travel between 'Ulster' and the 'UK' which is doubly nonsensical; and for years we have had to endure the sloppy use of 'Britain' to mean 'Britain and Ireland'.

'Britain' is in any case an unstable word as well as being an unstable entity. It was brought in to placate the Scotch after the union of 1707. Down to my childhood people still habitually said 'England' which now one hears less and less. The adjective 'British' is stable enough, though of very variable meaning, depending on context. But the noun formed from it, 'Briton', is very unstable indeed and is never used in real life: only by journalists and media-persons.

As for me, I find that I keep the word 'English' for things I love or admire, as English poetry, English landscape, English law, while using 'British' for things which have seen better days: workmanship, railways, justice. . . . Another favourite misuse recently noted is to call a company formed by the agglomeration of a number of pre-existing companies the 'parent company' when the exact opposite is the case.

'The child is father to the man.'
It cannot be, the words are wild,
The man is father to the child.

I heard not long ago on the BBC the shameful admission that
there are more people in gaol per head of the population in
Britain than in any other Western country except Turkey. Do
you notice anything wrong with this assertion (apart of course
from the shocking state of affairs which it discloses)? Since when
has Turkey become a Western country? It is easy to see how this
absurdity came about. Turkey is part of – no, not Christendom,
nor yet the EEC, nor yet (except for a small part of it)
geographical Europe, but NATO. So that makes it all right.
Except that when the British have found themselves reduced to
comparing themselves with the Turks, things have come to a
pretty pass.

A great favourite of the users of adspeak is the word
'natural' which is always used by them to mean its opposite.
Otherwise why bother to use it? But here we are up against a
genuine difficulty which is not of the admen's making. Long
ago T.H. Huxley pointed out that the only possible meaning of
the word 'nature' is 'neither more nor less than that which is',
from which it follows that 'natural' can mean only 'existent' and
is therefore, as a word, virtually useless. But of course people
constantly use the word and know what they mean by it, and
so do you and I. So where is the fallacy?

The fallacy lies in making the mistake of thinking that
'natural', like 'unique', is a word of absolute meaning and does
not admit of being compared. In neither case is it true. People
will try to fault you if you say 'very unique' or 'almost unique'.
Do not let them. Everything is itself and not some other thing,
and therefore everything is unique, and therefore unique, by
itself, is a word without meaning. What we mean by calling
something unique is that it has a quality or a combination of
qualities so rarely found that the chances of finding it or them
again are virtually nil. In this sense there can legitimately be
degrees of uniqueness.

(This has practical bearing for me because in my job I was constantly badgered and harassed by administrators who, having employed me as an 'expert', wanted to be told whether a given thing was 'unique' or not. Instead they got a short lecture in semantics.)

Similarly with 'natural'. The word may be redefined as 'unmodified by human intervention' so that it can be used in an absolute sense only when the thing in question is *totally* unmodified: which is not very often. A pebble is natural, a piece of broken stone probably less natural, a block of dressed stone less natural still, followed, in ascending order of artificiality, by a brick, a concrete block and a block of some synthetic substance.

Once such words as 'unique' and 'natural' are freed from the strait-jacket of the absolute they are re-equipped to play a useful part in what we say. They must be allowed to have degrees.

VIII

It is quite untrue to say, as is fashionable nowadays, that 'there is no such thing as a free lunch'. Of course there is, and free fasts as well. To assert otherwise is to say that no uncovenanted benefit ever comes without its price, which is manifestly not so, any more than that all our misfortunes are, sooner or later, countervailed by some unexpected mercy. Some people are, quite simply, more fortunate than others. People are, understandably, reluctant to believe this. The hunger for equity and the belief that it is somehow satisfied in the real world, are wellnigh all-pervasive.

Those who are not prolific are tempted to believe, or to try to believe, that there is an inverse correlation between quantity and quality. There is in fact no such thing. Some people, in short, are not good for much, in either sense. Some are very good for a little; some are very good for a lot. And every gradation in between.

The theological obligation to regard all men as equal in one essential respect deludes us into thinking that they are or ought to be equal in others. Rolleston and Allingham must be content to live in two little poems each, out of all their output, and think themselves lucky.

When I was young I was the recipient of great generosity from some of my elders: Richard Rowley, Geoffrey Taylor, Joseph Hone, John Hayward. There was no question of my being able to pay them back. The most I can hope to do is to try to be as open to people younger than myself as they were to me, and to carry the debt, or part of it, forwards by something resembling an apostolic succession.

IX

Some people are as readily disconcerted by a sentence which is unusually short as by one which is unusually long. Henry Wheeler, Edgar Gillespie and I were once in the small back room on the first floor of the Bailey, in the company of a lady of a certain age who had British military connexions and had, on this occasion, had a certain amount to drink, as had we. She delivered herself of an opinion on the then current conflict which, though clearly enough expressed, was at variance with ours. 'I think', she said (and followed this opening with a formulation which may have contained a sub-clause or two: I do not remember).

'Erroneously,' said Edgar.

The lady was probably not accustomed to being replied to with an adverb qualifying the verb which she had herself used so long ago that she had by now probably forgotten it.

'I beg your pardon?' she said.

'You err,' said Edgar.

This did not much improve matters. She contemplated these two glum syllables, perhaps not recognizing that one of them was a verb and not just an interjection. Edgar came to her rescue.

'You are in error,' he said.

The penny dropped.

There is a deal of nonsense talked by people who ought to know better about the superiority of short sentences over long ones. When I was learning to drive, the instructor told me, after a few lessons, that I must learn to vary my speed. As I could only just, with difficulty, drive at all at that stage, this seemed to me extremely difficult. Later it became second nature: meaning that I never think about it.

It is the same with prose. Children may have to be taught to make their sentences a bit longer and to introduce subordinate clauses, though it is much better that they should learn this by osmosis, by reading good writers. Conversely, over-clever schoolboys, such as I was, need sometimes to be told to try and 'keep it simple'.

The first duty of a prose-writer, as of a speaker, is to persuade his reader/hearer not to fall asleep. The most potent way to do this is to vary the rhythm. The writer of expository prose lacks the advantage possessed by the writer of narrative, whose reader may be presumed to want to know what happens next. To supply this want, the texture can be salted with various tropes and even with jokes. Both the tropes and the jokes are better if they 'just happen': in other words if they slip out without too careful contrivance. It is better, if possible, not to think about it. How is this done? It is like taking no thought for the morrow. It is done by careful preparation: by constant practice, and above all by repeated reading of the best models.

So: the reader must not be allowed to fall asleep, and he must be kept amused. What else?

He must not be told untruths if it can possibly be helped. This is not as easy as it sounds. The truth, as Oscar Wilde observed, is rarely pure and never simple; while Burke (I quote from memory) said that it was a commodity so precious that it should be dispensed only in small quantities at a time. All engineering, alas, is compromise, and this is true of prose as well. It must be kept moving steadily in th required direction, carrying its freight of information with the minimum of qualification and parenthesis. Much, perhaps most, of what you know, you must not tell, because it would clog up the works. You are not there to show the reader how much you know or how clever you are. You are there to jolly him along, and if possible to instruct him in the process. Before you dances the spectre of the reader who will say 'But he has left out this,' or 'He has oversimplified that.' This spectre must be resolutely ignored.

It takes me all my time to perform these two elementary duties. If, as occasionally happens, the prose should take wing and soar for a moment or two, I have learnt to let it have its head, because I know that it will not happen often and that the reader will be grateful.

The three great masters to whom I return again and again are Landor, Swift and Gibbon. There are other prose-writers in whom I delight or have delighted but from whom I do not learn or rather should not learn: Yeats, Sir Thomas Browne, Lytton Strachey. Among my own older but still-living contemporaries two are outstanding for their ability to marshal large quantities of intractable facts and weave them into a texture both agreeable and elegant: Runciman and Summerson. I have tried and still try to learn from them, especially from Summerson.

Some foolish person at a cocktail party once asked me who my favourite writer was. Instead of laughing it off, as good manners perhaps should have dictated, I tried to answer it.

'Prose or verse?' I asked.

'Prose,' of course.

'In English?' (This was naughty of me: I was hardly going to nominate Bossuet or Lesage, was I?)

'In English.'

'Alive or dead?' This brought a pause.

'Oh, alive I suppose.'

This narrowed the field very quickly. It did not take me long to reach, by process of elimination, Steven Runciman. I can truthfully say that he is the living English prose master from whose books I have got most pleasure. Admittedly, I find the subject-matter interesting, which predisposes me to enjoyment, but that is only a small part of the story. There could hardly be a more tangled web of intrigue, dynastic ambition, jockeying for power and purposeless chance, than the history of the Frankish fiefs of Outremer, yet Runciman can hold my attention.

What I value most in Swift is the vigour and clarity of his style, his ability to endow common speech with urgency and force. I cannot imagine that any aspirant prose-writer could fail to benefit from studying and indeed imitating him.

Gibbon is a different matter. Many of the things I most enjoy in Gibbon are not for imitation. He is fond of yoking together two substantives or two predicates with a single verb, or vice versa. His preference for abstract nouns over concrete ones is legendary. Here is a beautiful example:

> Zeal might sometimes provoke, and prudence might sometimes correct or assuage, the superstitious fury of the pagans. (D & F, Vol. 2, p. 442)

It is a great pleasure to catch him at these tricks and a temptation to the unwary to copy them. Not to be yielded to. None of us is great enough to match that diminutive rotund figure as he marshals his magnificent periods, so aptly likened to the tread of the Roman legions marching through history.

Landor's rhythms are subtler than Gibbon's and his imagery tellingly concrete. I know of no prose-writer with a firmer grasp of the physical world. It is one of his greatest strengths. But even his admirers concede that his prose is deficient in forward movement. For some people this defect is fatal. All prose, they feel, should move forward. I do not see it that way. Just as there is some music which gives the illusion of being suspended in stillness, so there is a place for prose of a monumental stillness and repose. But it is not for everyday use.

X

'Hard pounding, gentlemen!' How is it possible for so much style to be crammed into a mere three words, and a style, moreover, so inimitably typical of their author, who was, of course, the first Duke of Wellington. Some of his utterances are even shorter: 'Sparrowhawks, Ma'am,' for example: but, long or short, they are all unmistakably his. 'I never saw so many shocking bad hats in all my life,' his comment on first seeing the new parliamentary intake after the passing of the Great Reform Bill, could surely not have been said by anyone else. *Le style, c'est l'homme même* is quintessentially true, here if nowhere else.

Some part of it, no doubt, is the period. It was an age when people said what they meant, forcibly and vividly. He had that advantage over us. But, though Creevey and Sydney Smith have each their characteristic flavour, that of the Duke is different. It is not necessary to agree with any of his opinions to savour his quality.

'Upon my soul, if Blucher had not been there, I don't think it would have done. It was a damn close-run thing.'

'I don't give a damn what becomes of the ashes of Napoleon Bonaparte.'

It is all a matter of style: the right words in the right order.

There are some expressions which, with the best will in the world, cannot be translated out of their original language without losing much of their bite. Thus, the devastating French sentence 'Il a perdu une bonne occasion de se taire' is cumbrous when rendered into English as 'He has missed an excellent opportunity of keeping his mouth shut'; and it is not merely that it is longer, both typographically and when spoken. The best English analogue to it is surely the anecdote of Disraeli, who is reported to have said to a political aspirant, 'Better that people should wonder why you do not make a speech than that they should wonder why you do.'

I have never been able to find a suitable equivalent in English for 'Gegen Dummheit kämpfen die Götter selbst vergebens.'* Part of the trenchancy of this observation comes from putting 'Dummheit' right up at the front of the sentence. But if you try to emulate this by starting off 'Against stupidity . . .' the impact is lost. At this point it is only one syllable longer than its German equivalent, but that is not why it is weaker. The two syllables of 'gegen' are so light that they serve only as grace-notes to the massive thump of the syllable 'dumm' which really does all the work.

* 'Against stupidity the Gods themselves strive in vain.'

XI

A sentence in one of Iris Murdoch's novels describing a helmetless hero 'wearing extremely brief fishscale armour beneath which a fancy undergarment fell in pleated flounces so as barely to cover his private parts' provokes speculation on two questions. Firstly, why is the word 'brief' of which the primary meaning denotes shortness *in time*, though by extension applied to, for example, a document (which takes time to read) or a journey (which takes time to accomplish), otherwise reserved only for garments which cover, or barely cover, the genital region? We do not hear of anyone having brief hair, or of a car having a brief bonnet, or even of anyone wearing a brief overcoat. 'Brief life is here our portion, brief sorrow, short-lived care.' If brevity is the soul of wit, is it not also the soul of sex? (Not always, for when a female journalist of my acquaintance visited Mr Paisley's church, in which all the ladies of the congregation were wearing calf-length skirts while hers went down to her ankles, she was immediately the object of suspicion because in that season long skirts denoted sexiness, as, for all I know, they may still do.)

Second speculation: can it really be the case that, as shown on hundreds of vase-paintings, classical Greek men wore cloaks, tunics, greaves and such clothing so disposed as to cover everything except their genitalia? And if not, what is the basis of the convention which so often showed them thus on the vases? We are familiar, in later Western art, with conventions whereby people wear either no clothes at all (as not in real life) or just enough drapery as, by happy chance, to conceal the critical area (as also not in real life). Did the Greeks depict their men thus precisely because they did not appear thus in real life?

XII

Why do so many Irish people pronounce the name of Verdi as 'Vurdi'? This is affectionately known as the Fur Hur accent, and much fun has been made of it. It is in fact a genteelism, something resorted to by a speaker who fears that he or she may be caught out in something which he or she thinks of as vulgar. It is not that the correct sound is beyond the range of Irish people: quite the contrary: you can hear Ballyfermot prounced Ballyfairmot any time you like. But the Fur Hur brigade are anxious to dissociate themselves from such a sound. The bur has more than his fur shur of the chur as Goldilocks might have said.

Kieran Hickey tells me that when Gerard Manley Hopkins was living in Dublin (which he hated) his poet's ear was both fascinated and affronted by what he heard from the mouths of the Dublin middle class, and devised a phrase by which to test it:

the marriage and the burial of the Orange barrister in Merrion Square.

In the same vein, I have devised a succession of hurdles for the bourgeoisie of the late twentieth century:

you will have to pay for your au-pair girl's air-fare

– which I flatter myself is topical in sense as well.

I hear the BBC babbling away about 'detonations in the Third World'. What can they possibly be on about, I wonder? Surely they have not started bombing the poor out of their so inconvenient existence, already? But no: after a while I realize that they are talking about debtor nations. In the same way I used to be at a loss to identify a Lord Dillon who was mentioned on the BBC from time to time. There is, of course, a perfectly good Lord Dillon, an obscure and retiring Irish peer who could not possibly be the hero of the various escapades in question. On closer scrutiny it turned out to be the man whom we Irish call Lord Dilhorne: none other than that farcical figure Sir Reginald Manningham-Buller as was, 'Mbulla' as Bernard Levin used to call him, the 'Reggie' at whose expense Lord Devlin had such fun in his wicked book about the trial of Dr John Bodkin Adams.

Many years ago I wrote a poem in which occurred the line

Our footsteps rang like iron on the road

where the play of the three 'r's was intended for effect, and it was published in *The Irish Times*. By the time the inclusion of it in my book of poems to be published in London* arose, I had noticed that English people do not sound the 'r' in 'iron', which they call 'ion'. So I changed the line to

Our footsteps on the road rang out like steel

which is weaker. Later still I discovered that the English have philological right on their side in pronouncing the word as though it were spelt 'iern' which, for them but not for us, would mean calling it 'ion'. It is 'jern' in the Scandinavian languages. Recently, though, I have noticed that on the BBC they give full value to the 'r' in the name of Mr Gorbachov. They do *not* call him 'Gawbachov'. Wonders will never cease.

Irish people suffer, I am afraid, from the same delusion as the English: that it is somehow unmanly to pronounce a foreign language correctly. There is a grain of sound sense lurking at the back of this. When a foreign *word* occurs in a context of speech in English, it can sound very affected if it is resolutely given its full value in its home language, and we all know the kind of person who does this. As Logan Pearsall Smith and others have pointed out, in the days when English-speaking people were allowed to do as they liked, they lost no time in assimilating foreign words and names to an English-sounding norm. Since the arrival of 'education', and largely because of print, more recent importations are left to hover uncertainly in a limbo of half-assimilation like 'renaissance' and 'naïve' and 'garage'.

I do my best to avoid using such words whenever possible, and when I do use them try for 'renascence' with pronunciation to match, 'naïf' (which defies anglicization) and 'garridge' which, I am glad to see, is at last making headway.

I would write 'barock' if I had the nerve. It is impossible to get very far without using words like 'cliché', 'kitsch' or 'pentimento', and quite often their English sense is not that which they bear in their own language. But we have no choice because there is no English equivalent. Unless we are to restrict the

* *Some Way for Reason* (1948).

range of discussion unacceptably, we are compelled to use them. Three hundred years ago they would have been ruthlessly anglicized and we can only guess at what their present form would be. In one case, as I now remember, we can make rather a good guess. Ernest Bevin's literary discernment far exceeded the scope of his formal education, which stopped at thirteen. 'Clitch after clitch after clitch' was his comment on a speech made by one of his colleagues.

There is a special difficulty in writing about such a subject as architecture or music, where there is a large technical vocabulary without which any kind of description is impossible. I am constantly being told that the average English-speaking reader's acquaintance with this vocabulary is much smaller than I can possibly believe it is. The ordinary reader may not know the difference between an astragal and an echinus, or a crocket and a quatrefoil, but surely he must be presumed to know what a 'gable' or a 'nave' is, or the meaning of the word 'Gothic'? Yet I have been asked to gloss these words, incredible as it may seem, and I have clear evidence showing that many readers do not know the meaning of the word 'rubble' and think it means rubbish. It is true that the two words have apparently a common origin, but their meanings have long since diverged. The fear of this kind of misunderstanding makes it very difficult to write for the common reader. Yet the thing must be done.

XIII

Language is not algebra. A word can have two opposites with completely different meanings: for example, uninterested and disinterested. Negatives are not always what they seem. If you are reproached for saying that someone is not fit to black so-and-so's boots, and if, by way of apology, you then say that he *is* fit to black those boots, you have not improved matters very much. Double negatives nearly always give me great trouble. In no time I become mentally cross-eyed trying to work out what cancels out what and where we now find ourselves after all those 'not's. This is especially the case when some of the negatives are concealed in the meanings of some of the words used. A good writer, writing about a now almost forgotten scandal, produced this sentence:

> Most politicians now would probably not rate the continued deception of their wives a higher good than uncorrupt administration.

Try as I will, I cannot puzzle out what that means. If it were indeed algebra I could set it out, moving things from one side to the other of the equation and changing the signs or cancelling pairs, till I was left with something simple which I could understand.

In conversation, people often throw in an extra negative or negative's-worth without noticing what they have done. I don't mean statements of the 'I didn't see nobody nowhere' type where we do not trouble to count the negatives because we know perfectly well that reiterated negativity is the essence of what is being said. I do mean statements of this type:

> He's not very far from wrong

which we constantly hear, and which are intended to mean 'He is right.' It is the little word 'from' which has slipped in and reversed the polarity of what the speaker has actually said.

Heard on the wireless:

> 'No matter how much money my mother didn't have, she couldn't have disinherited me.'

Even the best writers sometimes allow themselves to get tied up in nots. Consider the following sentence from Anthony Powell:

> It was by no means impossible that he was not collecting information. (*The Fisher King*, p. 237)

or this, from Logan Pearsall Smith:

> But to be remembered, or at least to save the places and people one has cared for from being totally forgotten, is not the least unworthy of human desires. (*Unforgotten Years*, p. 194)

In both these cases it is apparent, on close analysis, that the writer has said the opposite of what he intended to say.

Litotes, as the grammarians call it (description by contrary qualities), is a useful device, undeservedly derided by Orwell, who, as usual, did not play fair. 'A not unblack dog was running across a not ungreen field' and so on. All this is beside the point. 'Not unworthy of its position', 'by no means contemptible', 'not the least of his worries', 'not without value', 'not unexpected' – all of these express nuances which cannot be expressed otherwise, and are worthy to be retained and sparingly (it should go without saying) used.

What a useful device is that 'it goes without saying' dodge! 'It is unnecessary to enumerate [says, or might have said, Gibbon] the vices of this most contemptible of princes: his luxury, his malice, his esurience, his defiance alike of the precepts of scripture and the usages of polite society . . .': it is an intoxicating mode and almost impossible to stop.

XIV

Irony seems to me to be of three kinds:

(1) is when you say the opposite of what you think, expecting your hearer to discern what you are up to.

(2) is when someone does or says something which has a meaning, usually sinister, or at least untoward, not appreciated by the person doing or saying it. This is the *eironeia* of Aristotle, to be observed in Sophocles and Ibsen. (The audience, of course, knows better.)

(3) is where someone strives long and hard to bring about a desired result and in fact achieves something resembling its opposite. The historian is apt to preface his account with the word 'ironically'.

When the Turks insist on calling Constantinople 'Istanbul', without in most cases being aware that this is only the garbled Greek for 'to the City' (*eis tēn polin*) this is an example of category (3) above, with a tinge of category (2). In any case, the old city, that is to say the part which the Turks now call Eminonu, has been called Stamboul for centuries.

I have heard people who live in places such as Ealing and Acton talk about 'going up West' when they mean going East, as far as the West End. I see that some modish persons have recently decided that part of the right bank of the Liffey is the 'Left Bank'. And what are we to make of the movie tycoon who gratuitously christened his film *Krakatoa East of Java* when Krakatoa is, for what it is worth, some distance *West* of Java? What can have impelled him to such folly?

These are trivial instances, and perhaps not truly ironical. But when I hear a character in Ibsen say to his wife 'And how is my little dove today? happy in our nest? Is it not a great comfort to think that we are not in debt and that there are no secrets between us?', a shiver runs up my spine and I know what is round the corner and that we are in for the authentic Aristotelian jag.

Knowing what is round the corner is a large part of the point.

The *Edinburgh Review* critic, quoted (apparently with approbation) in Peacock's *Headlong Hall*, who questioned the aesthetic validity of the device by which the spectator in a landscape garden is suddenly confronted with an unexpected view, on the grounds that such a trick can be played only once: 'pray, sir, by what name do you distinguish this . . . when a person walks round the grounds for the second time?' was wide of the mark. He was confusing the experience of life with the experience of art. As Hans Keller pointed out, when such an effect, for example an unexpected modulation, is brought about in music, it works precisely because it has been prepared for. The hearer is simultaneously led to expect the expected and to know that the unexpected is coming, and the pleasure is not at all diminished by repetition; rather it is increased. As everybody knows, the Greek audience knew the plot beforehand. If this is irony in the realm of drama surely it is also irony in that of music or of landscape-gardening?

An impersonal agency can bring about a circumstance which, using the word in another, but legitimate, sense, we call ironical, as when we notice that the extreme Unionist leader Mr McCusker has, in its Irish form, the same name as that borne, in its anglicized form, by the Nationalist leader Mr Cosgrave.

Irony should be used only between friends of similar educational experience: otherwise it is apt to backfire. My immediate boss, the then Chief Inspector of Ancient Monuments, was given to making ironical observations on official papers. These were, as often as not, taken *secundum literam* by the leaden-witted inmates of the administrative side, and the resulting tangle sometimes took a bit of sorting out. Exasperated by the obstinacy of the chairman of a certain 'quango' who remained deaf to the appeals alike of sentiment and of reason, I wrote 'Assassination is now our only resource.'

Meiosis or understatement: Conor O'Brien told me once that the most uncomplimentary formula available in the language of diplomacy was 'We shall await another occasion on which to express our esteem for you.' This, it seems, is the equivalent of shouting 'Pig-dog! Hyena! Lackey! Lickspittle!' etc. I told this at lunch to two Quaker friends: I mean friends of mine who were Quakers: and one of them capped it by saying that the worst thing he had ever heard one Friend say, in public at least, about another Friend was when the name was suggested for membership of a committee: 'Not the first name that would have occurred to me.'

Have there ever, I wonder, been any Quaker diplomats?

XV

Surely one of the greatest of all mysteries is why some things are funny and others not. For example, Christabel Aberconway tells how, during the Scott-Sackville lawsuit, old Lady Sackville told the court how Mr Scott had proposed to her and followed her on his knees all round the room, illustrating this with her knuckles along the edge of the witness-box.*

The whole court, including the judge, dissolved in laughter, and is it any wonder? Even to read it in cold print makes me laugh aloud, but to have seen it . . . The secret here seems to

* See the memoirs of Lord Jowitt, *Some Were Spies* (1954).

lie in the crescendo. A middle-aged man proposing to a peeress, on his knees, is already a figure of fun. If she retreats and he follows her on his knees that is funnier still. But when the lady herself, against a background of hardwood panelling, the royal arms and judicial ermine, does her ingenious little mime, the effect is explosive.

There are some jokes which are so good, so durable and so obvious that I suppose they must have been on the road well-nigh as long as humour itself. The pantomime-horse, for example. I do not even have to see one: the mere thought of two men inside one skin, trotting along with the horse's head up in front, makes me smile every time. When it is used as a political metaphor, as a description of the yoking together in office of such an ill-matched pair as James Cousins and C. P. Snow, it is irresistibly funny. As a joke it is worthy to take its place beside the famous horse of Caligula.

Another joke which I have found very durable is only eight words long and is only a fragment: all I can remember of a larger whole. It comes, I fancy, from one of those monologues popularized and recorded on 78-disc by the late Stanley Holloway. It purports to explain why some muskets would not, on some occasion, fire:

The tooch-'oles were boonged-up wi' floof.

I do not often try it out on other people, but I repeat it to myself on suitable occasions, always with great satisfaction. For sheer felicity of expression it matches that quatrain by Frank Loesser, so much (and rightly) admired by the poet Auden, who used to do a little dance while reciting it:

Take back your mink
Take back your pearls
What makes you think
I'm one of those girls?

except that I think 'pearls' and 'girls' should be 'poils' and 'goils'.

Such things are what the Greeks called *ktēmata es aei:* possessions for ever. If I were ever in gaol I would divert myself by dredging up as many of them as I could remember.

Some of my most beautiful ideas have been killed by a change of circumstance. It happens to everybody. The one I most regret is the following:

In the 1960s (I think) the Queen of England made a royal progress through Canada. Many of her engagements were in French Canada, where she was resolutely ignored and cold-shouldered. She soldiered on regardless, which did her great credit. At her heels followed Richard Dimbleby, the royal tabby-cat who had a line in obsequious commentary which was all his own and quite inimitable. Never was his resource so tested as on this occasion. He got no more than his due when his biographer wrote that he 'did more than any other individual to secure the position of the monarch in the affections of the British people' (quoted by David Cannadine in *The Invention of Tradition*).

This inspired me to propose a subject for those clever people who used to enter and win the *New Statesman* literary competitions. The 'usual prizes' were to be offered for an extract from the radio or television commentary which Dimbleby would have delivered on any of the following occasions:

> The coronation of George IV *
> The decapitation of Charles I
> The public penance of Henry II

It would, I am sure, have produced some well-flavoured entries. But before I had time to send it, it was announced that Dimbleby had cancer and was dying, which he shortly afterwards did, thus translating himself to the level of the sacred, which must not be mocked. A pity.

When we used to stay in Las Palmas a quarter of a century ago we, and our German hosts, were greatly amused by an item

* To which his Queen, Caroline of Brunswick, was denied admittance, which caused an unseemly tumult.

which appeared week after week in the small ads of the *Diario de Las Palmas*:

Jesus y Tommy enseñan peluqueria señoras.

To our Nordic minds, the scene evoked was one of exquisite incongruity. We were, of course, perfectly well aware that in Spain Jesus is as common a name as Joshua (its doublet) is among the Jews. Hairdressing is not among the most apostolic of occupations. If Tommy and his partner had offered to teach carpentry, or fishing . . .

What we were observing was a unique moment of precarious, indeed unstable, equilibrium, even more vividly illustrated by a shop-sign which I noted and photographed at about the same time:

JESUS

SPANISH

SHOP

A little earlier, and the unselfconscious user of this Christian name would have had no occasion to use the English language to attract tourists towards his stock of folkloric souvenirs. A little later, and he would have – no doubt did – come to realize the oddity of its appearance in such a context.

The Spanish for 'hot dogs' is 'perros calientes' and indeed I have seen this written up in public over a stall. There is now, I read, a campaign in the Algarve to outlaw the use of English in publicly displayed notices. This does not surprise me, and indeed I approve; but no doubt it will fail.

'Decimate' is constantly misused to mean to 'reduce by a very large amount', to 'devastate'. In fact it means to reduce by a rather small but very exact amount, ten per cent, and by a very precise method, by executing every tenth man in a legion.

It will be remembered that Pétain, later famous for other reasons, used this old Roman method to stiffen the resistance of his troops before Verdun, and this was the subject of a very powerful and harrowing film made by Stanley Kubrick. Georges Clemenceau was the prime minister of France at the time, and was asked by someone whether he did not feel misgivings at the use of such methods in the name of the French people.

'Military justice, my friend,' replied the Tigre, 'bears the same relation to justice as military music does to music.' As good a black joke as I know.

The fundamental structure of this joke is similar to that of Wilde's 'Meredith is a prose Browning, and so is Browning,' or the quip of Beecham's when he called somebody 'a kind of musical Malcolm Sargent'.

XVI

The misuse of 'careen' in place of 'career' (as a verb) is by now endemic and almost certainly unstoppable. It seems unlikely that anybody except students of maritime history now knows what 'careen' actually means. (It means to turn a ship over on her side in order to clean or repair the bottom.)

I think I may perhaps know how the misunderstanding came about. In George Meredith's well-known sonnet 'Prince Lucifer in Starlight' (from which Eliot pinched a line without acknowledgment to put into 'Cousin Nancy') occur the lines:

> And now upon his western wing he leaned.
> Now his huge bulk o'er Afric's sands careened,
> Now the black planet shadowed Arctic snows.

Meredith is describing what we should now call space travel. The Enemy, *Der Feind*, the Fiend, is orbiting the earth, and half-way through the sonnet the poet needs a rhyme for 'fiend'. English is not rich in rhymes for this particular sound, so after 'screened' and 'leaned' had been used up, 'careened' it had to be. The sense worked reasonably well, as Satan could be thought to be heeling over as he changed course. But careless readers simply thought of him as zooming along through the stratosphere, and the damage was done.

Meredith has been much raided. In Stanza XLIII of *Modern Love* (the one beginning 'Mark where the pressing wind . . .')

the last three lines have furnished titles for, I think, four or five novels (Rosamond Lehmann got the title for *Dusty Answer* from another place in the same poem):

> In tragic life, God wot,
> No villain need be! Passions spin the plot:
> We are betrayed by what is false within.

XVII

The concept of purity is one of which I am deeply suspicious. It may have – no doubt it has – legitimate uses in the sphere of chemistry and chemical engineering. There are, I believe, processes in which the success of an operation depends on the complete absence of anything extraneous to the matter in hand. To make a compact disc, for example, you need air (or a vacuum?) in which there is no dust whatever. But in nearly every sphere of real life which I can think of, virtue inheres very largely in contamination. Distilled water is undrinkable because it contains no trace elements. Good whiskey and good wine are distinguished from ordinary hooch and plonk by the quality of their contaminants, which are so complicated that they cannot be synthesized – or more accurately, so complicated that the quickest and easiest way to make them (which includes first finding out what they are made of) is to let them occur in the traditional way.

'Pure poetry' is a chimera. It is a mixed art, compounded of sound and sense. The proportions may vary widely, but unless a little of each is present it cannot be poetry. In music the 'purest' sounds, that is to say those with the fewest overtones, are perhaps those of the flute and ocarina: all very well in their way and especially when contrasted with the richer timbre of oboe or violin. Occasions for the use of the flute all by itself are rare. Times when the use of bold primary colours in painting is called for do occur, but, again, they derive their value from the context in which they are set.

There is even less place for purity in politics and morals. Garibaldi was, perhaps, a rare example of the 'pure in heart', but a man of strictly limited utility. Right conduct, it seems to me, must be founded on the recognition that all human motives are mixed. And we do well, on the whole, to distrust those whose motives are not mixed. Those who see one great goal in life, one cause to be served, one enemy to be overcome, may sometimes be effective because of their intense concentration, but they are generally what the rest of us, with good reason, call mad.

XVIII

It now appears that Tom Driberg, whom I knew slightly, was some sort of spy. Whether he was a double or a triple agent is not very clear. Perhaps he was not quite clear about it himself. Since the function of spies is to make quite clear to each side the real intentions of the other side, they are, theoretically at least, not on anybody's side but on the side of the human race, and therefore we ought to approve of them. So I would, but for the fact that I cannot take them seriously. They are all players of charades, and I am not very interested in charades.

I have often been amazed at the recurrence, in the huge volume of commentary on Philby and Blunt and the rest, of the idea that there are, or can be, some people who can be expected to be 'absolutely reliable', who have an irreducible impregnable core of loyalty. It is a purely English idea, and it turned out, of course, to be mistaken. No Irish person, from the most extreme republican to the most extreme loyalist, and including those who call themselves Irish but believe them-selves to be bound by hereditary and educational ties to the British crown, has any allegiance which is not, ultimately, provisional or conditional. We all know that there are some circumstances in which we might turn our coats, like Alcibiades going over to the Spartans.

But, they will tell us, this is a serious matter. People do, after all, get killed, stabbed with a poisoned Bulgarian brolly, or strung up from Blackfriars Bridge, or electrocuted by the American government. So they do, but not in large numbers; probably no more, proportionately, than get maimed or killed playing rugby or even cricket, or hunting the fox.

CODA

I AM at home again, looking out of the window over Sandy-mount Strand. There is no wind whatever. Only meteorologists and others with special reason to know are aware that there are many more absolutely calm days in winter than in summer. I know because, though in general I prefer to sail my ship models in waves which approximate to scale, there are some special purposes for which still water is desirable. The water is hardly ever still when it is also warm. The ancients knew this, and believed that the halcyon, a kind of kingfisher, bred only on the still water of the ocean at the time of the winter solstice. Certainly the poetic qualities of the sea are more apparent during the winter than in summer, when it has so often a cheery bucket-and-spade appearance, ready to welcome and flatter the thousands who resort to it. But now it is winter.

The tide is about half-way out, and a quarter of a mile away, on the edge of the sand, a dog is racing madly along, from right to left. Presumably it is, at least in theory, chasing birds. Presently it turns round and runs back from left to right. Still chasing birds? Its owner is so far away as to be out of frame; with some trouble I locate a human figure to whom, probably, in the last resort, the dog must be related. But not yet. Another notional bird has caught its fancy and off it goes in another direction.

What, I ask myself, is the dog really at? In other words, is there some formulation of words which, if the dog could understand them, would agree at all closely with his idea of what he thinks he is up to? Is he, without thinking, running just because he feels like running? Has his body taken the decision for him? Are there any birds, real or imaginary, in the case? Nature has programmed him to behave like this. Has the programme operated, at any stage, through his conscious will? (I know that dogs do have a conscious will because sometimes they show it in their dealings with us.) How much can we learn about the dog's behaviour from observing our own? And how much about our own by observing that of the dog?

We give the name 'instinctive' to the behaviour of an organism when the organism does not know why it is doing something but only that it must be done. But surely it is we, with our huge top-hamper of rationalization, from whom the true springs of our behaviour are most effectively hidden. And there is, surely, a sense in which animals 'know' what they are doing, because for them the motive and the method are one and the same thing. Individuals can make tactical choices: to chase this antelope rather than that antelope, but strategic choices are made by the species. And so it is with us.

Yet why should a dog, running along the ground, be programmed to chase a flying bird which it has not the slightest prospect of catching?

Can an animal, for example, distinguish between actions which are 'for real' and actions of an 'as if' nature? The play of young animals, being educative, is of an 'as if' kind, and the ethologists tell us that all domesticated animals are fixed in a juvenile mode. So are artists. All art is play.

I look out again, and now there is a human being running along the water's edge: another animal fixed in a juvenile mode. But this is a matter of fashion, and man is the only animal subject to fashion. There were no 'joggers' fifteen years ago and there will be none fifteen years hence.

But dogs go on for ever.

INDEX